WORK AND WORKERS

A Sociological Analysis

To the Memory of

EVERETT CHERRINGTON HUGHES

1897–1983

WORK AND WORKERS

A Sociological Analysis

Lee Braude

ROBERT E. KRIEGER PUBLISHING COMPANY
MALABAR, FLORIDA
1983

Original Edition 1975
Second Edition 1983

Printed and Published by
ROBERT E. KRIEGER PUBLISHING COMPANY, INC.
KRIEGER DRIVE
MALABAR, FLORIDA 32950

Copyright © (original material) 1975 by
Praeger Publishers, Inc.
Transferred to Lee Braude April 16, 1979
Copyright © (new material) 1983 by
ROBERT E. KRIEGER PUBLISHING CO., INC.

Printed in the United States of America

Library of Congress Cataloging in Publication Data

Braude, Lee.
  Work and workers.

  Reprint of the ed. published by Praeger, New York in series: Viewpoints in sociology.
  Bibliography: p.
  Includes index.
  1. Work. I. Title.
[HD4904.B68 1983]   301.5′5   79-20996
ISBN 0-89874-017-7   AACR1

CONTENTS

PREFACE TO THE SECOND EDITION

The first edition of this book was favorably received. Reader reaction suggested, however, that the interpretive frame might well have been carried further, that more needed to be said. This coupled with dramatic changes in the world's economy and consequent shifts in national power relations that occurred since the publication of the first edition provided the stimulus for this new edition. It is thus fair to say that the thrust of the book remains as it was: work as a form of human behavior cannot be understood in isolation from other kinds of human behavior and from the values and social structures that characterize and give vigor to a particular society; at the same time the centrality of work in defining the outcome of the human condition implies that we gain insight into that condition through a grasp of this crucial and "central life interest." It is as well appropriate to say, or at least to hope, that those who objected to or took issue with the treatment of gender in work and with the space accorded work organizations in the *Urtext* perhaps might be appeased through the pages that follow. And I have certainly tried to maintain the stylistic lucidity that appeared to evoke positive reactions when the first edition appeared.

In the preparation of this volume I have been aided considerably by the comments and suggestions of Rudolf K. Haerle, Louis H. Orzack and L. Wesley Wager but they are in no way responsible for the final outcome; the sins of commission and omission, the excesses and the deficiencies are each and all my responsibility alone.

To Mr. Robert E. Krieger go my sincere thanks for his willingness to bring this edition into print and my thanks, too, for his patience and forbearance during the process. Ms. Caroline McCarty provided sage and perceptive analyses of role and career problems of the elementary school teacher. And my wife Norma once again contributed to the happy outcome of this venture not only through her unerring linguistic sense but through her sustained encouragement and—dare one say it?—her continual nagging that the project be completed. She is aware of the extent of my debt to her. So, too, my son Jeffrey amazes and perplexes, never ceasing to remind his father that the work we do is not ours alone but, like ripples in a stream, can touch others—who knows how distant? My work, indeed this work, is certainly for them. And for you.

As the galley proofs of the book were being read, word was received of the passing of Everett C. Hughes on January 5, 1983. His influence on the growth of the field of sociology and on generations of sociologists was profound. The pages to follow should in some measure illustrate the impact he had on me.

Hughes once wrote: "If we study man and his institutions with broad-sweeping curiosity, with the sharpest tools of observation and analysis which we can devise, if we are deterred from no comparison by the fallacy which assumes that some people and peoples are more human than others, if we do not allow loyalty to truth to take second place to department or academic guild, we will all be proper students of man."

This was his hope. This is his legacy.

Fredonia, New York   LEE BRAUDE

PREFACE AND
ACKNOWLEDGMENTS

THIS BOOK PROCEEDS on the assumption that the study of work can contribute significantly to an understanding of the variety of social fabrics in which human beings live out their lives, the value systems that legitimate these social fabrics, and the cultural frameworks that support them both. For work does not merely embody tools and techniques. Rather, it rests upon some consensus about what behavior is to be rewarded, what is worth doing—indeed, about the kinds of commitments of self and time people make or ought to make. A knowledge of work is ultimately a knowledge of the human condition itself.

The focus used in this endeavor is sociological. Because the human being is a product of, and continually enmeshed in, groups, it behooves him to make some sense of this involvement as a means of better comprehending his world and himself within it. I share with many of my colleagues the view that the study of work and workers constitutes an unparalleled laboratory for testing the propositions about conduct that sociologists propose. I hope to convince the reader that this is in fact the case, and, further, that the investigation of work is a fascinating and exciting adventure in its own right.

The approach taken here stems largely from the teaching and research conducted at the University of Chicago by Everett C. Hughes, his colleagues, and his students. While this is certainly not the only stance that one could take toward the analysis of work, the "Chicago school" has impressed several generations of sociologists with its ability not merely to clarify the complex relation among the individual, his work, and his society but to illuminate the varieties of human experience. Consequently, because I assume such illumination to be the goal of sociology in particular and education in general, I regard it as especially appropriate to a volume in the "Viewpoints in Sociology" series.

There is no question that my interest in the study of occupations was generated and shaped by my experience as a student at the University of Chicago. Exposure to the thought of Hughes, of Howard S. Becker, and of Anselm L. Strauss was an intellectual adventure of the highest order. Although their work was not within the Hughes tradition, the presence on the sociology faculty at Chicago of Robert Blauner and Mayer N. Zald further sharpened my interest in work, an interest that has not wavered in my post-Chicago years. It is a very real pleasure to acknowledge the debt I owe these individuals; whatever merits this book may have stem from their instruction, but responsibility for its faults rests solely upon me.

Thanks and appreciation are due as well to the Office for Research Administration of Wayne State University for the award of a faculty research fellowship and grant-in-aid in 1967, which permitted release from faculty responsibilities for one academic quarter and thus enabled me to develop ideas and perspectives that eventually coalesced into this volume. It should be emphasized that this support in no way implies endorsement of this volume or any other that may emanate therefrom.

Three of my colleagues at Fredonia—Paul Dommermuth, David Larson, and Edward G. Ludwig—at one time or another served as ready and willing sounding boards for some of my conceptualizations. Their comments and observations helped materially in sharpening some of the ideas I was trying to put on paper. It is personally and professionally gratifying to be able to acknowledge their assistance.

Jerry Rose is a colleague and friend. Because he knows the respect and affection in which he is held, no further words are necessary.

Some years ago, I met Louis H. Orzack quite by accident. When I discovered that he, too, was fascinated by the study of work, a friendship grew and flowered. In the process, I learned even more about work and workers and a good deal about the role and career problems of sociologists. It is a delight to recognize this friendship and to thank Lou Orzack for his aid and counsel—and for just being around.

To Arthur J. Vidich, the series editor responsible for this volume, go special thanks for his incisive and penetrating assessment of the work. His frank but friendly criticism considerably altered the texture of the book; whatever elegance it may possess is due in no small measure to the exercise of his critical sense.

And then there is Gladys Topkis, my editor at Praeger. Her role in this enterprise far exceeded that of the typical stylistic watchdog or one who innocuously represents the publisher to the author. Rather, at every step of the way this wonderful person encouraged, goaded, taught, befriended, so that there were times when she became a virtual alter ego. "What will Gladys think?" seemed to assume far greater urgency in recent months than the demands of those closer to home. In short, she was a very real partner in this effort, and I value the association with a genuine human being.

Finally, my wife, Norma, and my son, Jeffrey, have truly made me realize the importance and necessity of work. This book is for them.

Fredonia, New York   LEE BRAUDE

A WORD ON NOUNS,
PRONOUNS AND GENDER

In this book I follow traditional, and so far conventional, English usage in which the masculine nouns *man* and *men* and the pronouns *his* and *himself* are held to refer to any member of the human species, without the attribution, imputation or implication of gender. Adherence to this style should not be construed as in any sense denigrating or chauvinistic; it is simply one person's response to the demands of clear, readable prose—i.e., the avoidance of linguistic clutter.

1

AN APPROACH TO WORK

WORK LOOMS SO LARGE and so problematic in the lives of most of us that, as with other momentous things, we tend to take work for granted and calmly forget it. It is simply there, as illness and taxes and car payments are there, to be endured. But when concern about salaries or promotions or the job in general or the boss in particular intrudes on our thoughts, endurance may give way to polemics, and it becomes difficult to remain detached about behavior that so clearly structures our lives as work does. And, indeed, even in ordinary conversation it is not easy to divorce discussions of work from a moral or ethical perspective. Either an individual takes the view that honest labor ennobles the human spirit or he becomes resentful, regarding work as irksome, dehumanizing, in fact irrelevant. Certainly one cannot be indifferent to the work one does.

Because work does exert a profound influence upon us, the sociologist R. M. MacIver called work groupings one of the "great associations,"[1] human assemblages that by their ubiquity and their behavior form the very backbone of society. To know something about the work people do and the way they do it, apart from the intuitive knowledge we gain from going about our own work tasks, is to learn something about society itself and, in the process, about ourselves.

Sociologists have chosen to study work and workers precisely for these reasons. The sociologist argues that the human being is not an economic animal and that only, nor is he a psychological mechanism and that only, nor is he wholly political or exclusively cultural. The sociologist contends that the reality which is the human being cannot be split apart even for intellectual, analytic purposes without doing violence to this reality. If one is human at all, the sociologist says, this humanity stems from the necessary inclusion of individuals in groups and in the web of groups that make up society. All of us are born into and live out our lives in groups; this is perhaps the inescapable and irreducible fact of human existence. Thus in the study of work we encounter the confrontation of individual with organization, the way in which the person structures a major segment of his adult role and his adult identity. We come upon the processes by which people who work at different tasks are distributed through the population and, perhaps most important, the manner in which a society is permitted to continue beyond the lives of those who currently constitute it. The sociologist who studies work takes the view that such study becomes a stage on which society can perhaps best be observed, particularly as individuals come together and attempt to make some sense of the orderly but impersonal roles into which they are cast. In the study of work behavior we come firmly to grips with the human condition. To understand this condition should be the goal not only of the sociologist but of the educated layman who, whether he likes it or not, wills it or not, must work. This is the rationale that will guide the discussion to follow.

WORK IN HISTORICAL PERSPECTIVE

At first glance, it would seem simple to define work. We assume that someone on an assembly line is working. So might we grant that a

[1]Robert M. MacIver and Charles H. Page, *Society: An Introductory Analysis,* rev. ed. (New York: Rinehart, 1949); pp. 229–37, 468–83.

doctor with scalpel poised over an anesthetized patient in an operating room is working. And so, apparently, is a lawyer earnestly pleading a case before judge and jury. But what about a baseball player? Or a retired executive who spends every day in his accustomed office, often arriving earlier than the employees in the steno pool and leaving after the janitorial staff has emptied the last wastebasket? Perhaps we can better understand what work is today if we know how it has been defined in the past.

Throughout history, it appears, there has always been an underlying element of tedium in work, to judge from the terms applied to it. *Labor* derives from a Latin word signifying trouble, distress, difficulty. *Travail,* the French work likewise is of Latin origin; it originally denoted the *tripalium,* a three-pronged instrument of torture employed by the Roman legions. Similarly, *occupation* emerges from the Latin *oscupare,* to seize hold of or grapple with. In Greek, work and trouble are synonymous; in Biblical Hebrew, work and slavery are identical. Work was evidently not a pleasant sort of thing to many peoples of antiquity.

Certainly, the distrust of and disdain for work are rooted in the beginnings of the Judaeo-Christian religious tradition. We are told that "man's first disobedience," as Milton put it, resulted in the curse of work: "In sorrow thou shalt bring forth children . . . by the sweat of thy forehead thou shalt eat bread." One could argue that death and work were literally bestowed on man in the same Divine Breath. Nevertheless, however distasteful work may be, the Jew said that it must be borne, for it is part of God's inscrutable design of the universe; it is His will. Work well done honors God. The rabbis of the Talmud worked. So did Jesus and Paul, since diligent pursuit of a livelihood was deemed a religious obligation.

To the Greeks of antiquity, work was a symbol of human finitude, in contradistinction to the relative ease of the eternal gods of the Hellenic pantheon. In the Greek view, virtue—that is, prudence, morality, wisdom—was directly proportional to the amount of leisure available to the person. He who must work cannot acquire virtue, and work with the hands is especially degrading since it is the task of slaves. Certainly, one who would work when there is no need to do so runs the risk of obliterating the distinction between master and slave and, by implication, of subverting the state itself. Leadership in the Greek commonwealth rested upon the work one did *not* have to do:

"The subject may be compared to a flute-maker, whereas the ruler is like a flute-player who uses what the flute-maker makes."

The Hebrew and Greek themes, together with Roman thoughts on the subject, were eventually woven into a Christian conception, which dominated the European world of the Middle Ages. To the Christian of the fourteenth and fifteenth centuries, work was still a Divine imperative, but intellectual labor was to be preferred over work of the hands. The ideal of labor—as, indeed, of all life—was the contemplative existence of the monastery, a microcosm consecrated to the service of God and removed from the demands of an earthly existence. Since monastic discipline is not for the individual except at the express pleasure of God—the call—it must follow that all men are "called" by God to their particular work; that, like the cleric, once having embarked on a particular work course one is free neither to desist from working at that task nor to change tasks. Work, like the very social structure in which it is found, is ordered and maintained by the Deity.

Just as Protestantism profoundly transformed the Christian world view, so did it transform the Christian orientation toward work. For the Protestant, work became less an end in itself than a fundamental tenet of religious faith. It is the duty of the (Protestant) Christian to remake the world into the Kingdom of God, not through the hope of bliss in some far-off millennium, but through righteous living in the here-and-now. Of course, no one can know whether he does in fact live righteously, as God foreordains the destinies of all. One can only assume that he does indeed know the answer, that he does truly live a holy life and is therefore among the elect rather than among the damned. One must behave *as if* his fate is known. An important objective manifestation of the degree to which the person is behaving as a Christian and, hence, is living proof of God's "correct" choice is success in one's work.

In this Protestant view, it is true that the individual does not have his work literally chosen for him by God. But, once a person freely chooses a line of work, he is, like the Catholic Christian, not free to relax. He must work at his chosen field as intensively as possible—not simply to "kill time" in the long and traumatic passage from birth to death and the glories of Heaven beyond the grave, but because work is a part of life. It is in the eyes of the Protestant the very focus of life, for in work man joins God in the continuing process of His creation.

If the individual steadily earns more money, and if he uses the money judiciously, perferably returning it to his business so that even more capital results, he can be sure that he is a useful servant in God's vineyard. If, on the other hand, he works hard, even diligently, but nevertheless has nothing to show for it, such a man is well advised to consider himself a sinner and consequently damned. Hard work and the acquisition of wealth that stems from hard work become a religious imperative, and the circumspect display of gain becomes emblematic not merely of worldly well-being but of religious favor.

Today, there appears to be a blurring of the Protestant image. One must work, one must succeed. However, success rather than work has become the cardinal virtue. It does not matter by what means one succeeds as long as one does so. To retrench, to admit defeat—that is the ultimate and unforgivable failure. Like the Greeks, modern man works in order to acquire the wherewithal to relax at leisure. The Puritan notion that sloth is evil, that "the devil finds work for idle hands," has been retained, but with it has come the apparently contradictory idea that work must be made as easy as possible. Work is necessary, but it ought to be "fun." Coffee breaks, "canned" music in shop or office, and automation itself represent efforts to make work more tolerable. Our society looks askance at the "idle rich," so we take strenuous vacations and come back to our jobs to recuperate. The distinction between "work" and "play" is perhaps less clear than at any point in history, because work, like so many other areas of contemporary life, has become secular; it has been shorn of the religious overlay that presumably provided a rationale linking work with the Divine and consequently ennobled it. There is no such linkage now, and scholars are hard put to infuse work with significance over and above the monetary reward that accrues from it. Is leisure simply "nonwork," or do leisure and work each contain aspects of the other? Before we can discuss the ways in which people work, we must be clear about what work is—at least from the perspective of the sociologist.

WORK FROM THE SOCIOLOGICAL PERSPECTIVE

Sociology is one of many disciplines that study human behavior, each from a particular point of view. Although the field of sociology certainly makes no claim to having generated the "best" or "most cogent" way of looking at human behavior—and it is certainly not the "only" way—the sociological perspective does offer a way of understanding human behavior that (it is claimed) gets at the very heart of that behavior: sociability, gregariousness, affiliation, call it what you will. Sociology asks, first, what is true of man by virtue of the inescapable fact that he is a product of, and continually bound up in, group life. We achieve our humanity precisely because we are born into a society, live out our lives in that society, and are socialized by that society. The sociologist also addresses a second logically related question. Given that individuals are certainly products of their group existence, how is it possible that they learn to achieve concerted action with others of their kind? In other words, how is social control eventually achieved? When all is said and done, all the research, all the theoretical conceptualization ever done by those who call themselves sociologists ultimately revolves about one or both of these foci.

Central to sociological thought is the notion of interaction. Relations between individuals and groups imply reciprocal relationships, mutual recognition of one another, and response on the basis of that recognition. Thus, interaction is at the core of social relations, and it is to an understanding of the myriad forms of interaction that the sociologist directs attention in an attempt to develop a general sociological theory. That is, like any other scientist, the sociologist looks for uniformities in the interactions he observes and tries to generalize. Unfortunately, it must be admitted that sociologists have been only moderately successful in developing generalizations that extend beyond limited amounts of data; the hope for theoretical statements that link bodies of data, that are of general relevance, is still unrealized. Nevertheless, much has been learned about a wide variety of social forms and relations.

With respect to work (remembering, of course, that we have yet to define it sociologically), even a mildy astute observer of the human scene must recognize that most of us do work during a major portion of our lives. We may try to avoid it for a while by going to college; on the other hand, there might not be work for us at the time we want it. But eventually man and work do meet. Then, like it or not, the long arm of the job remains with us. If large numbers of a population work, it is reasonable to suppose that here is a ready source of data for the interested investigator. Therefore, from virtually the very birth of sociology as a coherent intellectual endeavor, work has been studied on several levels and with several ends in view.

On a grossly mascroscopic level, bare statistical data of men at work can tell us much about the relative openness of the American class structure, about changes in the class structure through studies of intergenerational occupational mobility and occupational inheritance. (Do bricklayers' sons become bricklayers or doctors? Do housemaids' daughters become housemaids, advertising executives, or college professors?) Analysis of census data can tell us about changes in the occupational composition of all those who work (the labor force) and changes in the labor force itself. Such information can help us to understand, for example, the spread of bureaucratic organization in American life, the impact of automation, and trends in the distinction between work and leisure.

Examination of statistical and case materials from other societies and other cultures can enable the sociologist to develop comparative analyses of cultural differentials in the distribution of occupations and of the forms of socialization and social control based on these differentials. Comparisons of the prestige accorded to particular work roles in other societies and our own can provide information on the basic perspectives or world views of these societies. In other words, by examining how people regard the work they and others do and comparing these evaluations we learn about the fundamental values of the societies themselves.

Less macroscopic but certainly no less interesting is the sociological investigation of particular occupations and classes of occupations—professionals, foremen, semiskilled laborers, the chronically un-employed. Several kinds of knowledge are derived from such study. First, since occupations comprise what the German sociologist Georg Simmel (1858–1918) called "forms of [as]sociation,"[2] we can attempt to generate patterns of interaction peculiar to classes of occupations with the obvious intent of generalizing to nonwork situations.

Second, sociologists are often interested in occupations as case studies, as illustrative of particular problems and specific organiza-

[2]Kurt H. Wolff, ed. and trans., *The Sociology of Georg Simmel* (Glencoe, Ill.: Free Press, 1950), pp. xxxvii–xxxix, 21–22; see also Rudolf Heberle, "The Sociology of Georg Simmel: The Forms of Social Interaction," in Harry Elmer Barnes, ed., *An Introduction to the History of Sociology,* abridged ed. (Chicago: University of Chicago Press, 1966), pp. 269–93.

tional forms. These illustrations can also be added to the fund of knowledge as a basis for possible future generalization. Thus, there have been studies of railroad engineers, furriers, realtors, jackrollers, doctors, janitors, and preachers. These and many other studies have contributed to awareness of particular social personalities and problems of interaction.

Third, and perhaps most important, by investigating specific occupations we gain profound insight into the internal dynamics of groups that exercise a significant influence upon us because we are involved in them during so much of our lives. We learn that an occupation, like a person, can have a career, and that this career involves all those within the occupation and those who come in contact with it—that, to put it briefly, an occupation is as much a social organization as is Park Forest, Illinois, or the Church of the Holy Innocents or the Brown Shoe Company. By analyzing the organizational dynamics of an occupation, its stresses and strains, we can discover at first hand, as if in a laboratory, processes that are usually less readily available for study in the larger society of which the occupation is a part.

Finally, on the microscopic level comes the research that most of us would probably find the most interesting and the most compelling of all: the study of the individual in and at his work, his problems and prospects, his journey through a life of work, and the events on that journey, the hopes and aspirations fulfilled and unrealized. For the humanist, here is the real *comédie humaine*. As if we were so many actors, each playing a part that is somehow integrated with others, we all come face to face with what has so aptly been called the "work drama." But this drama is played out in earnest.

To sum up to this point, it is our position that the occupational panorama is a crucible in which hypotheses about human social behavior can be tested and refined and in which new hypotheses applicable to other forms of interaction might be derived. In very few areas of sociological research is such a laboratory so readily available. Perhaps it is for this reason that some of the most fruitful efforts carried out by sociologists occur in this field within the discipline.

THE SOCIOLOGIST DEFINES WORK

We have tried to indicate why some sociologists study work so avidly; it now becomes necessary to characterize the nature of that phenomenon in order that we might have the common frame of reference that is necessary for subsequent discussion.

Work may be viewed as that which a person does in order to survive. Narrowly conceived, work is simply the way in which a person earns a living. From a broad perspective, a person works in order to maintain or enhance any of the statuses that are his by virtue of his membership in a multiplicity of groups. A person may be happy in his survival tasks or he may be woefully miserable. He may work merely in order to receive his weekly paycheck, or he may perform some activities for no reason other than sheer joy in the task. However, as long as the person defines, or has defined for him, the activities in which he is engaged as in some manner related to his survival, either physical or social, then we can say that person is working.

The work that any individual performs is articulated with that of others who work and with the containing social structure by its location within the division of labor. The idea of the division of labor derives originally from the writings of the economist Adam Smith.[3] It entered the sociologist's vocabulary primarily by way of the discussion offered by the French sociologist Emile Durkheim (1858–1917).[4] This idea is predicated on the observation that no individual is self-sufficient, since it is impossible for any individual to perform all the tasks necessary for his survival; it is therefore much more reasonable to distribute these tasks among the population than to expect the individual to do them himself. *Division of labor* refers to this distribution. As a consequence, production is rendered more efficient, output per task is increased, and the responsibility for survival is shifted from the lone individual to the entire productive population. So we have farmers and letter carriers and tool-and-die makers, doctors and teachers and computer technologists—all sorts of persons doing all sorts of things so that the work of the society might be accomplished efficiently and effectively. Think of all the people needed to see this book into print.

[3]Adam Smith, *An Inquiry Into the Nature and Causes of the Wealth of Nations* (New York: Modern Library, 1937), pp. 3–21.

[4]Emile Durkheim, *The Division of Labor in Society,* trans. George Simpson (Glencoe, Ill.: Free Press, 1947). Although Comte discussed the matter in his *Course in Positive Philosophy* and praised Smith for his contribution, the term is Durkheim's, and sociological discussion follows largely from Durkheim's treatment.

It follows that, the more complex the material and social technology of a society, the more complex will be its division of labor. We may expect a greater variety of occupational specialties in Russia or France or the United States than among the Yoruba of Africa or the Kwakiutl of British Columbia. Many of the problems of "emerging" or "developing" nations may be seen as the inability of the existing division of labor to utilize effectively, or to make room for, occupational skills not indigenous to the culture.

If there does indeed exist within a particular population aggregate a distribution of skills and specialties called a division of labor, the question may be raised as to the criteria for this distribution. How *are* occupations distributed within a society? The most general, although by no means the simplest, answer—one that must suffice for now—is that occupations are distributed, and the division of labor is organized, in terms of the functional scarcity of the occupation for total system survival. Such tasks as those of ditchdiggers, hod carriers, garbage collectors, or dishwashers obviously require few if any specialized skills, so that the people who perform them are easily interchangeable. The occupations requiring skills that are hard to come by, on the other hand, are scarce, precisely because those who are qualified to perform them are difficult to replace. Their absence from the work world would be dysfunctional to the system. In short, it is easier to find someone to mow your lawn than to remove the frontal lobe of your brain.

Now that we defined the division of labor in these terms, it can be seen that, whenever we discuss the division of labor as a *distribution of skills,* we are in effect talking about the *functional* division of labor.[5] In developing such a functional division of labor for a particular society, we simultaneously define a prestige hierarchy of those skills: The scarcest jobs, the tasks most essential to system survival, bring the most prestige. When we define the distribution of work tasks within a society in terms of their *prestige differentials,* we generate the *social* division of labor. Just as tasks differ in terms of the skills necessary to perform them, so do they differ in the prestige attached to them. The functional division of labor and the social division of labor therefore

[5]This discussion derives largely from Everett C. Hughes, "The Study of Occupations," in Robert K. Merton, Leonard Broom, and Leonard S. Cottrell, Jr., eds., *Sociology Today: Problems and Prospects* (New York: Basic Books, 1959), pp. 442–58.

refer to different levels of analysis of the same phenomenon: occupational distribution and differentiation within a population.

There is a third approach one can take to the division of labor: the moral or ethical. The use of these terms is not meant to suggest that the sociologist labels a given job as good or bad, or right or wrong; it is not his role as a sociologist to let his values and biases intrude upon his supposed scholarship. Rather, the moral division of labor refers to the distribution of differing moral power attached to the work tasks characteristic of a particular population. The question posed by the moral division of labor is: Who can do what to whom, and how severely?

The moral component in work is illustrated by the fact that attached to work specialties (at least in Western societies) is a license to perform a set of tasks specific to the specialty. Ostensibly, this license constitutes a stipulation by some governmental or quasi-governmental agency that the bearer is capable of performing the behaviors that are appropriate and relevant to the particular specialty. One need only think of a driver's license, a master plumber's license, or a license (certification) in the teaching of high school French. The possession of the license implies propriety in activity associated with the work specialty. I may know all there is to know about the installation and repair of sinks, drains, and toilet tanks, but to set myself up as a master plumber without appropriate documentation would be ethically indefensible as well as illegal.

Following from the idea of license is the equally important concept of mandate. A license implies that the person possessing it may perform in a manner in which others may not. A mandate further implies that this individual may tell others how to perform. Part and parcel of the doctor's role, for example, is the assumption that, in addition to treating the illness at hand, he must tell people how to behave if they wish to remain healthy—not only now but in the foreseeable future. And if the patient values his health—as it must be assumed he does, having chosen to visit a physician—he will listen to the doctor's admonitions and heed them, quite literally on pain of death.

The possession of an occupational mandate not only implies that the practitioner can tell the client how to behave but that the practitioner can structure the behavior of others he regards as appropriate to the effective discharge of his occupational role. Thus,

returning to the physician's role, it is obvious that the doctor can
order a patient with respect to immediate and future conduct—"take
this pill three times a day, call me on Tuesday and let me know how
you're doing, and while we're at it, you really ought to try to take off
twenty pounds; that should go a long way to alleviate the discomfort"—
but so can the physician tell others, like nurses, physical therapists or
even other physicians, how to behave toward that patient in a clinical
setting. Consider a hospital in general or an emergency room or an
operating room in particular. In order to accomplish a particular task
the practitioner must be in a position to structure a work setting,
including the interaction of others with each other and with the
practitioner. It is not enough for the practitioner to ask: "I wonder if
you'd be kind enough to . . ." or "Do you think you'd be able to . . ."
but he must be in a position to command, to order, and be sure of
having these directives obeyed. The recognition by all those involved
in the work setting (what we shall later refer to as the work drama)
that a particular individual does indeed possess that right, that
mandate, clearly defines rights, responsibilities and even work flow,
and work is rendered more efficient and predictable.

Part of this differential in moral leeway between license and
mandate is a corresponding variation in the amount of dangerous or
threatening information the practitioner of an occupation can know
about those he serves. For example, a doctor is in a position to do
great damage because the techniques of healing can also kill. Moreover, because of his intimate acquaintance with his patients, because
he has access to their innermost thoughts, it is possible for the
physician to maim psychologically as well as physically. Think of the
momentary shock all of us have had at one time or another when
meeting our physician unexpectedly, in an audience or at a party; we
imagine for a moment that we are being publicly undressed. Similarly,
the priest, who hears confessions and absolves the dying, is potentially
capable of blackmail. That he does not exploit this capability, or that
the doctor does not broadcast his patients' self-revelations about town,
is indicative of the fact that the relationship between the practitioner
and his client is essentially a bargain about the giving and receiving of
such information. The recognition on the part of the client that a
particular person has skills needed by the client implies that it is
appropriate for this individual to know things about the client that
others may not; the practitioner, on his part, accepts this harmful or

dangerous information with the tacit agreement that he will not misuse what he knows. But what happens when the bargain is broken or if one of the parties to it acts in bad faith? Although a detailed answer must wait for a more appropriate point in the discussion, it may here be noted that this lapse forms one of the crucial dilemmas in work behavior.

THE SOCIAL CONTEXT OF WORK

Ultimately, what makes any work task prestigeful or important is the readiness of the containing social structure to acknowledge its significance and legitimacy for survival. Work, then, is clearly a social product; it cannot be understood apart from group values, from social perceptions of what constitutes worthwhile and meaningful behavior. To see work in full perspective requires that we take account not only of what is done and how it is done but also of the normative and interpersonal patterns that surround the work task. This is why the sociologist does in fact study work and why such study interests him.

In order to see how work arises out of socially sanctioned needs and expectations, let us adopt a comparative perspective. We examine the performance of tasks within the divisions of labor characteristic of cultures differing in technical complexity. This includes our own, both in the recent past and as it was in the period known as the Middle Ages.

The pygmies of the Ituri Rain Forest. The BaMbuti (Mbuti, Bambuti), Black persons seldom growing more than four feet tall, live in a fifty-thousand square-mile area at the northeastern corner of a lush tropical rain forest that spreads like a green belt across half of central Africa. The portion known as the Ituri Forest takes its name from the Ituri River that runs from west to east through it. Lying roughly from 0°–3° N. Lat. and from 27°–30° E. Long. in the Republic of the Congo, it was described by its first White visitor, Henry Morton Stanley (of "Stanley and Livingstone" fame), who crossed the Ituri River three times in 1887 and 1888, "with poetic enthusiasm" (according to the *Encyclopaedia Britannica*). Towering trees, often with trunks of four feet or more in diameter, thick moss that appears to be green fur, give the place a towering but brooding magnificence. "But if it is magnificent," the *Encyclopaedia* article continues, "this is also an oppressive world, heavy with permanent humidity and silence, swarming with disquieting life: never a ray of sunlight, nor any rain or even mud. The creepers ooze latex and there are swarms of red and black ants. . . ." Some thirty to forty thousand pygmies call this forest home, a home that they love, with which they identify and in which they feel safe.

But the pygmies are not alone in this beautiful but forbidding environment. They interact with Bantu who may own the territory in which the pygmies live. Moreover, the Bantu live in permanent villages while the BaMbuti live in impermanent camps of the nomad. Yet, it is just these differences which make for an almost symbiotic interdependence, and it is this interdependence which is at the base of a very simple division of labor.

The relationship between BaMbuti and Bantu is interfamilial; the pygmies serve as scouts and hunters (particularly of elephants) and as providers of honey and fruit—indeed, anthropologists speak of pygmies as a "hunting and gathering" society—while the Bantu give them nets, axes, knives and arrowheads. The relationship continues over several generations and, should it be terminated, there are usually hard feelings on both sides. While the pygmies feel themselves to be inseparably attached to the Bantu villagers and believe it to be their duty (whose origin is lost in myth) to provide them with meat, honey, fruit bark for the making of cloth, they nevertheless eat all the food they can before arriving at a Bantu village. In fact, the pygmies regard this provision as something of a nuisance, even though they continue the practice year after year. They do not preserve or store the food so that, by the time a shipment gets to its destination, the Bantu village, it may well have completely rotted. Conversely, the Bantu do not give freely of their supplies of axe blades, arrowheads or mortars and pestles. What a BaMbuti wants he must wheedle or beg for. When once he gets what he needs, the items are neither protected nor preserved so that, like the food the pygmies gather, they often rot or mildew.

According to one student of the pygmies, Patrick Putnam, this grudging-wheedling relationship symbolizes a miniscule social division of labor in which the Bantu is deemed "superior" to the BaMbuti. For the Bantu makes tools while the pygmy does not, but rather borrows them. Therefore, while the pygmy possesses the skill to hunt elephants (by running close to the ground, coming up *underneath* the animal and jabbing a spear upward into the belly, aiming for the bladder) or other animals, he does not have the skills appropriate to the making of tools. And it is *these* skills that are deemed to be a more scarce commodity than hunting expertise, even though the village Bantus require the forest pygmies' skills as surely as do the pygmies need the Bantus'. Both need each other to survive.

The work performed by each of the parties to the relationship makes for both normative expectations of non-work interaction and for the moral division of labor. The Mbuti see the village as a noisy place and the people who live there as "empty" as the songs they sing. On the other hand, for them, the forest is quiet and is to be treasured therefor. To the villagers the forest is a forbidding, hostile place fit only for animals; the pygmies are viewed as fit creatures to inhabit the forest. Though the pygmies are not animals, say the Bantu villagers, they are not human either but a species in between—barbaric and uncultured, friendly and worth maintaining as one might a pet. The Bantu see pygmy women as excellent and knowledgeable sexual partners. Children of a union between a BaMbuti female and a Bantu male are seen by the villagers as "real" children and are raised as Bantu (the reverse relation does not appear to take place). Despite the conflict induced by differences in work performance, Bantu and pygmy hold each other in real affection; both Bantu and pygmy males are age-graded and go through the same circumcision school which serves as the major rite of passage for both (although even in this ritual, which the BaMbuti regard as "empty" as the villagers themselves, the pygmy male is made to feel inferior to the Bantu male). Each pair of boys "whose blood is allowed to mingle" is religiously "brothers"; they learn the same religious secrets and the pygmy-Bantu relationship is cemented thereby.[6]

[6]This discussion is based on Jean-Paul Harroy, "Ituri Forest," *Encyclopaedia Britannica*, 15th ed. *Micropaedia*, 9:1176–78; Colin M. Turnbull, *The Mbuti Pygmies: An Ethnographic Survey, Anthropological Papers of the American Museum of Natural History*, vol. 50, pt. 3 (New York: 1965); Turnbull, *Wayward Servants: The Two Worlds of the African Pygmies* (Garden City, N.Y.: Natural History Press, 1965); Patrick Putnam, "The Pygmies of the Ituri Forest," in Carleton S. Coon, ed., *A Reader in General Anthropology* (New York: Henry Holt, 1948), pp. 322–41. See also Turnbull, *The Forest People* (Garden City, N.Y.: Natural History Press, 1951); Turnbull, "Initiation Among the BaMbuti Pygmies of the Central Ituri," *Journal of the Royal Anthropological Institute, Great Britain* 87, pt. 2 (1957): 191–216.

The fishermen of Rusembilan. The village of Rusembilan occupies a
ten-square mile area in the delta of the Pattani River on the east coast
of Thailand just above the southern boundary of that country and
Malaysia (6° N. Lat., 102° E. Long.) The metropolis of the area is the
provincial capital of Pattani from which Rusembilan is separated by
3½ miles of secondary road. The name of the town, in Malay, means
"nine pines", the thousand people of the town speak Malay (while
surrounding people speak Thai) and are Muslim (while their neigh-
bors are Buddhist). Consequently, the inhabitants of Rusembilan feel
much more identification with the people of Malaysia than with
Thailand, even though the Royal Thai government has attempted to
assimilate them as rapidly as possible, even to erecting a national
university virtually at the outskirts of Rusembilan. Nevertheless, as
"one man of Rusembilan [put it], 'Thailand is not our country—it is
over there (pointing toward Malaysia). We are Malays. . . .'"[7] The
climate is tropical with a well-defined rainy season lasting from
October to January. When the rains come, the road between Rusembilan and Pattani floods, making it virtually impassable. A portion of the
village would also be inundated each year, despite drainage and flood
control projects instituted by the Thai government. (Just for the
record, it should be noted that, although my treatment of Rusembilan
is given in the present tense, the events reported by my source really
occurred between 1950 and 1964.)

Although every family in Rusembilan either owns or works a rice
paddy, the principal occupation and major economic orientation of
the village is fishing. Fishing is limited to the dry season and takes
place only at night, in order to see the phosphorescence of organisms
stirred up by the fish swimming in deep water. Fish are not taken on
Friday, the Muslim Sabbath. The chief fish caught is a small species of
mackerel, in Malay the *kembong,* although a type of bonito may also be
netted. Prawns are also caught but, though they bring a high price in
Bangkok and Japanese canning factories, their capture seems to be of
less interest to the villagers, apparently because their schools cannot
be sighted but must be detected aurally by a diver who listens for the
noise of the moving fish.

[7]Thomas M. Fraser, Jr., *Fishermen of South Thailand: The Malay Villagers*
(New York: Holt, Rinehart, 1966), p. 53. This discussion is based on Fraser's
fieldwork in Rusembilan in 1956, 1960 and 1964. See also his *Rusembilan: A
Malay Fishing Village in Southern Thailand* (Ithaca, N.Y.: Cornell University
Press, 1960).

Most of the boats used for fishing are individually owned or shared by partners; others are coöperative ventures. A boat crew numbers from twelve to eighteen men. The most specialized role in the crew is that of the steersman, who, in addition to a good knowledge of wind and weather, must know where to find the fish and must have, as people in the village put it, "good eyes" to sight the fish swimming deep beneath the ocean surface. The steersman is also responsible for the maintenance of the boat, which may range from thirty-five to fifty feet in length and is brightly painted with stripes and Islamic motifs, although he is not responsible for the cost of maintenance unless he happens also to be the owner. In most cases the steersman is an individual with a reputation for fishing ability who is chosen by the owner to take command of the crew. Two men of the crew are permanently stationed at the bow paddles. Their special job is to assist when the boat turns in a tight circle when the nets are dropped around a school or fish, and to be lookouts during scouting expeditions. The rest of the crew rotates at will or by agreement between oar and paddle; they rotate for the tasks of net-handlers or of bailer and fish-washer.

After the boats return to the beach with their catch and the nets have been spread on the drying racks, the men have finished their share of the work. As soon as the boats arrive, the wives and mothers of the fishermen start unloading the *kembong* into baskets. The women roughly estimate the total catch and approximate the size of each share, with steersman getting the largest share; in coöperatively-owned boats all shares are equal. The women also take care of the marketing of the catch.

The inhabitants of Rusembilan contend that coöperation in areas of communal life other than economic is minimal, and this in fact tends to be the case, according to Fraser. Social relations stem from the boat groups, which themselves retain remarkable stability over time, although the solidarity of these groups lessens during the non-fishing season. Authority within the village (other than political authority, imposed from the outside) is more-or-less absent and revolves, as one might expect, about age—the *orang baik* ("morally good men") are the respected elders of the village—and skill in boat or with net. Indeed, the steersmen are usually older men.

During World War II Rusembilan was a reception center for Japanese replacement troops headed for the South Pacific; a new railroad line runs nearby and, since 1963, Pattani has had airline service. Inevitably, intercultural contacts have intensified and the village is changing. Perhaps this change is best mirrored in the response of Rusembilan's fishermen to imported technological innovation. According to Fraser, the most strenuous part of the fishing expedition, from a purely physical point of view, is the towing of the boats to shore. In 1956 it was decided to introduce motor boats to do the towing. After much discussion four motor boats were purchased and all the fishing boats were absorbed into four tow groups. Now this situation represented a marked disequilibrium between the traditional individualistic and competitive perspective of the fishermen and the new, perforce coöperative, social system that developed in the tow groups. Individual tensions on the part of crew members and their families increased to such an extent that heated quarrels broke out in the village over the equal distribution of income even though the individual boats had unequal catches. Some tow groups were forced to remain on shore because some crews would not accede to the new method of payment. Even the religious leadership of the community was attacked for attempting to maintain the new fishing structure. Then it was decided to try day-fishing for awhile, but the tow groups were restructured to once more allow for fishing and marketing by the individual boats. Meanwhile, because the *orang baik* were involved in ownership and maintenance of the motor boats their focus as moral authority in the village diminished and they were no longer able to maintain the sort of communal harmony that had existed previously. By 1957 one of the motorized boats had been sold and the individual boats were being motorized; by 1959 the last of the boats previously used for towing had been sold and all the individual boats had motors.

Now that all the boats had motors and with the substitution of nylon for cotton nets, harmonious relations between people were restored but the nature of fishing in Rusembilan was irretrievably changed. To be sure, the activity was once again the province of the individual boats, but the involvement of all crew members as a collectivity had markedly deteriorated. The influence of the *orang baik* had ended and crews were now larger than necessary; they did not need to coöperate on shore in the inspection of nets and sails, and the nylon nets could be manipulated by five or six men rather than the nine or ten formerly required. The steersman in a motorized boat needed no assistance. Consequently, there was little or no reason for crew members to interact away from the boats since interaction on the boats was itself minimal. Attendance at the coffee shops of the community, the principal amusement and diversion for males, dwindled and the status of the steersman declined.

But with the triumph of motorized fishing has come changes in associated work behavior. The number of mechanics, tinsmiths, and electricians has increased in both Rusembilian and Pattani as has the number of gasoline truckers. Some of the men formerly employed in the boat crews have relocated in nearby rubber plantations or have joined their wives in cultivating rice. Still others commute to Pattani or other provincial capitals nearby to work. Others drive three-wheeled pedicabs for hire. The cultivation of the sea is giving way to the cultivation of the jungle and the future of fishing in Rusembilan is very much in doubt. According to Fraser, the "basic difference [in the acquisition of interior land for rubber cultivation by Rusembilanese] that appeared between 1956 and 1964 is that while the earlier owners, anchored in many ways to their coastal village, sought interior land as *another* way of investing capital, the new owners have staked everything on their plantations and have severed all ties, economic, social, and religious, with their former coastal villages. If these latter do not succeed at rubber growing, they will be left with nothing to fall back on. Therefore, it is reasonable to assume, as long as world rubber prices do not fall too much below their present level, that these people have made a permanent transition from fishing to plantation management and that others will be forced by the same reason to do likewise."[8]

The waitress in the restaurant. In 1945, the sociologist William Foote Whyte was given a grant by the National Restaurant Association to study ways of improving the social climate of the restaurant.[9] The turnover rate of waitresses in restaurants throughout the country was distressingly high. When under tension, many waitresses simply left their assignments and retreated into a lavatory or the nearest available corner and cried, often uncontrollably. The association wished to know why such behavior on the part of waitresses took place and to discover ways in which it could be minimized or at least controlled.

[8]Fraser, *Fishermen of South Thailand,* pp. 96–7.
[9]William Foote Whyte, *Human Relations in the Restaurant Industry* (New York: McGraw-Hill, 1948).

In essence, Whyte found through interviews and observation that the waitress was the victim of a highly complex division of labor that placed her in the unenviable position of having to serve more than one master, a circumstance that often led to severe tension, frequently manifested in prolonged crying.

At the time of the study, the typical urban restaurant—we are not speaking of the short-order "greasy spoon"—consisted of two large areas separated by a set (or sets) of double doors: the guest area, and the service or kitchen area. The waitress was required to move, almost as an intermediary, through both areas. In the guest area were the tables and the chairs for the diners and materials for setting the tables and for disposing of soiled dishes and utensils; this area was presided over by the hostess or *maître d'hôtel*. The service or kitchen area was composed of a series of waist-high counters, one for each of the meal courses (soup, salad, meat, fish, vegetable, dessert), each presided over by a chef, and a beverage-dispensing counter. The entire service area was supervised by the chief cook or master chef.

The usual sequence of waitress behavior was something like this: the customer (guest) is seated by the hostess, who gives him a menu, and eventually the waitress takes his order. As the waitress fetches the several courses specified in the guest's order she is required to appear before each of the service counters with the appropriate plate or utensil, get in line, and wait until she reaches the head of the line, at which time she orally transmits her particular need to the chef, who serves her. She then takes that dish back to the guest area and the customer. Thus, while occupied with a specific customer the waitress will essentially make a circuit of the several serving counters, in addition to walking back and forth between guest and service areas several times. Now, in order to serve her guest as expeditously as possible, the waitress must be relatively speedy in getting about the restaurant. But her progress is impeded both by the necessity to stand in line and wait at each counter, so that whatever food she may already have placed on her tray in an effort to increase her efficiency may become cold or warm (as the case may be), and by the fact that the waitresses themselves push and shove to reach the head of the line. Moreover, the chefs are not wholly impartial in the service they give the waitress. They may play favorites, serving one woman with special alacrity or even refusing to recognize a particular waitress when, after a long wait, she does reach the head of the line. In addition, the waitress must contend with the impatient customer (with the threat that he will reduce her tip—most of her wage—in the background of her thoughts), a demanding hostess, and a head chef jealous of the creativity of his associates in the kitchen. With all these competing pressures, Whyte found, it was no wonder that many of the waitresses simply buckled under the strain and resorted to the only means of rebellion available to them in that environment: They retreated from the work space and cried, or quit.

The problem was thus clear to Whyte. Somehow, the waitress had to be freed from the complex pattern of interaction to which she was subjected in the service area—the conflicting demands of placing the order and getting it delivered quickly, the necessity to be on good terms with chefs and other waitresses, the requirements of the guest himself for efficacious service—and which conspired to drain her emotionally, leading ultimately to that high turnover about which the National Restaurant Association was so concerned. The solution Whyte suggested was eminently sociological and had precedent within the restaurant industry; in fact, it was so simple that to the outsider it is surprising that it had not occurred to the restaurateurs themselves.

Who were the principal players in this work drama? The waitress and the several chefs. Theirs was the primary antagonism. Well, then, said Whyte, separate them. It had long been known that isolation is an effective method of keeping tensions within bounds and preventing persons and groups of differing status from upsetting orderly inter-action. The wide space that usually separates the professor in the classroom from the first row of students, for example, prevents status confusion; it restrains the professor from becoming overinvolved with the students and it keeps each student aware of his status in the information exchange, symbolized by the gulf that separates him and his fellows from the professor. Thus the educational venture can continue undisturbed (for the most part). To apply such a rationale to the problem of the waitress would be easy. Whyte took a cue from the short-order diner. He proposed to minimize the necessity for the waitress to interact with the chef, separating them by a neck-high counter on which one or several spindles would be placed. The waitress would simply leave the complete order on the spindle. One chef would fill one order as needed, and the food would be kept warm or cold until needed. The waitress would therefore have to talk little to the chef. Orders would be filled in the sequence in which they were placed on the spindle; favoritism or prejudice would be reduced or eliminated altogether, and the waitress would be free to serve the customer unafraid of the evils that had lurked behind the swinging double doors.

The "staffer" in the newsroom. Warren Breed investigated the ways by which newspaper staff, as distinct from newspaper executives, learned to conform to the journalistic policy of the newspaper, even though such policy is often at odds with the canons of "a free and responsible press," staff members often disagree with it, and formal techniques of enforcement are lacking.[10]

Newspapers do have a policy, a stance, through which they perceive the world of events and determine what from among the kaleidoscope of events is to be considered newsworthy, and in terms of which that "news" is to be reported, through "slanting" (Breed's term—not prevarication but omission, selection, and placement within the paper). Obviously, executives may determine policy, but they cannot write the news themselves; this task must be delegated to the "staffers," the reporters, rewrite men, copy readers, and the like. It is the implementation of this policy, the interface between executive and "staffer," that Breed investigated on the basis of interviews and his own newspaper experience.

While no newspaper that Breed studied has training sessions for new reportorial recruits, nor do they have style manuals, stylistic demands are assimilated through continual exposure to an informal communications network through which the neophyte is socialized to the normative expectations of the social structure and to role performance appropriate to a "staffer" in a particular interpersonal setting. The recruit becomes a member of an ongoing social system and, in so doing, learns what is expected of him and, by implication, what he is to expect of himself in that situation. In addition, the staff gains clues from a daily reading of the paper itself; consistency of presentation or placement further legitimates appropriate behavior. And finally, the actions of executives or more experienced staffers— in consistently blue-penciling material for revision or offering thinly veiled reprimands (always obliquely phrased, since policy itself is never explicitly stated)—serve to control conduct and shape attitudes.

[10]Warren Breed, "Social Control in the Newsroom: A Functional Analysis," *Social Forces* 33 (May, 1955):326–35.

Breed suggests that, once having become attuned to the policy of the paper, however covert it may be, newsroom employees conform to that policy for six reasons:

1. the power of the publisher to hire or remove an employee or to exert other sanctions, such as suggesting that an editor might altogether ignore a potentially embarrassing story or that a story be given to a "safe" reporter—one who will not make trouble—in preference to an individual who might be better qualified to cover the story but who could create difficulties
2. obligations toward significant others, role models, on the paper
3. mobility aspirations
4. group consensus with respect to policy
5. involvement with work (News is a value, it is worth getting and worth disseminating and thus tends to minimize any latent hostilities that might develop.)
6. involvement with colleagues (Because the newsmen like their work, there is a high level of identification with one another, a sense of interdependence in making a significant social organization "work.")

In other words, conformity becomes the line of least resistance because it brings in its wake associations with pleasant people, doing work that is inherently interesting with prestige in the eyes of "outsiders," and the realization that, except for turpitude or gross incompetence, one can be reasonably sure of job security and probably some mobility within the occupation over the long term. Moreover, the presence of role models promotes such a perception on the part of the "staffers." At the same time, however, Breed notes that, of the six factors, only the sense of obligation toward significant others (item 2) may be stronger on some papers, weaker on others. This appears to him to account not only for conformity to policy but for morale and performance as a newsman as well. Thus, while conformity to the norms of newsgetting and dissemination may be consistent from paper to paper, the greater the obligations felt toward role models, the higher may we expect the level of conformity to newsroom norms and morale to be.[11]

Having said all this, however, Breed adds that policy on the paper is not ironclad; it can be defied. In order to understand the conditions

[11]Although Breed does not state the relation in these terms, the hypothesis is apparent from his remarks; it has yet to be tested.

under which it can be transgressed, it is necessary to mention the
stages of a staffer's progress through his occupation (what will later be
referred to as his career). Breed suggests three such stages. First,
there is the "cub" stage, in which the recruit learns basic techniques
and policy; he may write short articles—an accident story or the
report of a meeting—but they have little to do with policy, so that at
this time his is a noncombatant role in relation to policy. The second
stage is what Breed calls "wiring in"; it involves further assimilation of
values and perspectives and the further solidification of interpersonal
relationships within the newsroom. The last stage is the "star" or
"veteran" stage, in which the individual defines himself as a fully
functional member of the newsroom group, "sees its goals as his, and
can be counted on to handle policy sympathetically."

Thus, the placement of an individual staffer in the occupation will
determine his position in the interpersonal network *and* in relation to
conforming behavior. Obviously, the veteran newsman will be better
able to flout policy, to initiate stories that have policy implications, and
to argue for specific positions with respect to a particular story than
will the cub or the person in stage two. The veteran will be better able
to select what ought to be told and what should be excluded when
pursuing a story or writing it. And, finally, the veteran will be better
able to survive any battle over policy that might eventuate because of
the secure interpersonal involvements that he has developed over
time.

Breed concludes that, when the publisher's policy, as communicated
by executives, is established, that policy is followed; and it is the milieu
of the newsroom, involving the interaction of staffers with one
another and with the common concerns with which they deal—the
news—that ensures conformity, even though the dissemination of
that news over time might be compromised in the name of conformity. Preservation of group ties may be more rewarding than the
canons of journalism or service to the reader.

The cathedral builders. For the final illustration we go back in history
to a time very different from our own, and yet very much like it too.
The period today called the "Middle Ages," from the eleventh
through the fourteenth centuries, was hardly "dark" nor was it a time
of waiting or preparation for a more "enlightened" period—the
Renaissance—that was to follow, as if history stood still, took a deep

breath, and made ready for the Reformation. Science, medicine, philosophy, all took great strides in a Europe dominated by a religious world view that saw human life as a herculean struggle between good and evil and believed that only through submission to the truth of the Church's deposit of faith and the consequent abasement of self could the individual attain the "peace that passeth understanding." This, then, was a world of essential piety; the Church attended at birth and at death and in all the events of the life cycle in between. Each person knew his place in a hierarchical and organically interconnected world. Each person owned allegiance to those who were superior to him in the hierarchy, and all ultimately owed allegiance to God; and each depended on the actions of others to keep the "organism" functioning.

> During the second half of the twelfth century, the baron in possession of his fief was the typical unit. A convenient portion of this estate was cultivated directly under the supervision of the lord's *maire*, or steward, by labor *corvées* of the lord's own serfs and by hired agricultural workers, or *botes*. This was the lord's demesne [land set apart for his exclusive use]. The rest of the baron's holdings were sublet to peasant tenants and to the serfs, who were responsible to a steward. Such tenants supported themselves and sold their produce, paying an annual rent of some kind. A free peasant owed, in addition to his rent, tithes and extraordinary payments. A serf paid these in addition to further obligations imposed upon him by his status. He was required to labor a certain number of days on his lord's demesne. If he wished to marry his children off the estate, there was a tax; for the privilege of moving about there was still another payment. There was a general feeling of dissatisfaction toward the institution of serfdom. At this time many lords were manumitting their serfs frequently in exchange for a large payment.[12]

Many serfs did not wait for manumission but simply fled from the manor; if they could elude their pursuers for a year and a day they were free. There was never sufficient coinage, so trade and sometimes salaries were by barter. The baron, like every knight, owed military service to the nobleman above him in rank; the baron often

[12]Urban Tigner Holmes, Jr., *Daily Living in the Twelfth Century* (Madison: University of Wisconsin Press, 1962), pp. 12–13.

owed rent ad other fees as well. In addition, in towns the lord of the
town and local clergy demanded their due. "There were also the trade
guilds, which had authority to define the hours of work, the number
of apprentices, and the precise articles that could be made or sold."[13]
Hard as such an environment may have been, precarious as survival
was, between 1050 and 1350 there was an outpouring of piety that
resulted in the great cathedrals which dot the European landscape,
especially in France. There was such a frenzy of building during this
time that one architectural historian has referred to it as the "cathedral crusade" and claimed that it paralleled in intensity the
pilgrimages that were being waged to win the Holy Land away from
the "infidel."[14]

This "creative outburst" drew together individuals of differing
talents who united their efforts toward the glorification of God and
the Church through stone. Although new approaches to building
design and engineering problems were one obvious outcome (the
development of buttressing to take the strain from the thin outer
walls of the cathedral edifice, for example), another outcome, of
much more interest sociologically, was the enormous proliferation of
specialized occupations that accompanied the cathedral-building
enterprise. In fact, there was even a medieval version of the *Dictionary
of Occupational Titles* to take account of this proliferation, Etienne
Boileau's *Livre des mestiers* (1268), which listed 101 separate occupational descriptions.

An especially cogent example is provided by masonry. We tend to
think of a mason as anyone who works with or on stone. But along
with masons, whom Boileau regarded as primarily stonelayers, he
listed quarrymen, stonecutters, dressers, cementers, mortarmen,
plasterers, and plaster mixers. A further distinction was offered
between those masons who worked with particularly hard stone
("hard hewers") and those who worked with softer varieties of stone
("freestone masons" (a term later contracted to "freemasons," from
which derives the fraternal organization of freemasonry)). Often rude
wood shelters were built on construction sites to shield the stonecutters from inclement weather. These shelters became a gathering
place for all those involved with stonework; there they ate their

[13]*Ibid.*, p. 16.
[14]See Jean Gimpel, *The Cathedral Builders* (New York: Grove Press, 1961),
p. 37.

lunches, took their afternoon siestas (a common medieval practice), and discussed common problems. Out of the interaction in these shelters, or "lodges," developed the lodges of freemasonry.

The statuses and prerogatives of these several occupations with respect to each other and toward outsiders were rigidly defined. Periods of apprenticeship, the penalties for communicating "trade secrets" (it should be remembered that medieval guilds conceived of themselves as organizations to protect the sancitity of their "mysteries"—that is, the secrets of their craft—from infringement by outsiders), and the ethics of the occupation were spelled out in detail in statute and royal decree. In some cases, even the very mixture of mortar or cement was prescribed, together with the penalties that could accrue to both buyer and seller for violation. And all of this *ad majoram gloriam Dei,* to God's greater glory.

Implications. However complex the division of labor in a given occupation may be, the five cases examined here suggest that the organization of work permits the survival of that social system in which the work takes place. Changing expectations regarding the requirements for the survival of a society can be expected to elicit changes in the division of labor, in the character of work, in order to meet these new needs.

Whether one takes a narrow view of work, as activity performed for monetary gain, or (as we prefer) a broader view, as activities related to individual and social survival, work is not an isolated behavior. It is appropriate to see work in a context of *people, position,* and *purpose.*

People. The very notion of division of labor implies that even the most simple task or skill requires the assistance of others. Mowing a lawn, which, in our society, is a relatively simple if onerous task, requires a mower, which took many people to make, all the way back to the extraction of the basic raw materials that were ultimately fashioned into the mower. To understand the work one must understand the people who work. For, as will be seen, work not only influences its practitioners but is influenced by them. People who perform the same tasks may see their jobs quite differently, and these differences in perception may generate different work stances. Consider, for example, the funeral director who sees himself as performing a service at a time of intense need as against the funeral director who prides himself on the facility with which he "moves 'em in and moves 'em out." We must understand the selection and recruitment processes that bring people and occupation together and the ways in which men learn work roles and create or modify them.

Position. It is a tenet of the sociological perspective that people do not passively react to stimuli from the outside; they initiate behavior, and in responding to the behavior of others they are, perhaps imperceptibly, changed. As people interact, whether in work or in other situations, the interaction proceeds in terms of similarities and differences in the participants. These similarities and differences may be *ascribed*, applied by others to the actors without any merit on their part (e.g., age, sex, kinship), or they may be *achieved* (e.g., the statuses of doctor, teacher, wife). The imputation of such likenesses or differences, whether by self or by others, gives rise to similarities or dissimilarities in position relative to the work involved. To understand the social division of labor is to understand the rationale behind these differences in position or status. But an understanding of the positions (or statuses) of the people who work is more than this. Differences in status imply differences in authority or responsibility; a Steno I and a Steno II in the typing pool of the XYZ Company may perform similar functions but, by virtue of experience, seniority, or a variety of other factors, may differ in status and, thus, in expectation of reward and view of the job and the work organization. The keypunch operator whose machine is nearer the entrance to the machine room may occupy an entirely different niche in the structure of that room than another whose machine is farther from the door but whose skill is no less. One cannot understand work in its totality or in a more narrowly circumscribed setting—junkyard, machine room, operating theater—without understanding the reciprocal influence of work and status.

Purpose. Finally, the student of occupations must be aware of the ideological constraints that surround work. In work as in any other human activity, personal and social norms and values provide a framework of goals or purpose in which work is conducted. A norm prescribes behavior, it sets bounds to behavior; a value expresses the desirability or worth of that conduct. It is assumed in our society that an individual will wear clothes in public—a norm—but whether the clothes he wears are at the height of fashion or are cast-offs constitutes a value (indeed, several values) of the wearer. The conflict of values and norms at either the social or the individual level often engenders social disharmony or personal deviancy.

Both societies and individuals define useful work activity. The society evaluates work with respect to its desirability and importance in ensuring the continuity and health of the social system; it sets the terms by which work can be recognized. When does work as we usually think of it shade into indolence? How idle can one be and still be thought to be working? "Goldbricking," or loafing, is a matter of social prescription. In addition, people choose occupations, change occupations, choose to work in particular places at particular hours, and undergo protracted and interminable training periods to reach their occupational goals, or else drop out of the occupational panorama altogether, because of the values they place upon work and the social and emotional context in which work is performed. Indeed, what *is* work is a matter of value; and this value may often conflict with societal norms about work. The male who wishes to be a fine artist (in contrast to a commercial artist) may alienate his parents and lose their aid because of the stigma applied to the fine artist in North American society. Painting and the artist tend to be sanctioned only when art is pursued as an avocation; if a fine artist is viewed as a "legitimate" worker it is only when that work is "safe," when it does not pose a personal or social threat to those around him. Consequently, the person who chooses art as occupation rather than preoccupation runs the risk of ostracism. Nevertheless, he chooses art because such performance is valuable at least to him, if not to others. It is seen as worth pursuing, regardless of the financial gain that may or may not be involved; it is no longer work but life.

As we have seen, changing conceptions of the place of man in the world have led to changes in the value attributed to particular occupations and to work in general. Increasing secularization of the American ethic has stripped work of its divine sanction and made the unremitting pursuit of gain a thing in itself. Those tasks which bring the greatest monetary success appear to assume greater value than tasks which do not. A rapidly changing technology and an expanding inventory of knowledge have made some occupations glamorous, all but obliterated interest in others, and certainly created still others. The village blacksmith is long gone, while the space technologist or computer programer are work roles that were relatively unknown twenty years ago. Changing fashions and motivations in work and workers arise, then, out of the changing purposes of and for work.

SUMMARY

In this first chapter, changing conceptions of work in history were presented, a case was made for the sociological study of work, and work was defined and related to the idea of the division of labor. Five examples of the division of labor were presented, and implications of this discussion for an understanding of work were set forth in the tripartite notion of people, position, and purpose.

2

WHO WORKS:
THE AMERICAN LABOR FORCE

IN CHAPTER 1, I contended, among other things, that work (however it may be defined) is carried out and that the functional division of labor is defined in terms of a normative and evaluational framework. There is no better way of illustrating this than to note the changing responses of the U.S. government toward work, as represented by the variety of ways in which the Bureau of the Census has quantified information about America's workers down through the years.

The conduct of a decennial census was mandated by the framers of the Constitution of the United States in order to provide for an equitable distribution of direct taxation and political representation. Article I, Section 2, states:

Representatives and direct Taxes shall be apportioned among the several states which may be included within the Union according to their respective Numbers, which shall be determined by adding to the whole Number of free Persons, including

those bound to Service for a Term of Years, and excluding
Indians not taxed, three-fifths of all other Persons. The actual
Enumeration shall be made within three Years after the first
Meeting of the Congress . . . and within every subsequent Term
of ten Years in such Manner as they shall by law direct.

Thus enabled, the census of population came formally into being
through enacting legislation on March 16, 1790, signed by George
Washington as President. Thomas Jefferson, who was Secretary of
State, attested to the authenticity of the first census, in 1790. The
United States and its census of popuation were born literally together.

The first census adhered closely to the constitutional mandate; it
hinted at the work behavior of the American population of 1790 in
broad terms in the distinction between slave and free males, and in
the very simple distinction between those engaged in agriculture as
opposed to those involved in manufacturing, construction, and hand
trades (an aggregate listing). The unit of enumeration was the family.
The data were collected by U.S. marshals and their assistants, who
used whatever paper they could lay their hands on and who did not
attempt to verify their information.

By 1890 work was being treated in more detailed fashion, with
enumeration by industry or profession but not by actual employment.
Whether or not a person was actually working at a particular task at
the time of enumeration made no difference; what was enumerated
was whether he had *ever* worked at the occupation in which he
claimed proficiency or competence. Unemployment was thus a residual category.

In 1929 the financial base of the United States collapsed, the
economy was severely dislocated, the unemployment rate rose
sharply, and the nature of American occupational disruption loomed
not merely as an academic question for the Bureau of the Census but
as a problem of major political import. The 1930 census introduced
the concepts of the "gainful worker" and "gainful employment." It
was hoped that the use of these concepts might soften the picture of
economic havoc, which steadily rising unemployment figures might
create. Building upon previous assumptions about employment,
gainful workers were persons reported as having an occupation in
which they earned money or a monetary equivalent or assisted in the
production of marketable goods, regardless of whether they were

working or looking for work at the time of enumeration. Their willingness to work at the job was all that was important.

With the outbreak of World War II, American became first an "arsenal of democracy," producing matériel for England and those European countries that were resisting the onslaughts of a revived Germany; after the Japanese attack on Pearl Harbor in late 1941 the United States became an active participant in that war. Employment rose as industry geared for war and large numbers of males entered the armed forces. Beginning with the 1940 census, the "gainful worker" concept was replaced by the perspective that is currently in use, that of the "labor force."

The term "labor force" describes the aggregate of overt individual occupational activity at the time of enumeration for the decennial census or in the week containing the twelfth of each month, the date on which the Bureau of the Census conducts its monthly sample survey of population. On the basis of responses to questions about current work activity—either actively employed or actively seeking employment—persons are classified with respect to employment in the following categories:

Employed includes (1) all persons sixteen years of age and older—originally age fourteen—who worked for pay or profit in either agricultural or nonagricultural pursuits, or who worked at least fifteen hours during that week as an unpaid worker in an enterprise, either farm or nonfarm, operated by a member of the family of the respondent; and (2) all those sixteen or over who neither worked nor sought work but were temporarily absent from employment because of illness, inclement weather, vacation, labor dispute, or the like. Volunteer work and housework were excluded from the accounting. A person working at more than one job is counted only on the job at which he or she worked the greatest number of hours.

Unemployed includes all persons sixteen years of age and older who, during the week of reference, did not work but were available for work, except for temporary illness and (1) had actively sought work within the preceding four weeks; or (2) were waiting to be called back to a job from which they had been laid off or were waiting to start new jobs within the next thirty days. (The unemployment rate represents the number of unemployed as a percentage of the civilian labor force).

In 1974 the Bureau of the Census and the Bureau of Labor Statistics specified the content of full-time as against part-time employment. Full-time workers are employed at least thirty-five hours a week; part-time workers are employed less than thirty-five hours a week. Workers on a part-time schedule for economic reasons (such as slack work, material shortages, termination of or beginning a job during the week of reference or inability to find full-time work) are counted as being on full-time status on the assumption that they would be at work full-time if conditions permitted. Unemployed persons are further classified as full-time or part-time unemployed by their reported preferences for full-time or part-time work. Once again the Federal Government responded to increased unemployment occasioned by both inflationary trends and the impact of petroleum shortages upon industrial output; as before, in its use of the "gainful worker" concept, the Government treated the politically potent variable of unemployment as a residual category: it is a temporary matter, people would be employed if they could be; and if they are at work less than thirty-five hours a week this, too, is only a temporary setback, and they will be treated, for statistical reporting purposes at least, "as if" they worked full-time.

The *labor force* consists, then, of civilian employed and unemployed persons over sixteen years of age, in addition to members of the armed forces of the United States (obtained from official sources). Those *not in the labor force* include all persons sixteen years of age and over, not in institutions, who are not classified as employed, unemployed, or in military service. These individuals are further classified as "engaged in own-home housework," "in school," "unable to work" because of protracted illness or other disability, and "other"—retirees, the voluntarily idle, seasonal workers who were enumerated in an "off" season, and those working less than fifteen hours in unpaid family work. When inmate populations are sampled annually, they are also included. The conception of the labor force thus provides, given the present state of the census-taker's art, the most accurate picture we have of the participation of Americans in the labor market. But at the same time it is important to recognize—and this is the burden of this section—that the approach of the U.S. Government to work is a reflection not only of the need to know about work and workers but of political and ethical considerations about what *ought* to be known. (See Table 1.)

TABLE 1. THE LABOR FORCE

Total labor force
  Armed forces
  Civilian labor force
    Employed
      Agricultural
      Nonagricultural
    Unemployed
Not in the labor force
  Keeping house
  In school
  Other

WHO WORKS?

To get some idea of work in America, let us look first at bare labor-force statistics. In the thirty years between 1950 and 1980 the total noninstitutionalized U.S. population above the age of sixteen climbed from approximately 106 million to approximately 170 million. In that same period the total number of participants in the labor force climbed from approximately 64 million to approximately 109 million, with the percentage of the total labor force to the total noninstitutionalized population above the age of sixteen rising from approximately fifty-nine percent to approximately sixty-four percent. Of the approximately 110 million in the labor force in 1980, approximately 107 million were in the civilian labor force. Of these, about 96 million were employed in non-agricultural pursuits, approximately 3.4 million were involved in farm-related activities, and about seven million, or seven percent, of the civilian labor force were unemployed.[1] Data for the year 1981 are presented in Table 2.

WHAT KIND OF WORK?

We have seen who works. We must now ask what members of the American labor force do. The Bureau of the Census describes labor-force participation by industrial groups (Table 3) and in terms perhaps most easily grasped by the layman: the occupational status of

[1]Table 2, *Monthly Labor Review* 105 (June, 1982): 74.

38 *Work and Workers*

TABLE 2. LABOR FORCE BY AGE, SEX AND RACE, SEASONALLY ADJUSTED
ANNUAL AVERAGE, 1981

Total labor force	110,812,000
Civilian labor force	108,670,000
Employed	100,397,000
Agriculture	3,368,000
Nonagricultural industries	97,030,000
Unemployed	8,273,000
Unemployment rate (per cent)	7.6
Not in labor force	61,460,000

Men Aged 20 Years and Over

Civilian labor force	57,197,000
Employed	53,582,000
Agriculture	2,384,000
Nonagricultural industries	51,199,000
Unemployed	3,615,000
Unemployment rate (per cent)	6.3
Not in labor force	15,222,000

Women Aged 20 Years and Over

Civilian labor force	42,485,000
Employed	39,590,000
Agriculture	604,000
Nonagricultural industries	38,986,000
Unemployed	2,895,000
Unemployment rate (per cent)	6.8
Not in labor force	39,012,000

Both Sexes, Aged 16–19 Years

Civilian labor force	8,988,000
Employed	7,225,000
Agriculture	380,000
Nonagricultural industries	6,845,000
Unemployed	1,763,000
Unemployment rate (per cent)	19.6
Not in labor force	7,226,000

White

Civilian labor force	95,052,000
Employed	88,709,000
Unemployed	6,343,000
Unemployment rate (per cent)	6.7
Not in labor force	52,856,000

Black

Civilian labor force	11,066,000
Employed	9,355,000
Unemployed	1,731,000
Unemployment rate (per cent)	15.6
Not in labor force	7,133,000

SOURCE: Adapted from "Table 2: Employment Status by Sex, Age, and Race, Seasonally Adjusted," *Monthly Labor Review* 105 (June, 1982): 74.

TABLE 3. THE LABOR FORCE, BY INDUSTRIAL GROUPS

Nonagricultural private wage and salary workers
  Mining
  Construction
  Manufacturing
    Durable goods
    Nondurable goods
  Transportation and public utilities
  Trade
    Wholesale trade
    Retail trade
  Finance, insurance, and real estate
  Services (including medical and educational)
Government
Agricultural wage and salary workers

the worker (Table 4). But to understand the impact of statistics using the variables indicated in these two tables we must draw back a bit for a historical perspective.

Despite their differences in religious persuasion, the Puritans, Congregationalists, and Catholics who came in the seventeenth and eighteenth centuries to build a fledgling nation saw themselves as possessing boundless potential to harness a boundless land. The American would be a new race, combining the best of the European peoples, but the amalgam would be unique. This new being would be shaped by the unparalleled opportunity inherent in the undiscovered breadth of the North American continent. For land, land to be sown and tilled and settled, was a sacred gift of God, which called for the best men and women had to offer. On the other hand, the city was seen as an evil congregation of social castoffs and those who would

TABLE 4. THE LABOR FORCE, BY OCCUPATIONAL STATUS

White-collar workers
  Professional and technical
  Managers and administrators, except farm
  Sales workers
  Clerical workers
Blue-collar workers
  Craftsmen and kindred workers
  Operatives
  Nonfarm laborers
Service workers
Farm workers

profit from the sweat of the honest farmer. Cities breathed vice; the worker on the land was felt to be the American incarnate. In 1790, at the time of the first decennial census, 95 per cent of the American population lived in rural areas. Only two cities—New York and Philadelphia—had populations as large as 25,000. By 1850 only 15 per cent of the American population lived in urban communities of 2,500 people or more (the census definition). But by 1920 the picture had irreversibly changed; we had become an urban nation, with 51 per cent of the national population in urban areas. America had ceased to rely on the land either for its wealth or for its self-image.

In order to explain this transformation sociologically we must look to the values that first led Europeans to emigrate to an unknown continent. Obviously, colonization could open up new sources of wealth for the "mother countries," Spain, France, and England; Columbus, Vasco da Gama, Jacques Cartier, and John Cabot all sought the wealth of what they thought was the East. The settlement of new lands could as well serve as a springboard to win new souls for Christ. But the Protestants who formed the first great wave of immigration saw their task as more than the enrichment of monarchs or bourgeois speculators, even more than the conversion of the "heathen." In the territory that was to become the United States, the Kingdom of God, a new Jerusalem untrammeled by past traditions, could be built. Here one could find himself by finding a calling congenial to God. Patient, industrious effort at one's work could more clearly show God's favor and blessings on that "new order of the ages," which America was conceived to be. God's "election" of Americans, both individually and collectively, would be demonstrated (according to the tenets of the Protestant ethic) in the acquisition of wealth measured in strictly monetary terms. Achievement meant monetary achievement, and, since nothing succeeds like success, the larger the amount of money one could accumulate, the surer could one be that the Lord was indeed smiling upon him. And the more confident could the individual be in such a situation that he was included among the saved, that in his afterlife he would sit triumphant at the right hand of God the Father.

Once money was perceived as religious capital, the cultivation of land as a medium of capital formation became increasingly suspect. Blight, storm, flood, or drought could ruin the farmer or wipe out the rancher within a short time. Nevertheless, the land could provide other yields. A developing technology required metals, coal, oil, lumber. These commodities could be extracted relatively easily to generate wealth far in excess of any provided by cultivation and without regard for the productive future of the land itself. The "robber barons" of the late nineteenth century and the practitioners of strip mining in our own day are excoriated for just this despoilment of land for private gain. The conservation efforts of Theodore Roosevelt and Gifford Pinchot at the opening of the twentieth century or the current interest in ecology represent responses to the unbridled exploitation of the sacred land of the United States.

As greater reliance was placed on the extractive industries—mining, lumber, fishing, and the like—at the expense of agriculture, the pursuit of money and the success that presumably was contingent on monetary attainments became ends in themselves, shorn of religious implications. Bartholdi's statue of "Liberty Enlightening the World" (the Statue of Liberty), erected in 1884 at the entrance to New York Harbor, symbolized the hope of America for millions from other lands. Emma Lazarus articulated this hope in a poem engraved in bronze on the pedestal of the statue, "The New Colossus."

> Give me your tired, your poor,
> Your huddled masses yearning to breathe free,
> The wretched refuse of your teeming shore.
> Send these, the homeless, tempest-tossed to me.
> I lift my lamp beside the golden door.

Success was at every hand, because, so the supposition went, America's streets were paved with gold, the embodiment of the Biblical "land flowing with milk and honey." Generations of Americans dreamed of the well-being that could be theirs, if the response to the success-oriented tales of Horatio Alger is to be believed, so long as they were willing to work hard and to husband their resources.

Ironically, perhaps, it was the city that offered the best hope for fulfillment of that dream. Despite the persistence of the tradition that a city was a haven for the depraved, despite fulminations against urban life by none other than Horatio Alger himself, the city came increasingly to be seen as the place where work could be found—perhaps demeaning or oppressive, but work nonetheless. And the city came to produce what was required not so much by agriculture as by an increasingly technical, mechanized, and urban-oriented economy.

Consider, for example, the fact that in 1910 one-third of the American labor force earned its living through agriculture. By 1940 this had dwindled to less than 20 per cent, by 1950 it had fallen to 14 cer cent, and by 1970 it had reached 4 per cent. In a kind of self-fulfilling prophecy, as cities grew, more goods and services were required. The increase of these goods and services, however, necessitated the further growth and intensive use of the central city and later generated the exurban sprawl.

Thus, as the United States moved from the nineteenth into the twentieth century, the country was increasingly urbanized and more and more dependent upon the city for goods, services, and the underlying technological base. In the city at the turn of the century the worker lived near his work—within walking distance or a short streetcar ride away. This was the "zone of workingmen's homes" that the sociologists who studied urban growth were to write about later. There were relatively few labor-saving devices in the home or outside the home.

Most of the labor force in 1900 worked at manual occupations. In fact, 30 per cent of the 1900 labor force was unskilled labor.[2] In 1900, the workers in some six trades—metal molders, bricklayers, engravers, blacksmiths, locomotive engineers, and shoemakers—accounted for 20 per cent of the "craftsmen and kindred" group.[3] And the worker worked long hours—nine or ten hours, six days a week—for little wages (in 1909 a production worker in manufacturing earned, on the average, $9.84 a week; in 1940 such a worker earned $25.20; in 1960 he earned $89.72; and in 1970 he earned $133.73).[4] He had little job security, for survival was predicated on productivity. The last hired was frequently the first fired in time of exigency, and members of some ethnic groups were not hired at all.

Although racial and ethnic discrimination was widespread at the turn of the century, bias against the female worker was perhaps even stronger than other forms of bias. In 1900 women constituted only 18

[2]Seymour Wolfbein, *Work in American Society* (Glenview, Ill.: Scott, Foresman, 1971), p. 46.

[3]*Ibid.*, p. 48.

[4]Data for 1910 and 1940 are from *The Statistical History of the United States*, Series D. 626–634, "Hours and Earnings for Production Workers in Manufacturing: 1909–1957" (Stamford, Conn.: Fairfield, 1965), p. 93. Data for 1960 and 1970 are from *Statistical Abstract of the United States*, 93d ed. (Washington, D.C.: U.S. Department of Commerce, 1972), p. 235, Table 376.

percent of the labor force.[5] The office as well as the factory was the province of the male, for the belief was widely held that women were neither intellectually nor physically capable of operating what business machines there were. Women sewed, knitted, pressed, taught school, served as nurses, and performed domestic tasks.

Finally, it can be noted that the traditional professions—doctor, lawyer, minister—predominated over newer technical specialties at that time. It was as well the heyday of the employment of children in the United States. Children worked as office boys, errand runners, and messengers, in sweatshops, on boats, and even in brothels. Of the 29 million people who were at work or looking for work in 1900, 1.75 million (or about 6.75 percent) were between *ten and fifteen* years of age.[6]

The years that separate 1900–1910 from our day do not simply tick off the passage of time. Two world wars and several less global conflicts, economic depression and economic recessions, changes in consumption and production, the development of urbanism as a way of life (beyond the confines of the city itself), the harnessing of the energy of the atom, the change in approach toward the fossil fuels—all these have operated to produce changes in the nature of American work far greater than in any similar period of time in the history of this nation and, perhaps, in the history of the human species.

Consider, for example, how the development of the internal-combustion engine, which led to the development of the automobile and the airplane, has altered our conception of distance. We think in terms not of mileage but of time. Commuting time from urban fringe to central city has progressively decreased, so that the commuter (even with lowered speed limits) may live three to five times farther away from his job today than was possible in 1910. We are told today that the world is our neighborhood. In 1910 only five cars were registered per 1,000 population, but in 1970 there was one car

[5]*Statistical History*, Series D. 26–35, "Civilian Labor Force, by Color and Sex, and Marital Status of Women: 1890–1957," p. 72; Donald J. Bogue, *The Population of the United States* (Glencoe, Ill.: Free Press, 1959), p. 423; and National Manpower Council, *Womanpower* (New York: Columbia University Press, 1954), pp. 110–42.

[6]*Statistical History*, Series D. 36–45, "Gainful Workers by Age, Sex and Farm-Nonfarm Occupations: 1820–1930," p. 72.

registered for about every two persons in the U.S. population. Consequently, the coachman, the livery-stable operator, the wheel-wright, and the farrier (a blacksmith who shoes horses) have all been supplanted by more than 5 million engaged in the manufacture, maintenance, and operation of transportation media (not including licensed drivers of passenger vehicles). The teamster no longer drives a team to deliver his wares, and the railroad fireman no longer stokes a locomotive boiler, although the names survive.

Perhaps the most striking developments during the period 1900–1980 have been (1) the increase in craftsmen and kindred workers; (2) the development of diversification of professional specialties and those occupations aspiring toward professional status; and (3) the increase of women in the labor force.

The necessity to operate and service new machinery to meet new industrial and consumer demands is of course responsible for the increase in craftsmen. The development of radio and television and the use of electronic and automated equipment account for a con-siderable portion of this increase, as does the proliferation of new forms of transportation and construction techniques. Thus, the expansion of heavy construction requiring the use of concrete, particularly the pre-stressed form (concrete molded in place to a steel core), and the use of mechanical equipment in excavation, con-struction, and materials transfer required new skills. At the same time, however, the employment of stonemasons and paperhangers dropped because it was no longer fashionable to use ornamental stonework on buildings or to paper the walls inside them. The growth of aviation and the emergence of new techniques in the production of food—fast freezing, dehydration, precooking—further illustrate this change.

Professions have increased in number and have diversified since 1910. Only since the second decade of the century have medical schools offered opportunities for medical specialization. Prior to that time such training was usually acquired in Europe. The "general practitioner," the family doctor who knew his patients from birth to death, who came out at all hours to treat the sick or the potentially ill, was the normative picture of the physician until medical school curricula were altered under the influence of the Flexner report (1910) on medical education and specialized training began to be offered in the large medical centers of New York and Chicago. The prestige accorded to specialists led to a decline of interest in general practice until very recently, when, out of concern for the improvement of medical care available to the poor and to ethnic minorities, some medical schools began to offer specialization in what was now referred to as "family medicine." So, there are today not only physicians who deal with the entire body (the internist) but also others who deal with every conceivable facet of it, from head (neurosurgeon, neurologist, neuropsychiatrist) to bones (orthopedist) and so on.

So also has the legal profession proliferated. As Justice Holmes put it, the lawyer is not God and is therefore not omniscient. But as life around him has become more complex, so have the problems with which he has had to deal. There are now the criminal lawyer, the constitutional lawyer, the lawyer in corporate real estate or in patents or in labor, to name a few. If the reader wishes further examples, an examination of the compendium of courses offered by a single college or university department should be sufficient to illustrate the extent of this specialization. In addition, the quickening pace of social life has led to the appearance of wholly new professional technologies, perhaps unanticipated in 1900, in such areas as social work, library science, operations research, personnel and employee relations, and the like.

The third major development in this century is the increasing utilization of women in the labor force. Not only has the absolute number of employed women increased but their employment has become a great deal more diverse as well. Over half of all women at work in 1910 were employed in operative and service occupations; today over half of all women at work are found in the clerical and professional sectors. When World War II brought forth the now legendary "Rosie the Riveter," representing women who took over on the assembly line when males were inducted into military service, antagonism toward women in industry began to wane, aided by the equal-opportunity legislation that eventually followed.

LABOR FORCE EXPERIENCE
OF SELECTED GROUPS

The Bureau of Labor Statistics periodically reports the fortunes of particular population aggregates in the labor force, but especially

TABLE 5. EMPLOYMENT TOTALS AND UNEMPLOYMENT RATES,
SEASONALLY ADJUSTED, FOR PERSONS 16 YEARS AND OVER,
BY MAJOR OCCUPATIONAL CATEGORY, ANNUAL AVERAGE, 1981,

	Employment Totals	Unemployment Rate
Total employed	100,397,000	7.6%
White-collar workers	52,949,000	4.0
Professional and technical	16,420,000	2.8
Management and administrators, except farm	11,540,000	2.7
Sales workers	6,425,000	4.6
Clerical workers	18,564,000	5.7
Blue-collar workers	31,261,000	10.3
Craft and kindred workers	12,662,000	7.5
Operatives, except transport	10,540,000	12.2
Transport equipment operatives	3,476,000	8.7
Nonfarm laborers	4,583,000	14.7
Service workers	13,438,000	8.9
Farm workers	2,749,000	5.3

SOURCE: Adapted from Tables 3, 4, *Monthly Labor Review* 105 (June 1982): 75, 76.

those coming under affirmative action and equal employment legislation. And certainly no treatment of the American labor force would be complete without at least some consideration of the experiences of a few such groups within it. The order in which they are discussed is arbitrary.

Persons of Hispanic origin. As part of its continuing Current Population Survey, representatives of the Bureau of the Census ask respondents "What is your origin or descent?" The respondents are shown a flashcard and if they indicate any of the following categories—Mexican-American; Chicano; Mexican; Mexicano; Puerto Rican; Cuban; Central or South American; Other Spanish—they are identified as being of Hispanic origin. Persons reporting themselves as Mexican-American, Chicano, Mexican or Mexicano are grouped into one category, Mexican origin, while those who choose Central or South American or Other Spanish are grouped into the category "other" Hispanic origin. It is on the basis of such indications or perceptions that data on persons of Hispanic background are generated and reported.

Persons of Hispanic origin numbered over twelve million, or 5.6 percent of all those living in the United States (excluding Puerto Rico) in March, 1978. Persons of Mexican origin formed the largest ethnic

TABLE 6. EMPLOYEES ON NONAGRICULTURAL PAYROLLS,
BY INDUSTRY DIVISION AND MAJOR MANUFACTURING GROUP,
ANNUAL AVERAGE, 1981,

Total	91,543,000
Mining	1,104,000
Construction	4,307,000
Manufacturing	20,261,000
Production workers	14,083,000
Durable goods	12,136,000
Production workers	8,316,000
Lumber and wood products	679,300
Furniture and fixtures	476,600
Stone, clay and glass products	650,200
Primary metal industries	1,128,200
Fabricated metal products	1,583,600
Machinery, except electrical	2,512,600
Electric and electronic equipment	2,133,900
Transportation equipment	1,837,800
Instruments and related products	718,000
Miscellaneous manufacturing	415,300
Nondurable goods	8,125,000
Production workers	5,766,000
Food and kindred products	1,684,100
Tobacco manufacturers	71,100
Textile mill products	839,300
Apparel and other textile products	1,255,800
Paper and allied products	692,300
Printing and publishing	1,288,000
Chemical and allied products	1,107,300
Petroleum and coal products	210,800
Rubber and miscellaneous plastic products	744,400
Leather and leather products	232,300
Transportation and public utilities	5,151,000
Wholesale and retail trade	20,738,000
Wholesale trade	5,343,000
Retail trade	15,395,000
Finance, insurance and real estate	5,331,000
Services	18,598,000
Government	16,054,000
Federal	2,772,000
State and local	13,282,000

SOURCE: Adapted from "Table 10: Employment by Industry Division and Major Manufacturing Group," *Monthly Labor Review* 105 (June, 1982): 80.

category (over seven million people), with 1.8 million Puerto Ricans, 700,000 Cubans and about 2.4 million persons of other Hispanic origin comprising the balance of the Hispanic population. According to M. J. Newman, the source for this discussion,[7] the Hispanic

[7]Morris J. Newman, "A Profile of Hispanics in the U.S. Work Force," *Monthly Labor Review* 101 (December, 1978): 3–14.

aggregate grew rapidly in the five years from March, 1973 to March, 1978—nearly fourteen per cent as compared with a growth of only 3.3 per cent of the non-Hispanic portion of the U.S. population. The Puerto Rican segment of the population grew by 18 per cent, "other Hispanics" by 19 per cent and the Mexican component grew by nearly fourteen per cent; only the Cuban group failed to expand in the period, in fact declining by six per cent. The median age of Hispanics ranges between 20 years (for Puerto Ricans) and 23 (for "other Hispanics") as compared with a median age of 30 for non-Hispanics (although, to be sure, Cubans exhibited a median age of 37 owing to their immigration for political reasons during the sixties; older and better-established persons saw their existence threatened by the ascendancy of a Marxist government in their homeland and, hence, fled the country).

Although persons of Hispanic origin appear to participate in the labor force to a greater degree than do non-Hispanics (as measured by respective labor force participation rates, by sex—i.e., the percentage of persons age sixteen and over who are at work or who are actively looking for work), Newman contends that the statistics are "illusory"[8] because Hispanics are, by and large, younger than the population in general and (of course) younger adults, both males and females, tend to higher rates of participation in the labor force than do older adults. Nevertheless, the participation rate of Puerto Rican females has declined in recent years, primarily due to the declining economy of New York City where, in 1977, fully one-half of Puerto Ricans in the continental United States resided.

The unemployment rate of Hispanics continues its long-term trend of exceeding that of all white workers (10.1% as against 6.2% in 1977), but it is still below that of black workers (13.0% in 1977). "Puerto Rican workers had the highest rate of unemployment among the Hispanic ethnic groups in 1977, 13.6 per cent, compared with 10.1 per cent for workers of Mexican origin, 8.8 per cent for those of Cuban origin, and 8.6 per cent for persons of other Hispanic origin. The higher overall rate of unemployment for Puerto Rican workers, and lower rates for workers of Cuban and other origin, generally held true for most major age and sex categories as well."[9] This can be

[8]*Ibid.*, p. 4.
[9]*Ibid.*, p. 7.

attributed to the fact, Newman argues, that Mexican and Puerto Rican Hispanics are both younger and less educated than Cubans and Hispanics of other origins; for, in general, unemployment is greater among workers below thirty-five years of age precisely because they exhibit less educational attainment and, hence, have fewer marketable skills and experiences.

Workers of Mexican origin are subject to frequent but relatively short spells of unemployment (averaging 5.1 weeks in 1977), while adult male Puerto Ricans endured extraordinarily long periods. The average annual median unemployment duration for this group was 16.4 weeks, as compared with the duration for unemployed Mexican men, 7.3 weeks, and with Cuban males, 9.6 weeks. Newman argues that Puerto Rican-Mexican unemployment duration differences are less related to the ages of the two groups—the Puerto Ricans are no older than the Mexican group—but rather to the residential distribution of the populations. Most Puerto Ricans live in New Jersey and New York, states with relatively liberal unemployment laws with less restrictive coverage provisions (and, hence, longer unemployment durations for all males); while Mexican-Americans reside primarily in Southwestern states with more restrictive eligibility requirements for unemployment coverage, lower coverage for those who meet legal requirements and, consequently, shorter unemployment duration for all males, including Mexican-Americans.

Finally, Newman observes that, "although there was some shifting in the Hispanic occupational mix in the 1973–77 period, Hispanics have improved their occupational distribution only marginally, relative to the overall work force."[10] In 1977 persons of Hispanic origin were more concentrated in occupations requiring fewer skills and, thus, were paid less than the population in general; this was especially true for females who were largely employed as clerical workers or as nontransport operatives—dressmakers, machine operators, assemblers. One-third of employed Cuban and Puerto Rican women were so employed in 1977, compared with approximately twenty per cent of employed Mexican females and about 11.1% of all employed women. Perhaps because of their youth and low educational preparation. Mexican and Puerto Rican males are underrepresented in high-skill occupational categories—professional, technical and crafts-

[10]*Ibid.*, p. 9.

workers—(although they were more likely to be working at these levels in 1977 than in 1973) and overrepresented in low-paying nontransport operative and farmworker occupational categories. What movement there has been between 1973 and 1977, Newman attributes to "a reflection of overall changes in the American labor market, as lower skilled blue-collar employment opportunities decline[d] because of increasing use of automated techniques, and white-collar office jobs increase[d]." [11]

Newman suggests that the status of the various Hispanic groups in the labor force results from different histories of migration to and settlement in the United States. For example, Cuban immigration after 1959 was primarily political in nature, the immigrants had been largely successful in Cuba, as professional, technical or skilled blue-collar workers, prior to the Revolution, and, so, these migrants successfully penetrated and were integrated with the non-Hispanic population. Puerto Rican Hispanics, on the other hand, immigrated much as did groups before them. They settled in large cities along the East coast, notably New York, and accepted employment requiring little or no skill. But machines took over many of these tasks, and performed them more efficiently and cheaper than could human workers; and many employers moved from the Northeast and did not take unskilled, and therefore expendable, workers with them. Consequently, in 1977, some thirty-nine per cent of all Puerto Rican families lived below the poverty level, compared with nineteen per cent of the Mexican families and nine per cent of all U.S. families.

Given the virtual cessation of migration of persons from the rural South to the urban, industrial North, it can be expected that Hispanic immigration, particularly from Mexico can be expected to continue and to exert an ever greater impact on the transformation of the American cultural fabric.

Women in the labor force. In 1957 the National Manpower Council observed:

> The remarkable increase in the employment of women has come about because more and more women have made a personal decision to work. Before the turn of the century, women worked primarily before marriage. Older women worked only if they were forced to by adversity. Today, of course, some women

[11]*Ibid.*

work because they must support themselves and others, but ever larger numbers work because they choose to.

The changes which have occurred in the role of women in paid employment since the turn of the century can be explained only in terms of the many developments in American life which have provided women with vastly expanded opportunities to find their own place in the economy. In the future, as today, the personal decisions of individual women will determine how many will work, at what time in their lives they will work, how intensively they will work, and what goals they will seek to realize through work. Undoubtedly, the environment in which women will grow up and live—especially with regard to education, marriage, family structure, and employment opportunities and practices— will continue to change and to present them with new and varied choices concerning work. [12]

That prediction offered almost a quarter-century ago has come to pass both faster and to a greater extent than its framers then might have realized. Certainly, the changed status of women did not come unbidden; following World War II women in Western countries grew increasingly restive about being accorded a status inferior to that of the male and, provided an impetus and a perspective by such writers as Simone de Beauvoir [13] and Betty Friedan, [14] they organized to work actively for full, complete and equal participation of women in every facet of interpersonal life. Though victory is far from complete, largely through their own efforts women have achieved a level of parity with men that (perhaps) could hardly have been envisioned by the National Manpower Council back in 1957.

In the United States changes in existing laws and new laws facilitated the absorption of larger numbers of females into the labor force: the Equal Employment Opportunity Act of 1972, which amended the Civil Rights Act of 1964; amendments (1972) to extend coverage of the Equal Pay Act of 1963 to occupations that recruited females primarily; Women's Educational Equity Act (1974, amended 1978); Public Law 95-555 (1978) that prohibits discrimination based on pregnancy; tax legislation in 1976 and 1978 that made a tax-

[12]National Manpower Council, *Womanpower, op. cit.,* pp. 55–56.
[13]Simone de Beauvoir, *The Second Sex* (New York: Knopf, 1952).
[14]Betty Friedan, *The Feminine Mystique* (New York: Norton, 1963).

deductible item of monies paid by an individual for care of dependent children while the person is at work; amendments to the Comprehensive Employment and Training Act (CETA) of 1973 making funds available for the development of jobs and training for disadvantaged women, single parents. The Equal Rights Amendment to the Constitution must be considered in this context as well for the ideological support for integration of females into the work force provided by the very possibility of such an amendment, even though it has yet to be ratified.

Given the greater legal legitimation accorded females in the labor force (quite apart from changes in the overall normative structure of the country) the labor force participation rate of females increased from 43.3% in 1970 to 47.3% in 1976, with a slight downturn in 1977 at 46.4%. At the same time, the participation rates (computed to approximate the U.S. concept) of other countries in the industrialized world similarly increased during the same 1970–77 period: Canada, 38.3% to 46.0%; France, 40.0% to 44.1%; Great Britain, 41.1% to 46.8%; Sweden, 49.0% to 55.9%), although Germany and Japan were both notable exceptions (Germany's rate declined from 38.6% in 1970 to 37.4% in 1977, and Japan's fluctuated between 49.3% and 45.0% during the period). [15] "Against this background, more than a million women per year, on average, joined the [U.S.] labor force; the greatest percentage increase in women's labor force [participation] rates occurred for those with children under age 6. The dual-worker family became a more solid part of American life, and the number of women maintaining their own families, very frequently with young chidren in the home, rose to the highest level ever recorded in [the United States]." [16]

Certainly, later marriage, postponement of childbearing, the increasing willingness on the part of parents to limit family size—from 1970 to 1978 average number of children in families either with both partners present or in families maintained by females dropped from about 2.3 to about 1.9 [17]—have contributed to the increased participation in the labor force both of women in general and of women with

[15]Joyanna Moy, "Recent Labor Market Trends in Nine Industrial Nations," *Monthly Labor Review*, 102 (May, 1979): 11.
[16]Elizabeth Waldman, *et al.*, "Working Mothers in the 1970's: A Look at the Statistics," *Monthly Labor Review*, 102 (October, 1979): 40.
[17]*Ibid.*, p. 41.

children. Given the decreasing social stigma borne by the working mother, it has become less of a problem for mothers to continue in the labor force during childbearing years or to re-enter the labor force sooner than was the case in previous decades. Moreover, as women have improved their educational status they have chosen to work; for, other things being equal, the higher the educational level, the greater the likelihood of labor force attachment[18] as well as the greater likelihood of the feeling of relative deprivation of the female vis-à-vis males with similar educational attainments.[19] Thus, "[i]n March 1978, there were 2.1 million more wives with children under 18 in the labor force than there had been just 8 years earlier. . . . This growth in the number of working married mothers—almost all of which was among white women—took place despite the fact that the total population of wives with children declined by nearly a million over the period."[20] Not only has there been an increase in this labor force participation rate but also an intensification of attachment to (or involvement in) the labor force. Between 1970 and 1977 the percentage of mothers in two-person families who were working 50–52 weeks a year and who were caring for children under eighteen years of age increased from thirty-two per cent to almost thirty-five per cent; if we look only at mothers in two-person families working 50–52 weeks a year and who were responsible for chidren between the ages of six and seventeen, we see a percentage increase from 39.5% to 41.3%.[21]

Between 1970 and 1978 a dramatic growth in the number of one-parent families of some two and one-half million was experienced in the United States, a growth that "was far greater than that registered during the preceding two decades."[22] In March, 1978 there were 5.7 million single-parent families, of which only 540,000 were maintained by fathers. Forty-two of 100 families maintained only by the mother had incomes below the poverty level (approximately $6,200 in 1977) as compared with fifteen of 100 families maintained solely by the father. "White mothers [maintaining one-parent families] were considerably more likely than their black or Hispanic counterparts to be in the labor force; nearly 68 per cent of the white,

[18]*Ibid.*
[19]*Ibid.*
[20]*Ibid.*
[21]Waldman, *et al., op. cit.,* p. 44.
[22]*Ibid.,* p. 45.

compared with 60 per cent of the black and just 30 per cent of the Hispanic mothers maintaining families either worked or looked for work in March 1978. . . ."[23]

Bowers[24] points out, that while the labor force participation rates of white females has increased markedly, particularly for those females in the 16-24 year age group, the participation rate for black females of the same age range has "dropped sharply" *relative* to whites, even though there has been no downward trend as such for young adult black females. The percentage of white females age 20 to 24 with some work experience increased steadily from about 60 per cent in 1958 to 79 per cent in 1977, while there was little change reported for black women in that twenty-year period; about 62 per cent of black women reported some work experience in 1958 and 1977. Bowers also notes[25] "that prior to 1965 female teenagers had lower unemployment rates than their male counterparts, whereas the reverse was true from 1965 on. Among young adults age 20 to 24, the differential also widened, but not consistently." He explains this by observing that, as we have seen, while the labor force participation rates of females have increased substantially this has produced not so much higher unemployment rates among women but, rather, what he calls "occupational crowding: women tend to be employed in a relatively small subset of occupations."[26] Then, the more females who contribute to the labor force could as well contribute to a relative increase in unemployment; there are simply not enough places for the new participants to fill. According to Fullerton[27] this can be expected to hold true through 1995, regardless of whether one uses a high-, medium- or low-growth scenario.

FUTURE TRENDS AND PROSPECTS

But what of the future? The prediction of events in social life is a difficult procedure at best, but it is rendered still more problematic in

[23]*Ibid.*, p. 48.
[24]Norman Bowers, "Young and Marginal: An Overview of Youth Employment," *Monthly Labor Review*, 102 (October, 1979): 9.
[25]*Ibid.*
[26]*Ibid.*
[27]Howard N. Fullerton, Jr., "The 1995 Labor Force: A First Look," *Monthly Labor Review*, 103 (December, 1980), 11–21.

the present instance by the unstable state of the international situation, by expected changes in energy consumption and their impact on both the productive mechanism and individual life-styles, and by long- and short-term fluctuations in the economic cycle. Nevertheless, available data do permit some guesses.

The first edition of *Work and Workers* relied on Bureau of Labor Statistics projections of labor force changes and alterations of the occupational spectrum through 1985; the interested reader is referred to that discussion if only to assess its predictive adequacy as 1985 moves ever closer.[28] As this edition is prepared, BLS attention is directed to 1995. Howard N. Fullerton, Jr. suggests that, as a result of fluctuations in the birth rate since the 1930s (and, thus, the changing age composition of the population), by the middle of the present decade, "persons in the labor force are projected to exceed those not in the labor force—including babies."[29] As earlier data predicted for 1985, Fullerton asserts that, by 1995 "this labor force would have a greater proportion of women and minorities; indeed, about two-thirds of the labor force growth would be generated by women, reflecting their continued labor force participation."[30]

Of one thing we can be sure: the 1985–95 labor force will consist of experienced individuals. The baby-boom generation of the 'fifties will be in the prime earning years, while the relatively small cohort of persons born during the Great Depression will begin to leave the labor force. The youth labor force will decrease further between 1985 and 1995. Women will comprise about forty-seven percent of the labor force by 1995, while fourteen to fifteen percent would be black. Since more than half of all married women were already in the labor force in 1979, as were 45.2% of mothers with preschool children, it can be expected that both groups (which of course overlap) will contribute significantly to labor force growth in the 1990s.[31] This greater continuity of women in the labor force coupled with higher educational attainment of all age, sex and ethnic components will enhance the productivity of the labor force in 1995, according to Fullerton.[32] If there is not to be a shortage of skilled and professional

[28]Pp. 47–51 of the first edition.
[29]Fullerton, *op. cit.*, p. 11.
[30]*Ibid.*
[31]*Ibid.*, p. 17.
[32]*Ibid.*, p. 20.

workers in 1995, Fullerton argues that they will have to be recruited
in greater numbers from women and blacks than they are at present.

By 1995 employers may experience difficulty finding young
workers. As the United States debates the wisdom of reinstating
compulsory military service as opposed to an all-volunteer force, it
would be well to note that, as the largest single employer of youth, by
1995 the military may be especially hard-hit by the scarcity of
youthful workers. Moreover, given projected increments in education
levels for all population levels, it is still the young worker who brings
the least experience to the work task; hence, as the youth component
decreases, employers will find it more difficult to obtain unskilled
workers.

Valerie Personick[33] attempted to project "the outlook for industry
output and employment through 1990." Her projections "assume"
lower unemployment and taxes, higher investment and productivity,
and continued oil scarcity."[34] She suggests that by 1990 we shall be
firmly rooted in the electronic age; computers and peripheral equipment, optical equipment, typewriters, communication, scientific and
controlling instruments, as well as medical and dental apparatus are
projected to head the list of durable goods that will be demanded as
the 'eighties are transformed into the 'nineties. In fact, the computer
industry "is expected to lead all industries studied in terms of output
increase. . . . New uses and markets for computer technology will
continue to spur output in the coming decade, at projected rates of
increase ranging from 7.6 to 10.1 per cent a year."[35] Considerable
impetus will provided by the projection that Federal defense spend-
ing will rise considerably and sharply and at the expense of nonde-
fense Federal purchases of goods and services (even though the size
of the military forces is predicted to remain about the same).[36]

As in previous decades, service industries are projected to be the
most rapidly growing employment sector, with health care being
expected to lead the advance in that sector. Although employment in
the offices of health care practitioners is expected to grow considerably, Personick projects the most rapid gains for "other related

[33]Valerie A. Personick, "The Outlook for Industry Output and Employment Through 1990," *Monthly Labor Review* 104 (August, 1981): 28–41.
[34]*Ibid.*, p. 28.
[35]*Ibid.*, p. 33.
[36]*Ibid.*, p. 32.

medical care services, such as nursing homes, medical laboratories, therapists' offices and nurses' services."[37] Having said this, however, "[t]he greatest increase in employment opportunities over the next eleven years is expected to be in the trade sector, primarily because of its initial large size."[38] And, as in the past, it is expected that the number of farmworkers will continue to decline through 1990. As previously observed[39] "[e]mployment of farmworkers had declined for decades as farm productivity has risen as a result of larger more efficient farms, improvement in mechanized equipment, and technological innovations in seed, feed, and fertilizer."[40] The trend continues.

Max Carey observes that, even if one adopts a scenario of low occupational growth coupled with low productivity, some twenty occupations among those surveyed by the Bureau of Labor Statistics can be expected to exhibit rapid growth through 1990.[41]

Occupation	Percent Growth in Employment 1978–90
Data processing machine mechanics	147.6
Paralegal personnel	132.4
Computer systems analysts	107.8
Computer operators	87.9
Office machine and cash register servicers	80.8
Computer programmers	73.6
Aero-astronautic engineers	70.4
Food preparation and service workers in fast-food restaurants	68.8
Employment interviewers	66.6
Tax preparers	64.5
Correction officials and jailers	60.3
Architects	60.2
Dental hygienists	57.9
Physical therapists	57.6
Dental assistants	57.5
Peripheral electronic data processing equipment operators	57.3
Child-care attendants	56.3
Veterinarians	56.1
Travel agents and accommodations appraisers	55.6
Nurses' aides and orderlies	54.6

[37]*Ibid.*, p. 37.
[38]*Ibid.*
[39]See above, pp. 41-42.
[40]Max L. Carey, "Occupational Employment Growth Through 1990," *Monthly Labor Review* 104 (August, 1981): 47.
[41]*Ibid.*, p. 48.

The implications of this analysis are obvious. As our population becomes older, the population at work will be older. Yet there will be relatively more workers aged twenty to thirty-four as the "baby boom" cohort of the 'fifties and 'sixties is absorbed into the labor force. What do we do, then, with the relatively older worker when those who are younger clamor for employment? This is a problem fundamental to the life of the United States whose parameters are only now beginning to be defined. Of course, the federal government anticipated the problems of an aging population as far back as 1937, when the Old Age and Survivors' Insurance Program (Social Security) was introduced. However, the surplus built over the years by employer and employee contributions has become a deficit as increasing numbers of older workers dip into the fund. Labor unions and, increasingly, business are emphasizing retirement and annuity programs as one way to help meet the needs of older workers, but even as this is written the rights of workers under such programs are being challenged and are the subject of controversy. It is clear that this problem has yet to be solved.

But an even more important item on the agenda of the older worker is a confrontation with some basic values regarding age. As the age of majority has been lowered in many states from twenty-one to eighteen, bespeaking changed attitudes regarding the capabilities of this age group, so must we ask the question: At what age is one "old"? At what age ought one to be automatically retired, despite demonstrated ability on the job? Can we as a nation afford to continue an arbitrary retirement policy no matter how extensive our old-age assistance program? Is any human being simply "surplus"? If so, when does he become so? A manpower policy that more efficiently utilizes older persons is absolutely critical.

At the same time, however, the younger worker, who is apt to be far better trained and, far more strongly oriented toward serving others than his older predecessors, requires a renewed interest in tapping his potential at a time when the labor force is anticipated to grow faster than available positions. Current declining college enrollments at all levels suggest not only a response to the energy crisis or to the increased costs of attending a college but also an apprehension or a perception, buttressed by some hard empirical evidence, that a higher education may no longer be the primary route to enhanced socio-economic status, as a degree has traditionally been thought to be. Why sweat, sacrifice, and endure when a diploma in hand no longer guarantees that the doors to middle management will open? We are seeing an interest in self-employment, a return to handicrafts, the "cottage industries" of an earlier time—almost a disenchantment with the organizational structuring of work on the part of those who could conceivably bring the keen mind and the enthusiasm of the young to the work place. The disillusion of those just entering the labor force is every bit as pernicious as the disillusion of the older worker. This matter, too, requires the best efforts a nation can muster to arrive at solutions.

It is perhaps in the case of the underemployment of women, blacks, and other minorities that the development of a coherent policy has been most evident. Governments at all levels have exhibited a strong commitment to programs guaranteeing equality of employment opportunities to all and requiring that employers take "affirmative action" to find qualified members of those groups heretofore underrepresented in their organizations. But it may well be that the interest of government in increasing opportunities available to these groups was an expedient response to the pressures exerted by spokesmen of such groups rather than to the disjuncture between the American dream as expressed in judicial decisions and public documents (like the Declaration of Independence) and the American reality of slums and segregation and attendant job discrimination. Rapid as progress in this area has been, there is still more to accomplish to minimize the discrepancy between aspiration and fact.

Finally, at least for present purposes, labor-force statistics that detail the diminution of agricultural workers over time may be symptomatic not only of disenchantment with rural life but also of a progressive replacement of the farm worker by more efficient ways of agribusiness. Technological displacement of the worker by machines or new organizational or productive formats is also a growing national concern. How will the market absorb those displaced workers, or will it absorb them at all? We will have more to say about this in the last chapter of this volume.

3

DIMENSIONS OF
OCCUPATIONAL ANALYSIS

So FAR WE HAVE considered general conceptions of work. We have examined the notion of the division of labor. We have also looked at work through an examination of U.S. labor force statistics—yesterday, today, and perhaps tomorrow. This discussion has been primarily descriptive; we have tried to suggest what the situation is now and, occasionally, how the present emerged from the past. However, the sociologist not only describes but also seeks to understand. He wishes to make some sense of work as a social phenomenon, an activity that brings people together for individual and social survival, usually with reference to some sort of gain accruing to the persons involved. In order to achieve this understanding, we must see how the techniques and concepts of sociological analysis are applied to work and workers.

The approach we shall take here stems largely from the studies of Everett C. Hughes, his associates, and his students, begun at the University of Chicago in the early decades of this century. Their approach assumes, first, that the sociologist is an intensely curious individual who attempts to understand the social worlds in which he is interested by describing fully and completely what he sees. Like a reporter, the sociologist tells the news. However, he tells it by means of a special set of descriptive and analytical categories that place the description of the particular within an ongoing research enterprise, transcending the particular because it looks both backward and forward in time—backward to what has already been learned, forward to prediction, to action, to new frontiers of knowledge.

Second, such an approach argues that, whatever categories are used to subsume the raw data, these categories cannot be generated in splendid isolation, apart from the real world of flesh-and-blood human beings.

Third, this real world is one in which apparently unique inter-personal events will eventually sort themselves, through the "socio-logical eye,"[1] into recurring forms of interaction; even social struc-tures are no more than recurring, and therefore predictable, associa-tional forms that have, so to speak, crystallized.

Therefore, fourth, the imagery of the sociologist must be that of process. How do these forms come to be, how do they change, and how may the event of the moment be seen within a larger temporal perspective?

Finally, this approach assumes that, wherever people come to-gether, there are data that the sociologist can use. Nothing human is alien to him, so long as his inquiries do no damage to those he studies.

In some ways, this approach may seem anachronistic in the day of the computer. At a time when sociological studies may utilize hundreds or thousands of cases, concern with a small number of cases treated with an analysis that is admittedly simple mathematically or conceptually "fuzzy" smacks of an impressionistic orientation de-cidedly out of fashion with many sociologists. Yet such an approach "works." We learn much about occupations that we did not know before, and in so doing learn as well about ourselves. As Hughes put it:

Social science appears to have a double burden laid upon it. The one is to analyze the processes of human behavior, and especially of persistence and change thereof, in terms relatively free of time

[1]See the collection of papers by Everett C. Hughes, *The Sociological Eye,* 2 vols. (Chicago: Aldine-Atherton, 1971).

and place. The other is to tell the news in such form and perspective—quantitatively and comparatively—as to give clues for the taking of those chances of which action consists. The balance between these two functions varies from man to man, from time and place to time and place. Social science thrives on the strain between the two. . . .

[F]or an understanding of human work one must look at a wide variety of kinds of work and their social matrices. Only so will he get that relative freedom from time, place, and particular circumstance that is required of those who would analyze processes. Even that part of social science which is a telling of the news for action's (prediction's) sake depends for its efficacy upon putting of the particular into some larger perspective of other cases described in generalized terms.

. . . In so studying work, we are not merely applying sociology to work. We are studying work by sociological methods. We do not learn our method in some pure or generalized society or part of society and then apply it and the findings to industry, crime, or religion. Rather, we study group life and process where they occur, learning our method and developing our knowledge of society as we go. We may learn about society by studying industry and human work generally. In our particular society, work organization looms so large as a separate and specialized system of things, and work experience is so fateful a part of every man's life, that we cannot make much headway as students of society and of social psychology without using work as one of our main laboratories.[2]

Because our imagery as sociologists is one of process, we must assume that the interaction that is carried on with reference to work tends over time to take on recurring interpersonal and structural forms. Through the investigation, again and again, of how this happens, general statements are possible. Interest in industrial work as against professions, or in work in large-scale organizations or bureaucracies as against less structured work forms (musicians, Nobel prize winners, stripteasers) are all ultimately reducible to the documentation of variations on that recurring theme of process. This is the focus of the discussion to follow.

[2]Everett C. Hughes, "The Sociological Study of Work: An Editorial Foreword," *American Journal of Sociology* 57 (March, 1952): 423–26.

THE "NATURAL HISTORY" OF AN OCCUPATION

One way of understanding social groups and structures is to treat them as one might a newly discovered tribe on some faraway island. We begin as if we know nothing and attempt to discover as much as we can. In the manner of the anthropologist, we try to develop an ethnography or "natural history" of the group or structure. What is this group? Where did it come from? What are its history, its ideology, its hopes and dreams? How does it behave, and how is it organized to fulfil the demands made on it by its members and by the larger society surrounding it? Such a method has been employed to generate information on everything from the social order of the slum to criminal careers to the indoctrination of Polish peasants into the complexities of American urban life.

The "natural history" viewpoint is historical in outlook and descriptive in technique; consequently, it provides a convenient bridge between reportage and analysis, because the researcher has at least the sensitivities of the sociologist to guide his observations. But simple though the method may be, it is not unsophisticated, precisely because the sociologist is trained to observe and to dig beneath the surface of interaction by asking the appropriate questions. This is the way occupational analysis usually begins, and there are many sociologists who regard this approach as perhaps the most meaningful information-gathering strategy available.

In developing the "natural history" of an occupation, the investigator assumes (for the purposes of his study) that the occupation is a self-contained entity; he studies it without considering its location within the social structure. Obviously, of course, no grouping can be abstracted from its social matrix; however, the questions the sociologist "puts to" the occupation make this abstraction possible at a heuristic, analytic, or comparative level.

The sociologist begins, simply enough, by describing the occupation as it is. What name do the practitioners of the occupation give to their work? By what names do others in allied fields, or those not in the occupation at all, call the area being studied? Then, of course, one must ask what the people practicing the occupation do—their craft, if you will—as well (perhaps even more important) as what they *think* they do. What skills, both technical and social, are required to engage in the work? What implements are necessary? How or what do the

practitioners think of their occupation? How do practitioners respond to the evaluations of their occupation that may be made by
others? For it must be remembered that the worth people or groups
attribute to each other is always reciprocal, as are the interactions on
which such attributions are based; hence, the internal valuation of an
occupation depends upon the values imputed to it by the containing
social structure.

After description comes *comparison*. The sociologist assumes the
posture of the historian for this purpose. What occupations preceded
or gave rise to the particular field under study? What is the technical
and social history of the occupation? More interesting, however, is
what members of the occupational group conventionally (or con-
veniently) *assume* its history to be. In other words, who are conceived
as the real or mythical founders, heroes, and villains of the occupation? Who are the real or imagined enemies and friends of the
occupation? And what are—or are thought to be—the turning points
or historical landmarks along the course of the occupation, from its
origins to its present state?

Finally, current trends, problems, and conflicts within the occupation are considered.

The fruitfulness of this admittedly simple dimension of occupational analysis is well illustrated in the use made of it by Joseph
Bensman and Robert Lilienfeld, although nowhere do they use the
term "natural history."[3] They suggest that, out of the development of
the skills, techniques, and symbol systems of a particular occupation,
there comes to be attitudes and perspectives indigenous to that
occupation, which gives it a unique consciousness of itself, as well as a
resulting unique world view. Although the authors argue that one
cannot deduce these occupational "habits of mind" from the linkages
between the occupation and the larger society, such attitudes and
world views must inevitably feed back upon and color the containing
social structure. The orientation that a member of an occupation
takes toward himself obviously infuses his occupation-related interpersonal behavior and would therefore "rub off" on those who utilize
his services or on the practitioners of other occupations who interact
with him. Bensman and Lilienfeld then go on to consider a variety of

[3]Joseph Bensman and Robert Lilienfeld, *Craft and Consciousness: Occupational Technique and the Development of World Images* (New York: Wiley-
Interscience, 1973).

(largely professional) occupational specialties, ranging from the composer through the performer (including the athlete) to the psychiatrist, philosopher, and sociologist. Although they limit their treatment to what they regard as occupations that are singularly capable of articulating their attitudes and world views and of disseminating their perspectives to wider audiences, they nonetheless assert, "There is no doubt . . . that such occupations as medicine, architecture, teaching, law, steamfitting, cobbling, taxicab driving, and ragpicking produce unique and peculiar combinations of attitudes appropriate to the craft as well as to the societal and social position, ideological and material interests, and commitment to the society at large. Every occupation, every skill at every substantive level produces such attitudes."[4]

Similarly, Anselm L. Strauss attempted a "natural history" of nursing.[5] He begins by observing that the "structural profile" of the nurse in the United States is unlike that of any other occupation. Nursing is almost exclusively the occupation of women. It is predominantly and increasingly a salaried occupation with relatively open recruitment; a woman can gain admission to a school of nursing—of which there are several kinds—and, if she can graduate and be licensed, may legitimately practice nursing. The market for nursing is also relatively open, and the skills are easily transferable from one locale to another. Besides bedside nursing, nurses teach or administer in hospitals and public health agencies and to some extent in homes. But in all cases, nursing is not an autonomous occupation but exists in a status and authority system such that the nurse waits for orders from others above her and looks to the others—the doctor, primarily—for the determination of her behavior as nurse, even to the establishment of possible specialties in role performance. This is to say, the nurse is controlled by others rather than free to chart her own course. These characteristics are not fortuitous, according to Strauss, but flow directly from the history of nursing.

Stated briefly, the history of nursing in the United States parallels the increasing industrialization of the country at large. It was assumed that an increasingly complex technological base would require better-

[4]*Ibid.*, pp. 337–38.
[5]Anselm L. Strauss, "The Structure and Ideology of American Nursing: An Interpretation," in Fred Davis, ed., *The Nursing Profession: Five Sociological Essays* (New York: Wiley, 1966), pp. 60–108.

educated individuals to run and to administer this technology. In addition, the reformist orientation at the close of the nineteenth century, under religious and other auspices (the Christian social gospel movement, for example), sought change in many facets of American life. Urban renewal, immigrant education, and labor legislation are indicative of the changes proposed. Nursing, too, was affected by these currents. There were demands that nursing be "upgraded" by attracting women who were better educated and who came from a higher class background than that of those who usually chose nursing. Further impetus was provided by similar demands for the reform of legal and medical education.

The response to these concerns can be measured by the emergence of schools of nursing attached to either hospitals or universities, but with their own administrations, which did more than simply funnel cheap female labor into the hospital setting, and by conferences on curricular reform, the development of special programs for nursing administrators, and the proliferation of nursing specialties akin to those developing in medicine. The drive was toward professional status, toward the sense of calling or *noblesse oblige* advocated by Florence Nightingale. But, as successful as this push was, according to Strauss, it was not so successful as it might have been because of the unwillingness of physicians, educators, and others to accord full professional status to nursing. Moreover, university schools of nursing were often amalgamated with schools of education, which tended further to slow down professionalization. The degree to which nursing can control the recruitment of those who wish to be nurses and the willingness of doctors to grant equality to nurses in the medical-decision network will ultimately determine the professional character of the occupation of nursing. Like any occupation, nursing is a "victim" of its history. And this is what the "natural history" dimension of occupational analysis permits us to understand.

THE SOCIAL ORGANIZATION OF
THE OCCUPATION

As we move up the level of analytical complexity we begin to place the occupation within the context of the larger society when we look

at the organization of the occupation—the associational and pro-
cedural frameworks that characterize the occupation.

There is, first, the *institutional complex* in which the work is done.
The investigator would look at the formal licensing systems, the
training systems, and the procedures governing relations within the
work situation itself, including both formal and informal communication networks (the communication of news and information about the
occupation through newsletter or journal, on the one hand, or
through gossip or rumor or other face-to-face interaction, on the
other). The researcher would also be interested in the sources of
supply for both technical knowledge and procedures, for clients and
for the practitioners themselves. How is one recognized within the
occupation (awards, prizes, medals) and how can be be ejected from
the occupation? In short, our interest here is in the interplay between
the procedures of the occupation and the people who carry them out,
and also in the impact of this interplay on the clients of the
occupation.

Then there is the *economic complex* in which the work is done. Who
owns and controls the tools and facilities of the work? Does each
worker own his own tools or purvey his own skills, or is the work
carried on by a corporation of similarly skilled persons, by a nonprofit
organization, or by a public body? Is it possible to change the nature
of ownership of tools, skills, or ideas involved in the work? How much
does the work cost? Following this, of course, is the important matter
of the method of payment. Are fees paid by individuals for services
rendered, or are they paid by others? Are these fees paid in a lump
sum or over time, in cash or in kind (barter)? Or does payment take
the form of salaries or commissions, bonuses, or profits from sales?
Is haggling or bargaining over payment possible? What kinds of
economic incentives are held out by the occupation to its practitioners
or to potential recruits ("Own your own business. Become a _____."
"Earn big money as a _____.")? The investigator of the economic
complex is interested in competition within the occupation, within an
interacting network of occupations, or between occupations. For
example, considering within-occupation competition, salesmen compete for customers, lawyers compete for clients, and bricklayers
compete for openings on a new low-rent housing project. If we
consider an interacting network of occupations, we see the competition of clinics with private practitioners or graduate school

professors for student protégés. As far as the competition between occupations is concerned, one need only think of the tension between medicine and osteopathy or between social workers and lawyers relative to the counseling function of both.

Crucial to any analysis of an occupation is an awareness of the *system of authority, ranking, and status* in which the work is done (another way of looking at the relation among people, position, and purpose). Any work involves categorizing the people who do it in terms of the three divisions of labor involved—the functional, the social, and the moral. When one categorizes, he implies differences, which eventually result in some sort of hierarchy of work skills, responsibilities, and breadth of license and mandate with respect to the client. The investigator of an occupation would want to study these hierarchies in detail; in fact, this may be all he studies. If we think of the public schools, for example, there are school boards, voters, other community agencies, administrative officers, and teachers of various ranks (tenured and nontenured, to mention just two), parents, and, last but certainly not least, pupils. And think of the gradations, both formal and informal, among *them*! If we think of industry, there are the corporate owners, line and staff people of various specialties and ranks, supervisors, inspectors, union officials, and workers of various grades. Each of these rankings in the authority system has attached to it formal prerogatives (what Max Weber called "status honor")[6] and is attached to other rankings by ties that are both specific and formal as well as diffuse and informal. There is obviously the formal arrangement of interaction as specified in bulletins and rulebooks and contracts and wall-size organization charts. But perhaps more decisive for the occupation is the unwritten organization: the set of informal understandings and obligations that underlie any occupation or set of occupations. Formal and informal "pecking orders" are not necessarily the same, and it often takes little sensitivity to discover the relevant differences. Who *really* runs the office? To whom does one *really* go for advice? Who *really* does the hiring and firing—who is the "hatchet man," and who is the fellow who, despite his pretensions, should have been fired years ago as deadwood?

[6]Max Weber, "Class, Status, Party," in H. H. Gerth and C. Wright Mills, eds., *From Max Weber: Essays in Sociology* (New York: Oxford, 1946), pp. 180–95.

There are three components of the status and authority system of an occupation. First, *power determines position.* By "power" we mean simply the ability of one individual to control the behavior of another despite the wish or will of that other. Thus, there is the power of the machine gun, the fist, the loud voice, or (one would hope) the pen. Now, a power relation does not depend upon the agreement of those who interact; as long as one individual is controlled by another and acknowledges by his behavior his recognition of that fact, whether he likes it or not, a power relationship exists.

With respect to an occupation, the power of an individual is determined by such factors as:

(1) range of knowledge or ability to practice appropriate social or technical skills
(2) longevity or seniority within the occupation
(3) degree of control over entry into and progression through the occupation by others
(4) kind and extent of formal and informal social relations developed within the occupation

Power also derives from the presumption of the essentiality of the individual's particular role performance for the conduct of the occupation or, for that matter, its very survival. In those occupations where skill is at a premium or where particular kinds of jobs are scarce, the person becomes more powerful as his special or more highly developed skills are seen to be scarce, and therefore essential. Thus, a brain surgeon may be presumed to have more power than, say, a general practitioner, because there are fewer brain surgeons and because his skills are harder to come by.

Now that this has been said, it follows that still another determinant of occupational power is the degree of interchangeability of man for task. Where a skill is practiced by one or few, these persons can be thought to have a high level of power. However, where many persons perform the same task, so that it is always easy to find someone to fill the slot, the power attaching to this task is low and those who easily perform it have a low level of power. Two examples should make ths clear. In small offices it is not uncommon for one female to serve as secretary, clerk, and file girl. Her particular approach to the organization of the filing system may be idiosyncratic to the point where no one else can ever find anything in the files. But she can put her finger immediately on any material that may be needed. While the technical skills required of this woman may be low, she is nonetheless indispensable—essential—and her level of power is high. The second example involves six men digging a trench. The heat under which they work is intense, and on an especially hot day one of them faints. As he is carried off to be revived under the shade of a nearby tree another man is dispatched by the foreman to take up his shovel. These shovel-wielders have a low level of power precisely because they are so easily replaceable.

Still another aspect of power is the ability of an individual to control the behavior of others directly, in contrast to the indirect control we have been talking about. Obviously, to the extent that a person is able to tell other practitioners what to do and have his demands obeyed, to that extent does the individual have power. The possibility of direct control depends less on power-generating factors within the occupation than on the location of the person in the social structure in which he operates. For example, in the days when the academic market place was a seller's rather than a buyer's market, professors often moved from one college to another solely for increments in rank and salary—from assistant professor to associate professor, or from associate professor to full professor or department chairman. The newly appointed associate professor may not have known any more than an "older" assistant professor at his new university, may not have been so well known in his field or even so alive intellectually, but his new rank permitted a greater degree of control over his colleagues of lower rank and, hence, power, than did his old one. He occupied a higher position in this new social structure than formerly.

Thus, to the degree that a person can perform a task relatively independent of constraints by other occupational members, he can be presumed to have power and therefore to occupy a higher status in the authority system than many others. However, it should be obvious in any discussion of power that it makes little difference for the investigator whether the person does in fact have power. The possession of power need only be presumed; that is all that is necessary. As the sociologist W. I. Thomas said many years ago: "If men define situations as real, they are real in their consequences."

The second component of the status and authority system in an occupation may be suggested by the notion that *performance determines position*. This means that the complexity of the task performed by an individual with respect to others in the occupation may be roughly indicative of the person's position within that occupation. Of course, this assumes a variety of skill and performance possibilities; in an occupation requiring little variation in performance we could expect a relatively flat authority structure, or authority lying outside the occupation altogether. On the other hand, the greater the range of alternative performances, the more evident a system of authority would be. Or, from another point of view, the broader the mandate, the higher may we expect the person's location within the status and authority structure of the occupation to be.

So far attention has been directed to determinants of status that can be more or less objectively appraised. Now, however, we become much more clearly interactionist as we turn to the interpersonal component of role performance within the status system of the occupation. Roles and the statuses to which they are tied are reciprocal: doctor-patient, teacher-student, mother-child. Each of the roles in the reciprocal relation has a set of claims on and expections of the behavior of the other in the relation. A mother expects her child to be dutiful and submissive, to grow and thrive in terms of the values appropriate to the particular subculture in which mother and child live; the child at the same time expects to be fed and watered, clothed and protected, and have his wounds tended by the entity he comes to perceive as "mama." In an occupation, skill, seniority, loudness of voice, or size of muscles, or location of office—i.e., power and position—are not wholly determinative of status. Consciously or not, the person must convince others in the occupation (and outside of it) that he *legitimately* occupies his particular niche in the occupational hierarchy. He must provide cues for behavior that indicate his perception of his status to others as well as to himself and that constrain those with whom he interacts to perceive his status in the same way. So we encounter the third aspect of the status and authority system: *Perception determines position.*

Often these perceptual cues are simply highly visible aspects of behavior or appearance or position—a custom-tailored suit; a private, full-length locker in the plant; a covered parking space near the entrance to the office building in which one works; a carpet on the floor to go with the title on the door, or the like. If individual practitioners see each other as peers, if they use the same language and look at the world in essentially the same way, there is probably agreement on their relative status. If, however, there is a perception of status differences between the parties, then we shall find manipulation present. Often a worker will attempt to change his job title or classification in order to raise his status. While titles are partly descriptive of the work done, they are equally descriptive of the status attaching to the work. A typist, stenographer, and secretary may share many job tasks but differ enormously in status. The use of the jargon or special language characteristic of the occupation may serve to provide an aura of greater expertise and thereby enhance the person's status. "Name-dropping" is still another example.

In illustrating the "social organization" dimension of occupational analysis we draw upon the penetrating and insightful analysis of advertising provided by Joseph Bensman, who worked for more than eight years in an advertising agency.[7]

Advertising is like other industries in many respects. It is organized in separate firms, or agencies, each of which has its own distinctive internal structure for dealing with separate clientele, organizations outside the agency (the government, subcontractors), and the larger population (the "public"). The agencies are organized into several associations, like the Association of Advertising Agencies of America, and the agency staffs coalesce into several occupational associations that are specialty oriented (e.g., the American Society of Cinematographers). In addition, personal relationships and informal communication networks cut across departmental or agency lines and spread to the occupation as a whole and to the world of the clients served by the occupation.

Expanding on the capsule commentary, Bensman observes that advertising is a service industry, and it is this service orientation upon which advertising men and agencies capitalize: All we have to sell, they say, is our skill, our creative intelligence. To the extent that our ideas sell, to that extent are our fees, salaries, and commissions justified. If the agency can convince clients of the legitimacy of this claim, agency profits rise on very little capital investment; should the client question the claim, the agency's profits fall to the point where it may cease operations.

While salaries vary within the creative and managerial hierarchies of an agency, the possibility of acquiring stock in an agency, based on

[7]Joseph Bensman, *Dollars and Sense: Ideology, Ethics and the Meaning of Work in Profit and Nonprofit Organizations* (New York: Macmillan, 1967), pp. 9–68.

management's assessment of the individual's worth to the agency, represents additional incentive to the motivated person. It is not so much that one might become a millionaire—a perennial advertising myth, according to Bensman—but that he might be able to live as if he were rich, even though he might be only moderately successful within the agency in particular or advertsing in general. This possibility occurs through a number of "fringe benefits" available to the person: wining and dining clients and being wined and dined by them (Bensman notes here that anything can influence a client's decision, even the ambience in which the "free lunch" is proffered, since advertising buying is not centralized, while industrial buying is), the free magazine subscriptions and Christmas "loot" that comes to him, or the gifts that may be showered on him if he can "really" convince a client of the vitality of his "sell." There is an etiquette to the "wining and dining complex," and woe unto him, whether advertiser or client, who proves gauche. The practitioner accepts the myth of occupation-associated largesse as fully as does the layman. Bensman describes how agency staff look forward to lunching at the cream of New York restaurants, how they literally keep score on the gustatory jaunts of their peers, and how they piteously accept their fall from grace when a luncheon is suddenly canceled and they find themselves eating at a coffee shop rather than in the anticipated elegance.

But all is not bliss. Account losses in an agency mean personnel terminations up and down the status and skill ladders, and the job market becomes flooded. But should an agency win an account, requiring that it "staff up," it will probably utilize more intensively those workers it has rather than hire new ones. (Those who lost their previous jobs along with the lost client would hardly be wanted when the account shifts to the new agency because they represent a danger to the new agency.) So it may be that precisely those who are the most creatively able may, through no fault of their own, be the least employable for some portion of their work lives and may, in fact, never return to advertising. A variety of fictions is constructed to justify this termination of role performance.

In addition, the advertising marketplace appears irrational, and the anxiety that advertising men feel—their powerlessness in the face of an adamant client or a changing economic picture, their resentment at excessive demands often made by an agency ("we're paying you enough to take the heat, so if you can't then get out of the kitchen!")—can never be overcome by the dedication of advertising to "research." Advertising personnel assume that science, even sociology, can give a sense of market and of client. In practice, such an assumption turns out to be a myth. The client expects infallibility, and the agency, which knows this to be but a myth, behaves as if it were fact. Only the individual who sees himself as a participant in the theater of the absurd can remain unscathed.

Although the product of the advertising agency—an "ad"—is an unstandardized product (Bensman likens an advertisement to art produced under a patronage sytem, the patron "client" being able to determine the nature of the final product), the necessary skills—writers, painters, musicians, photographers, animators—and the strategy of their coordination tend to take on a characteristic form within advertising. The account supervisor is responsible for major supervision of the account; he serves as liaison between agency and client. The account executive is responsible for the internal operation of the agency relative to the account. The account group, consisting of creative, technical, and staff personnel along with sales staff, is an agency in miniature, working for and with the account supervisor and executive. There are as many groups as there are accounts. Because of this double hierarchy within the agency, conflicts are many and must be resolved by the over-all agency officers, the president and the chairman of the board of directors. Conflicts by and large center upon the distribution of time spent by individuals on accounts and differences in perceptions between the "creative staff," who regard account executives as "business types" beneath contempt of "the brains," while the account executives and supervisors see themselves as self-effacing, knowledgeable businessmen best able to represent the interests of both agency and client, even when the client is hell to work with, in contrast with the "academics" on the creative side of the house, who continually have their heads in the clouds and are devoid of practical sense. Occupational specialists feel themselves isolated and often required to operate with several sets of conflicting loyalties—to individuals, organizations, and subgroups within them. And, of course, each specialty feels itself to be functionally indispensable to the success of the entire operation, jockeys for position within the hierarchies at the expense of other groups, and creates additional conflicts that must be resolved.

The occupation of advertising has no fixed career line; the ladder

of ascent is open to those with the requisite skills. Obviously, judg-
mental, creative, and business skills are necessary if the individual
wants to rise in the agency hierarchy. But if the person has *only* these
qualities, he may find himself fixed at some relatively senior staff
rank. A further rise—let us say to account supervisor or even agency
president—requires less visible qualifications, which Bensman describes as:

(1) nerve: the ability not to crack under pressure
(2) likability: the ability to exhibit, regardless of pressure, those
    qualities of tact, deference, loyalty, and calm assurance that
    please both bosses and client (An agency is rather like the court
    of a king, and the ability to exhibit the demeanor proper to a
    courtier, such that the "king client" smiles and accepts the
    courtier, brands the individual as a "comer.")
(3) realistic toughness: being likable within limits, knowing when to
    say "no"

These qualities result in three types of agency personnel. The
"creative genius" attempts to create the impression that has ability
more than makes up for his insensitivity to the business character of
the agency enterprise. Though usually viewed as "irresponsible," if
his presentation of self is successful he can go far. The "likable chap"
is so likable, in fact, that he is likely to destroy the agency in a desire to
please. He is unable to work without structure and is utterly devoid of
nerve. He will rise no higher than account executive. Finally, there is
the "tough realist." He may not be creative, but he knows how to
please when necessary and how to be tough when necessary. He can
assess situations and manipulate them so that, whatever else may
happen, he will come out on top. Like all typologies used by
sociologists, these three types are "ideal" (as Max Weber called them)
in that they represent models, not found in the real world, which
sensitize the observer to the qualities to be investigated and serve as
benchmarks for observation. Any "real" advertising person will be a
composite or synthesis of these three "pure" types.

This discussion should indicate, therefore, that one way of understanding work is to see it as a network of claims and obligations among
individuals who operate in formal and informal structures. The
relationships specified in organization charts and manuals of procedure tell only part of the story. The intimate relationships formed

between workers on and off the job provide a context in which formal norms and the structure from which those norms emanate can be manipulated and reinterpreted to provide a work situation of greater meaning for the participants. In other words, work should be understood not only as a structure but as a process. The treatment of the advertising executive sheds light on both, for the agency employee operates both in a world of clearly defined jurisdictions, rights, and responsibilities and in the world of interpersonal loyalties, demands, and duties that may be coterminous or in conflict with the structured world of the agency. It is to a detailed consideration of process that we now turn our attention.

THE WORK DRAMA

When investigating an occupation from the perspective of the "work drama," one is at the other analytical pole from the approach represented by the "natural history of the occupation." In the "natural history" viewpoint we look at the occupation as a self-contained social fact, isolated from the world around it, at least for investigative purposes. In the "work drama" we encounter the occupation in its structural and interpersonal context, its social setting. It is in this kind of analysis that the sociological imagination can be given full play, and such analysis appears to attract a considerable number of sociologists who are interested in work and workers.

The term "work drama,"[8] coined by Everett C. Hughes, is but one manifestation of a long and honorable tradition extending at least as far back as Shakespeare, who, in *As You Like It*, has one of his characters comment:

> All the world's a stage,
> And all the men and women merely players:
> They have their exits and their entrances;
> And one man in his time plays many parts,
> His acts being seven ages.

[8]Everett C. Hughes, "Work and the Self," in John H. Rohrer and Muzafer Sherif, eds., *Social Psychology at the Crossroads* (New York: Harper, 1951), pp. 313–23.

Or read Alexander Pope in his *Essay on Man:*

> Behold the child, by nature's kindly law,
> Pleased with a rattle, tickled with a straw:
> Some livelier play-thing gives his youth delight,
> A little louder, but as empty quite:
> Scarfs, garters, gold amuse his riper stage,
> And beads and prayer-books are the toys of age:
> Pleased with this bauble still, as that before;
> Till tired he sleeps, and life's poor play is o'er.

The imagery of life as a drama (think of the ubiquitous afternoon "soap opera") has intrigued not only the poet and the dramatist but also philosopher Kenneth Burke,[9] philosopher—social psychologist George H. Mead,[10] early sociologists like Robert E. Park[11] (Hughes's teacher), and more recent sociologists like H. H. Gerth, C. Wright Mills,[12] and Erving Goffman (who has devoted several volumes to an explication of the dramaturgical model of human behavior).[13] Certainly, the intensive use made by social scientists of the concept of "role" connotes the stage and the parts that each of us try to carve for ourselves in the drama that is our lives.

We focus on the drama of work when we look at the individual in the work situation, the individual doing his job, whatever that may be. And with respect to work, the theatrical analogy is really quite apt. Work involves the individual in a number of role relations, and since role relations are always reciprocal, the individual is involved with others who are involved with still others. The "script" and the "cast of characters" are indicated by the nature of the task performed. The "stage" is the place where the work is carried on.

[9]Kenneth Burke, *Permanence and Change,* enlarged ed. (Los Altos, California: Hermes Publications, 1954), esp. pp. 274–94.

[10]George H. Mead, *Mind, Self and Society,* ed. and intro. Charles W. Morris (Chicago: University of Chicago Press, 1934).

[11]See Robert E. Park, "Human Nature and Collective Behavior," *American Journal of Sociology* 32 (March, 1927): 733–41, and *idem,* "Human Nature, Attitudes, and the Mores," in Kimball Young, ed., *Social Attitudes* (New York: Holt, 1931), pp. 17–45.

[12]Hans Gerth and C. Wright Mills, *Character and Social Structure* (New York: Harcourt, Brace, 1954).

[13]Erving Goffman, *The Presentation of Self in Everyday Life* (Garden City, N.Y.: Doubleday Anchor, 1959); *idem, Behavior in Public Places* (New York: Free Press, 1963); and *idem, Interaction Ritual* (Garden City, N.Y.: Doubleday Anchor, 1967).

We may approach the work drama on several levels. The *extensive work drama* involves interaction in the complex of work situations within the total organization and with institutions and associations outside both the work site and the organization in which the work is performed. Here we would consider such things as the actual conception of what the work is and how it is perfomed *vs.* the ideal—the "is" and "ought" of work, the actual and the desired. Here, too, we would be forced to examine the formal arrangements governing entry into the occupation as a whole (insofar as they impinge upon the individual's particular performance status) and into the person's particular status; socialization to the techniques relative to the task, and processes of recruitment, hiring, promotion, discharge, and the like. The *intensive work drama* refers to the more common day-to-day interaction in the work site under observation. For example, were we to study waitresses on the job, as Whyte did, we would be interested in the interaction between the waitress and the customer in the guest area of the restaurant, but this would also involve the chefs and kitchen help in the service area and the relations of both groups with the head waitress, *maître d'*, or owner as each (or all) of them flit between the guest and service areas, encountering the waitress in each. We would be much less concerned with relations involving the restaurant with the National Restaurant Association, the local chamber of commerce, food distributors, unions, and governmental agencies; we would be even less involved with farmers and food processors, since they affect but little the particular role performance of the waitress.

As a script is basic to the production of a play, so is what might be called the *work script* basic to the drama of work. Obviously, the character of the script derives from the work being performed. The script defines the boundaries of the work site and sets forth the work roles appropriate to both task and site. Even more important, the script assigns priorities to these roles. Some roles converge upon the work site and are central to task performance and accomplishment, while other roles merely intersect the site at greater or lesser degrees of tangency. Part of the knowledge that an aspirant to a work role *must* learn is an awareness of which of the other roles with which he interacts are important to his own work performance and which are only auxiliary or supplemental to it. A carpenter, for example, is concerned with his foreman and with other carpenters, for he most often interacts with them; he is less concerned with the electricians or bricklayers on a construction job unless they happen to interfere with his own activities. The architect or the building owner or the city planning commission or zoning board are still less of a problem for him. Thus, in analysis of the work drama, the sociologist is concerned in part with the specification of the priority of roles in terms of their relevance for any worker in the situation under study.

The ordering of roles in this fashion implies that the boundaries of the work site are sufficiently well structured to be known by all the participants (and of course discernible for the sociologist). Ordinarily, this would present no great challenge, since work site and ecological location are usually synonymous: an operating theater, the fifteenth floor of a skyscraper under construction, the "junior shop" of a large department store. However, this ordering and, consequently, the delimitation of the work site prove more difficult when one approaches the work drama at a social-psychological level. Allegiances and loyalties may intrude over mere physical presence. Others who are socially significant, though not necessarily by virtue of superior status, may exist far removed from the work site. And here the authority system enters. We may really feel loyalty to the boss, so that we might report goldbricking even though to do so means disloyalty to our co-workers. Then just where does one bound the region? How much of the authority system may one include in the intensive work drama? Perhaps one rule of thumb might be this: The greater the degree of authority a exercises over b, the smaller the sphere of action involving both a and b. Practically, this means that we tend to focus in the work drama on equalitarian relations or possibly on those involving superior-subordinate relations only one or two hierarchical levels removed from each other within the social setting under investigation. Even were we to focus on the suite of the company president, we would be concerned with relatively few interactions of people situated more or less equally within the hierarchy. The extensive work drama, of course, involves another order of interactions altogether.

Long-term observation of interaction in the intensive work drama will elicit three kinds of behavior as the people involved perform their specific work tasks. First, the workers attempt to present to an outsider, the audience (i.e., anyone who is not a worker participating in the drama, as distinct from a nonworker participant, such as

patient or client or customer), an image of cohesion, ease of interaction, and the possession of knowledge unavailable to "outsiders."
Second, one will observe a continuing process of inculcating in those
already on the job and in newcomers a sense of identity, of team
enterprise. Of course, this is also part of an image of cohesion. Finally,
there are attempts to modify and circumvent existing work rules and
formal guides to conduct by substituting informal, but usually more
powerful, norms governing conduct, output, appropriate use of tools
and techniques, and participation in role behavior extending outside
the work site and perhaps even extending to nonwork behavior. Since
these activities depend on the ways in which individuals on the job
relate to one another, a greater understanding of the work drama can
be gained if we examine these relations.

WORKERS AND COLLEAGUES

A work group is characterized by intimate face-to-face contact in a
work situation. It tends to be physically delimited and organized
about specific tasks that bind together the people performing them. It
may be, and usually is, composed of people of differing statuses and
possibly of different occupational specialties as well. It is often a
rather unstable group, with rather fluid composition due to the
movement of people in and out of the group. And though the group
may be highly structured in terms of the differential statuses within it,
it nevertheless tends to be highly informal. Because the group often
arises informally and spontaneously, it continues informally and
spontaneously. While there is no optimal size for such a group, it
often splits apart when it becomes too large to support its spontaneity,
thus giving rise to another work group on the same site.

Work groups not only induct newcomers into an occupation by
teaching them the necessary skills and the identity associated with the
skills. The members of the group also assist and protect others in the
group. Roethlisberger, Dickson, and Mayo report in their studies of
the Western Electric Hawthorne plant that members of a work team
would "cover" for another member who was tired. There would be
job trading and unusual aid to make up lost time or, for that matter,
to slow down. Most important, the work group serves as an informal
communications network. Informal practices and procedures that

might be disruptive of production, discipline, or decorum from the employer's perspective, but quite beneficial to the employee, are communicated through the "grapevine" of the work group. Donald Roy, for example, studied a machine shop in which output was fixed by a union-employer agreement—a daily quota called a "bogey." But the state of technology in the plant was such that the workers could easily exceed the daily "bogey." In order not to do so, and thus to adhere to the contract, goldbricking (intentional slowdown) became accepted practice. Certainly, activity contrary to management policy would not be communicated by the company; it could be disseminated only through the informal structures within the work situation. And so it was. Roy reports that an individual who once did exceed the quota was effectively ostracized by the constituent groups in the shop. This illustrates still another function performed by the work group. The group controls worker behavior by exercising sanctions against people for inappropriate conduct and by providing rewards for the maintenance of cohesion through the variety of friendship relations that result.[14]

A colleague, however, is not necessarily a co-worker, nor are co-workers necessarily colleagues. A colleague is a worker judged capable of sharing knowledge with his fellows which is not shared by others; the colleague has information that others do not have. This knowledge is acquired through training and apprenticeship, both formal and informal. The colleague-worker is permitted to use this knowledge in group-sanctioned ways for monetary gain, status increments, or both. He is the possessor of secrets and is literally part of a secret society. To be sure, such "secrets" may not be of much greater magnitude than where the best wheelbarrow is kept or the location of a nice spot to snooze unnoticed by the foreman, or the source of supply for drill bits of better quality than that supplied by the toolroom. Yet all this is information shared by few, and when one has been permitted to share it he has "arrived"; he is, to all intents, a colleague.

But only in part. There are both formal and informal criteria for colleagueship. The formal criteria may include graduation from an accredited training program or passage through a series of rituals

---

[14]Donald Roy, "Quota Restriction and Goldbricking in a Machine Shop," *American Journal of Sociology* 57 (March, 1952): 427–42.

designed to test the knowledge of the presumptive colleague, which may range from formal examinations to informal tests akin to fraternity hazing—e.g., sending the new man on the job for a left-handed monkey wrench or striped paint. Also included among the formal criteria may be licensing or naming, the granting of a diploma or certificate, the presentation of special garb or insignia, even the laying on of hands. The informal criteria are many. Fundamentally, they involve auxiliary, non-work-related character-istics of the aspirant to collegial status and may include age, sex, social-class membership, ethnicity, religious identification, hair length, or the cut of one's clothes. The existence of informal criteria for colleagueship implies that there is a group or groups within the larger colleague group that can be described in formal terms. Thus, groups grow up in work situations that can and do reject as members those who might otherwise qualify if only the more formal criteria for colleagueship were strictly applied. Let us call those individuals who meet the formal criteria for colleagueship *categorical colleagues*. Those persons who meet the informal criteria as well—who could perhaps be considered as colleague-like as possible—will be called *sociological colleagues*.

Oswald Hall's discussion of medical practice in an Eastern U.S. city nicely illustrates this distinction, although Hall does not use the two terms.[15] A group of doctors in this city constitutes what Hall called the "inner fraternity" (sociological colleagues). Because of age, length of practice, location in the city, "appropriate" ancestry, and the like, these doctors were able to "corner the medical market," controlling the sort of physician who could practice in the city, the sorts of patients attracted, and access to favored hospitals. What this inner fraternity, these sociological colleagues, did was effectively to limit practice in the city to those doctors they approved of and therefore sponsored and "admitted" into this particular group, just as the members themselves had previously been sponsored and "admitted." In this case, the group consisted of physicians who were white, Anglo-Saxon, Protestant, and male. Doctors from racial and ethnic

[15]Oswald Hall, "The Informal Organization of the Medical Profession," *Canadian Journal of Economics and Political Science* 12 (February, 1946): 30–44; *idem*, "The Stages of a Medical Career," *American Journal of Sociology* 53 (March, 1948): 327–36; and *idem*, "Types of Medical Careers," *American Journal of Sociology* 55 (November, 1949): 243–53.

minorities, although certainly colleagues in the formal sense, what we have called categorical colleagues, were consequently read out of the professional pale. Without the approval, albeit tacit, of physicians of impeccable WASP lineage, categorical colleagues of non-WASP backgrounds were denied the choicest plums of practice, ecological location, or hospital affiliation. All that these essentially economically disfranchised physicians could do was to segregate themselves in their own sociological colleague groups—the Italian group serving Italian patients, blacks treating blacks, and the like. Each group occupied its own little cell and was limited to interaction within this cell, despite the norms of the profession, which each doctor had sworn to uphold and which presumably were to guide the profession as a whole, internally as well as in its external relations with the laity (patients).

In a statistical study of the career crises (sociologists speak of them as "contingencies") of a sample of Chicago doctors, David Solomon demonstrated that even the sorts of residencies served by medical school graduates or the places in which they eventually established practices were in large measure determined by the physicians with whom they were able to associate in medical school (as students and protégés) and after (as sociological, as well as categorical, colleagues). It may very well be that the old adage, it's not what you know but whom you know, is more valid than our equalitarian ideology suggests.[16]

If, as appears to be the case, colleagueship rests primarily on informal determinants, the very real, if unwritten, distinctions between categorical and sociological colleagueship present dilemmas and contradictions in behavior for the worker. For one thing, what is "ethical" conduct? Is it that which is informally understood and informally agreed upon, or is it behavior that is formally prescribed by one's peers in codes or rules? In the face of obfuscation and protection by an ingroup, how can the delegated representatives of an occupation prevent malpractice or misfeasance? For example, if feesplitting is ethically indefensible but is nevertheless practiced by influential members of the occupation—members who serve as significant others to many practitioners—is this behavior then *really*

---

[16]David N. Solomon, "Ethnic and Class Differences Among Hospitals as Contingencies in Medical Careers," *American Journal of Sociology* 65 (March, 1961): 463–71.

unethical, despite official pronouncements, and perhaps sanctions, against it? Who, in this case, interprets norms, and who enforces them? What members of an occupation are thought fit to judge the competence of others? What criteria govern the selection of the "judges" and the assessment of competence? These are questions to which the student of occupations must attend if he wishes to understand the collegial relationship within a particular occupation. It may safely be said, by way of summary, that colleagueship can be viewed as the resultant of two vectors of colleague status: formal and informal, categorical and sociological.

COLLEAGUESHIP AND OCCUPATIONAL CULTURE

Simply stated, the idea of colleagueship is a sense of occupational consciousness that unites those who practice the craft. Colleagueship rests on both formal standards and informal perceptions. But, whatever standards may govern collegial relations, it is through the existence of such groups that an occupation perpetuates itself.

Like every other social system, every occupation has a culture. This culture involves the specialized knowledge, the lore and secrets and folkways of the occupation, the kind of material a sociologist would try to discover as he develops his "natural history" of the occupation. To be a colleague in the *formal* sense requires that the novice demonstrate to the satisfaction of judges or licensing officials that he has indeed assimilated this specialized knowledge.

However, there is more to the culture of an occupation than knowledge or even secret knowledge. Within the culture is contained the ethos of the occupation—a generalized philosophy of the occupation in terms of which it considers its place within the occupational firmament and views its problems and prospects and the world, and through which it presents to the "outside" its image of itself and of those it serves. On the surface, this intimate relation between craft and consciousness (as Bensman and Lilienfeld put it) appears to be occupationally prescribed, interpreted in codes of ethics or union charters or the handbooks of occupational organizations. In reality, however, this ethos is interpreted by the way in which sociological colleagues conduct themselves in the performance of their work tasks.

Consequently, an occupational member may face the dilemma of deciding which view he ought to accept as his own—the formal or the informal constraints on and evaluations of conduct. The very course of his career may depend upon the choice he makes, particularly if the formal and informal perceptions appear to diverge markedly. Unless the person is able to gauge the position of respective groupings within the occupation and then choose intelligently, even at the point of his very induction into the occupation, between groups that seem to represent categorical- or sociological-colleague positions, he may be shunted aside in favor of less pepared or capable but more astute practitioners. Consider the individual who finds "buttering up" the boss's secretary personally reprehensible and demeaning. However, he soon discovers that the key to the executive washroom figuratively as well as literally lies in the secretary's desk drawer. "Everybody does it," he is informally told. Our aspiring individual reluctantly does so, too, doors heretofore closed are opened to him, and his rise in the company hierarchy is assured. Or, again returning to medicine, the choice of major teaching professor in medical school or the choice of a particular hospital for internship or residency may enhance the career potential of the young doctor or dash it before it has even had a chance to get started. Suppose the physician chooses a field of specialization and the field proves to be short-lived. He is out in the cold, and in terms of collegial orientation he has judged inappropriately with regard to his future mobility.

Colleague groups attempt to generate an occupational identity or consciousness and an awareness of the occupational culture by using *esprit de corps,* morale, and/or collective representations.

Esprit de corps—literally "group spirit"—may be understood as efforts by colleague groups, especially those that see themselves as members of the "inner fraternity" (sociological colleagues), to organize feeling on behalf of the occupation. As students of collective behavior and social movements have observed, *esprit de corps* gives participants a sense of unity and collective involvement in a common enterprise. This may be accomplished through the development of in-group—out-group relations ("we're the good guys fighting a heroic struggle against *them*"; "*we* wear the white hats"). The generation of such a dichotomy is meant to suggest that the occupation may be open to attack from both incompetents within (as defined by the sociological-colleague group) and antagonists without. Such a construction of reality serves as a rallying point about which identification with both formal and informal occupational values can be developed and intensified.

Esprit de corps can also be heightened, and a sense of collegiality thereby intensified, through the development of groupings that foster informal relationships. So we often find in occupations the conscious use of many informal groups; in face-to-face contact people will unconsciously assimilate the gestures, attitudes, and values of the groups of which they are a part and, ultimately, the values of the occupation as perceived by these groups.

The common identification of occupational participation can as well be engendered through formal occasions of ritual and ceremony. Here the formality and dignity of ceremony can be combined with the repetition, rhythm, and emotional contagion of ritual to make of any occasion for interaction a situation in which loyalty to occupational norms and views may be further inculcated. Ritual and ceremony invest the otherwise routine with an importance and inevitability that coming together might not otherwise have. When song, speech, and gesture are coupled with a judicious use of such trappings as uniforms and banners and badges, the participant will be likely to expand his chest and exclaim: "Look at me! I'm a practitioner of x! Isn't that wonderful!"

If *esprit de corps* develops identification with the occupation, morale comprises those factors that rationalize the continuity of the occupation. An occupational ideology not only includes a specification of those persons who would defend the occupation from those who would attack it. It also contains some statements about the lofty purposes of the occupation itself—why it is worthy to continue, why it deserves support, and why its defenders will ultimately carry the day. The task of the colleague is in part to maintain and develop such an ideology.

The term "collective representations," although an old term in sociology, having been coined by the French sociologist Emile Durkheim at the turn of the century, is still useful. Collective representations refers to the verbal and nonverbal symbols that groups build up in order to segregate and differentiate themselves from others. Groups frequently develop special languages, or argots, to set themselves off from others. Sometimes these terms enter common usage, so that the group becomes less isolated and differentiated from other social groups and in effect loses its exclusive aura. (Consider terms like "hangup," "stoned," "turned on.")

It has been argued that the development of argots is a rough approximation of the institutionalization of the groups that use them, as well as of the segregation of these groups from the rest of the society. All sorts of occupations have argots—prostitutes, watch-makers, doctors, railroaders. For example, the funeral industry speaks not of a "coffin" but of a "casket"; a "hearse" is a "coach" or "professional car"; a corpse is "the (dear) departed"; and the area where the coffin lies before burial is variously referred to as the "slumber room" or the "reposing room." And the occupant didn't "die" or "kick off." He "passed on" or, occasionally, "expired." Similarly, the name of the person who provides for the care and disposition of the dead has changed from "undertaker" to "funeral director" to "mortician" over the past seventy-five years.

In like manner, the teacher speaks of "learnings" or "understand-ings" (in the plural), of "meaningful experiences" and "forward thrusts," on the assumption that another teacher not only knows what is meant by these terms but is also aware of their connotative implications. Finally, a student once provided the author with the following sampling of advertising-agency argot:

Run it up the flagpole and see who salutes.	See who likes the idea.
Nod on the diagonal.	Try to appear definite while remaining indefinite.
Lay it on the carpet and walk around it awhile.	Think about the matter be-fore a decision is reached.
Put a spot on the wallpaper.	Make the advertisement dis-tinctive.
Just blue-sky it.	Fake it; talk "big," but say nothing.

Unless one can understand the argot, can catch the perceptions evoked by the set of symbols of the occupation, one has not assimi-lated the culture of that occupation. Physicians write their pre-scriptions in an illegible hand—and in Latin at that—in part to maintain social distance between occupation and laity.

To summarize, the sociological-colleague group sets an occupation's cultural tone. The members communicate a perspective on the occupation and define standards of performance and excellence. Whether they themselves meet these standards is, of course, another matter. This group presents to occupational members a generalized picture of desirable occupational conduct. By the same token, membership in the sociological-colleague group legitimates the right of the member to whatever informal privileges and perquisites the occupation may offer. In fact, one could argue that such membership is the stuff of which success in the occupation is constructed.

ILLUSTRATION: THE VOUCHER CAGE

It is appropriate to pause here and attempt to draw together some of the strands of our previous discussion in as concrete a fashion as possible. Accordingly, we offer the following illustration: the work drama and attendant collegial relations in a unit of a large insurance company, as reported by Cara B. Richards and Henry F. Dobyns.[17]

According to the authors, one of whom (Richards) was a part-time worker in the unit, the Voucher Check Filing Unit, as it was officially known, formed a miniature social system within the insurance company. The task of the group was twofold. First, its members were to file checks and vouchers written by the company as they were cashed and returned and to do so in such a way that, once filed, any check could be retrieved on demand. Although there were usually eight to ten requests a day from as many different departments, the most frequent reason was to determine whether checks in payment of claims against the company had in fact been cashed. The work of the unit thus directly affected customer satisfaction, for complaints about failures to make payment could not be answered by the company until the document in question had been located; consequently, efficiency in the unit in part determined the speed with which the company responded to customer queries and, hence, customer good-will.

In late 1952, the period covered by the observations reported in the study, nine workers manned the unit, although the number actually

[17]Cara B. Richards and Henry F. Dobyns, "Topography and Culture: The Case of the Changing Cage," *Human Organization* 16 (Spring, 1957): 16–20.

at work during the day varied from six to nine, depending on the
number of part-time workers who were there and on whether one of
the permanent employees, who was receiving on-the-job training as
an IBM operator, was present. The part-time and permanent workers
were supervised by an Assistant, akin to a foreman in a factory,
named Miss Dunn.

The work site was so clearly defined that it symbolized the Voucher
Check Filing Unit to other workers and provided a ready source of
identification for the unit workers themselves. The work site was
bounded by walls on the north, west, and south. The north wall was
an exterior wall with windows; a door opened into the corridor from
the south interior wall; and the west interior partition was solid. The
east side of the work site consisted of steel mesh running from floor to
ceiling and from wall to wall. A sliding door through the mesh
separated the unit from the rest of the company's Agency Audit
Division, of which it was a part. The presence of the mesh barrier
suggested the name by which the unit was familiarly known—the
Voucher Cage—and gave the workers within the "cage" a sense of
uniqueness and self-sufficiency, which they cherished. Far from
feeling isolated, they regarded their situation as a "microenviron-
ment," a kind of separate culture.

This feeling of uniqueness or separateness was further reinforced
by the ecology of the work site. A rank of metal filing cabinets for
filing the checks stood just inside the mesh barrier and effectively hid
the unit workers from those on the other side of the barrier and,
especially, from the supervising Section Head. Further minimizing
the visibility of workers in the cage, a number of fiberboard single-
unit file drawers, used to transport the checks to the unit's work area,
was stacked on top of the files. Although the equipment within the
cage area, from desks and chairs to stamp pads, rubber "fingers," and
paper clips, were legally company property, the workers regarded
these materials as "theirs" because no one else had access to them.
Locks on both doors, always fastened, kept the work site closed to all
but those who were authorized to enter by Miss Dunn. The door
through the mesh was used for departmental business, while those
from other departments came through the corridor and pressed a
buzzer for service.

The ecological separation led to the development of a set of
conventional understandings—the norms of this social system—not

shared by those outside the unit, and an informality and camaraderie that were envied by outsiders. The existence of a private doorway to the corridor made it possible for cage workers to stand and talk to messengers and workers from other departments without being observed. The members of the unit could send out for a snack whenever the mood struck them without fear of being seen by the Section Head, Mr. Burke. They could even slip out themselves if necessary. The work area could be as neat or as untidy as the workers wished, uncompleted work could be left on the desks at the end of the day, workers could talk as much as they wanted so long as they worked, and they could even shoot rubber bands at each other— apparently their favorite recreation while at work—secure in the knowledge that their relative invisibility shielded them from reprisal by Burke. And Miss Dunn was one of their own.

However, unknown to the participants in the drama of the Voucher Cage, trouble was in the offing. Prior to 1952 it was becoming increasingly apparent to company officials that the Controller's Office, including the Agency Audit Division, could not meet its own standards of efficiency, thus jeopardizing the customer good-will that had been generated during the rapid growth of the organization following World War II. It was felt that the primary cause was the spatial diffusion of components of the Controller's Office over the entire twenty-two stories of the company headquarters. The time spent on communication through telephone calls or personal visits was staggering. While such a waste of space, time, and manpower might well have been tolerated when the company was small, its vastly increased size now made it unconscionable. So, in November, 1952, consolidation began. Two divisions were to be relocated on one floor; one of these was the Agency Audit Division, with its constituent Voucher Check Filing Unit.

As soon as the decision was made, lower-level supervisors were called in to help with the planning. Workers were not consulted but were kept informed by assistants. Although the assistants were responsible for equipment placement, they could be overruled by their section heads. This gave Mr. Burke just the opportunity he wanted for rearrangement of the cage to his liking so that he might now be able to see what was previously hidden. He vetoed Miss Dunn's attempts to maintain the vision barrier of filing cabinets. Accordingly, every piece of equipment in the cage was numbered, and a master chart was constructed. Employees removed their personal possessions on a Friday evening, were briefed on how to reach their new quarters on Monday morning—and that was that. A physical move was to be made, and it was made efficiently and expeditiously. But the implications for the workers in the unit were far more than physical.

The new quarters of the cage workers were similar to the old site. As before, they were to work within three solid walls and one wall of steel mesh. But the site was considerably smaller, attested to by the fact that a bank of filing cabinets had been ordered left behind. And now the unit possessed only one door—the sliding door directly into the Agency Audit Division. No longer was there a private doorway. And no longer were the workers invisible. Since Burke had insisted on rearrangement of the files, he could see very well into the work area. And with this altered site, behavior altered as well.

No longer could the people in the cage talk freely to each other or to those outside the unit. Interaction was severely limited, and the autonomy of Miss Dunn to determine the work situation was undermined by Mr. Burke. Because the unit workers could send out for and bring back snacks only through the Audit Division work area, workers there agitated for the freedom that had been unique to the Voucher Unit. Because of insistence by Miss Dunn, Burke did not terminate the snacking procedure altogether; however, he not only made the practice more rigid, by permitting only one worker to leave the cage at a particular time during the morning or afternoon, but also extended the practice to all in the Division. The cage workers thus lost one of their overt symbols of uniqueness along with the uniqueness guaranteed by the arrangement of the site itself.

Further, no longer was an untidy work area permitted. The fiberboard drawers had to be cleared by the end of the day and could not be piled atop the files. So newly arrived checks were put out of sight, whether filed or not, by being stuffed into desk drawers or unused file drawers. Workers reacted to their restriction by dubbing Mr. Burke "Old Grandma" and ridiculing him behind his back. No longer could Miss Dunn be trusted to defend her co-workers, and her ability to enlist cooperation deteriorated. Morale declined, especially when Burke began to "raid" the unit and reassign some of its personnel. The arrival of new metal desks to replace the wooden ones previously used, which decreased the drawer space available to the survivors in the cage, further depressed morale, as was evidenced by the increased fatigue and nervousness, reported by the workers, increased absenteeism, and a marked upswing in rubber-band sniping, which was now seen not as a way of relaxing or as playful exchanges between workers but as a technique for releasing frustrations. In the process, efficiency in the cage dropped, much to the surprise of Miss Dunn; when an inventory of unfiled checks on hand was taken at the beginning of calendar 1953 it was found that the workers in the unit were filing much more slowly than before the move.

What have we seen? We have developed a sense of the dynamics and the interface between the extensive and intensive work drama; we have seen how work site influences the development of collegiality and occupational culture, and how both can be modified by tampering with the stage on which the workers work out their particular drama.

OCCUPATIONAL CONTROL

Before our excursion into the world of the Voucher Check Filing Unit, we were giving some attention to the importance of colleagueship. Earlier mention was made of work groups, and in Chapter 1 the idea of the division of labor was introduced. Although these concepts are different orders of phenomena, they do have one characteristic in common. Each of them has something to do with control over occupational members. Work groups and colleague groups order and define legitimate role performance within the occupational specialty, while the division of labor defines the legitimacy of work performance in general with respect to its survival value for the social system. In other words, just as social control in the larger sense is fundamental to the orderly meshing of the parts of a society, so does control within an occupation ensure the functionally relevant interaction of the participants in that occupation.

Let us expand on some ideas presented earlier. When we first discussed the central sociological idea of the division of labor, we suggested that one of its components is what has been called the *moral division of labor*. This refers to the distribution of differing moral functions among a population. These differences in moral leeway are implied in the formal or tacit *license* accorded a specialty. This license not only legitimates a person's right to perform specific tasks but also gives him *permission to deviate*. This means that once a person is licensed he is no longer a layman in that area. He can now do legitimately, and more than likely legally, that which a lay person cannot do.

For example, one does not normally expect to be permitted to walk down a street, scalpel in hand, making incisions on anyone he might happen to meet; such an individual would be promptly locked up. But likewise, not just any individual can venture into an operating theater and make an incision on an anesthetized patient. However, if one is a physician he may do precisely that; he may deviate from societal expectations of moral behavior because of the right accorded him by licensing as a doctor to behave morally *in his fashion*, in terms of the normative constraints implicit in the role. What was improper or wrong before licensing is quite proper now. A little boy who gets Mother's spotless bathroom floor wet and dirty will be punished, and his father will probably be chastised for a similar act; a plumber is expected to behave in just this way, and his activity is treated benignly or ignored altogether.

If a license implies that an individual, in the course of his occupational role performance, may behave in a fashion in which others may not, then a *mandate* further implies that the individual may tell others how to behave. A priest charged by the canon law of the Roman Catholic Church with the care of souls not only confers sacramental grace, as guaranteed by his "license"—the act of ordination—with his ecclesiastical garb serving as a visible sign of that act, a visible "license." He may also tell others how to conceive of and aspire to the "good life." He has the obligation that flows from his license, his mandate, to legislate faith and morals. If one is a doctor, there is the implication that he may tell a patient how to behave, not only with respect to the ailment at hand, but also with reference to the patient's life course in time to come. Thus, the practitioners of occupational crafts attempt to define values and to establish and enforce sanctions over a particular area of life, to tell a society what is good and right for it in this area. The more license and mandate deal with values that are dearly held, that are felt to be central or crucial to the conduct of life, the broader the moral latitude accorded the specialty with respect to these values, the more prestigeful is the specialty, and the more it tends to take on the attributes of a profession.

In order to define their mandate and to carry out their tasks in their particular manner (license), occupations must have some order of guilty or dangerous knowledge. A janitor can tell much about the tenants in his building by noting the contents of their garbage cans. In order to advise and absolve, the priest or minister must become familiar with a range of behavior that makes him a connoisseur of the forbidden. This makes him dangerous to have around, for the information available to him could harm those entrusted to his care were it to be improperly applied. The opportunity to obtain and to keep secret some order of guilty or dangerous knowledge is the crux of occupational license; to act in terms of this information is the source of occupational mandate.

In the final analysis, however, the quality of "guilt" implicit in what the practitioner knows does not stem from the nature of the information—that it is in itself reprehensible or shocking or scandalous or even potentially damaging to customer or client. The "guilty" character of the knowledge is attributable to the fact that the practitioner can see this information in ways about which the lay person knows little or nothing. An occupation must look relatively at events and try to order them in such a way that future occurrences may be predicted. A technical language permits the practitioner to assume this detached, relative stance toward the layman. It is the realization that this relative, comparative approach has in fact been taken toward him that shocks the layman client. It is, to say the least, deflating to the ego to realize that one's own emergency is a routine affair to the practitioner.

The ideas of license and mandate not only permit an occupation's members to think of and perceive clients' problems in this relative and comparative and hence, to the layman, shocking way but also enable them to structure the occupation in such ways as to effectively discharge the mandate that has been set. Rules that govern conduct on the job, the relation of practitioner to client and (perhaps) to employing organization, do not derive solely from assumptions of technical efficiency but also from perceptions of what the occupation is ideologically committed to accomplish. Sometimes these rules are set forth in handbook or union contract, but more often they are unstated. Adherence to rules may simply be an outcome of the informal sanctions applied by categorical or sociological colleagues in order to elicit compliance. By effectively defining the nature of interaction in the work situation, a specialty ensures its autonomy and, depending upon its success in such definition, legitimates its mandate in the process.

But there's the rub! Not only does an occupation try to control itself, but it is in a way controlled by its clientele. Every occupation rests to some extent on a bargain between client and occupational member. The license or mandate of an occupation may not be accepted by a lay group. It may question the legitimacy either of the performance or of the underlying world view of the occupation. The laity may even arrogate to itself the right to participate with the practitioner in the determination of practice; it may challenge the boundary between practitioner and layman and thereby threaten the stability of the occupation. The conduct of work therefore rests on shared assumptions about the position and purpose of that work in the division of labor characteristic of a particular social system, and of the people who perform that activity. Unless the work role receives validation in the greater community, that role cannot be performed, regardless of the intensity with which the practitioners may be committed to a particular view of themselves and their world. Hughes has suggested that heightened questioning of license and mandate by varied segments of society may be indicative of social unrest in that society.

To illustrate, consider the military profession. While the Constitution authorizes the maintenance and provision of armies and militias, the same document stipulates that such groups ultimately shall be subject to civilian control. That an army can be an agency of repression as well as protection was all too clear to the framers of the Constitution. It was thought, or perhaps hoped, that civilian control would provide the same kind of "checks and balances" over the military that the distribution of powers among the executive, legislative, and judicial arms of the federal government would presumably provide for civil governance. In addition, the United States had no tradition of warfare as an instrument of national policy. Consequently, except in time of emergency, individuals who wished to pursue a career in the military were suspected of using such service to avoid or conceal their incompetence in civilian life. Since World War II and the Nuremberg war-crimes trials that followed it, and since the "undeclared wars" of Korea and Southeast Asia and the still more recent publication of the "Pentagon Papers," there has been an increasing (and increasingly vociferous) tendency to question the equity of any military action. Meanwhile, the military establishment has mounted increasing efforts to convince the citizenry of its necessity and its devotion to the cause of peace, even though armed conflict might at any moment be necessary to secure and keep that peace in the long run. The trial of Willam Calley for the alleged massacre of civilians at My Lai and the trial of General "Billy" Mitchell long before that (in the thirties, for advocating greater deveopment of the air power of the armed services), as well as the draft-card burnings and chants of "hell no, we won't go" by college students across America and the response of bricks and invective hurled by observers, were indicative of the dilemma posed by the presence of military might in a society that claims as its cardinal principle the pursuit of peace among men and nations.

At first glance, teachers may appear to be far removed from the soldier, but in the present context they face a similar dilemma. Throughout this nation's history the assumption has persisted that a teacher is some kind of unreal person, akin to a minister, destined to live a life of frugality and moral restraint that could attract only the less able in a society addicted to achievement measured in monetary terms. That the teacher was to be a woman—men were too good for that sort of thing—went without saying, and that her life both in and out of the classroom was subject to public scrutiny or censure was a common denominator of educational administration. Thus, the New York *Times* (October 19, 1964) reported that teachers in the New York City schools of 1872 were required to "fill lamps, clean chimneys and trim wicks, bring one bucket of water and one scuttle of coal to each day's session, spend time after school reading the Bible or other good books [and] lay aside a goodly sum from each pay for use during declining years so as not to become a burden on society." Men teachers, the report continues, were allowed one night per week "for courting purposes" while women teachers who married were dismissed. But there was hope. It was reported that the regulations stipulated that any teacher who behaved in seemly fashion for five years would be given a salary increase of *twenty-five cents per week,* "providing the Board of Education approves." In short, despite training, the teacher was an employee.

The teacher did not determine over-all educational policy but was the target of individuals and interest groups that saw her (him) as the embodiment of that policy and therefore fair game for their special, and frequently contradictory, pleadings. Her (his) only expertise was presumed to be in matters of pedagogy and classroom management, but her (his) field of operation, the classroom, was as open to outside view as a baseball diamond. What other occupation could boast of a "parent-teacher association"? Everyone but the teacher appeared to be able to define his or her mandate. And certainly the problems faced by the teacher in legitimating her (his) role have not diminished with time; while teachers are assuredly better compensated than at any time in history, while their extra-curricular life is no longer regulated so stringently as in the past, the occupation's practitioners still chafe at their status as employees, their openness to attack, and the instability of their occupational life. Particularly as the pressure to abolish job tenure has increased and as "performance-based accountability" appears destined to change traditional forms of teacher certification, the life of the contemporary teacher appears precarious indeed.

As a final illustration, consider the American minister. Regardless of denomination, he is committed to providing an interpretation of the life and destiny of man in terms of a framework, often embodying supernatural elements, that cannot be tested empirically but that, rather, must be accepted by the believer "on faith." In our secular world, such a perspective is at best difficult to communicate. In an effort to serve his parishioners and his commitment, the minister frequently finds himself called upon to play many roles that he finds uncongenial. He is neither interested in nor, he feels, competent as a fund raiser, an administrator, a janitor. He finds himself, as Sittler put it, macerated, chewed up, in his role performance, not knowing where to turn.[18] His congregants make demands upon him, which he frequently finds himself unable to meet because they are at variance with his identity as preacher and teacher, his commitment to a

---

[18]Joseph Sittler, "The Maceration of the Minister," *Christian Century* 76 (June 10, 1959): 697–701.

venerable tradition. As a result, the minister is often at odds with his congregation and, particularly among Protestant and Jewish clergy, is forced to move from congregation to congregation in order to establish some congruence between his parishioners' conception of his role and his own views.

We have used these illustrations in order to indicate the importance of the layman in providing a context in which the practitioner can perform. While an occupation may clearly define its mandate, it is validated in its dealings with clients to the extent that these clients accept the definitions presented to them. An occupation endeavors to structure client-practitioner interaction so that it can remain relatively unhampered in its operation. But occupations differ in the degree to which they can limit lay interference. The jazz musician literally erects a physical barrier, a row of chairs or a platform, to isolate him from his audience of know-nothing "squares." Other occupations are not so fortunate.

When the values that underlie a mandate are themselves legitimated within the normative framework of a society, an occupation can demand prerogatives for itself and get them, especially if the practitioners are few and the values they espouse are dearly held by both practitioner and laity. However, if the legitimacy of such underlying values is questioned, either because of their content or because the skills that implement these values are themselves widely available, then the occupation cannot claim autonomy for itself or a broad mandate in its dealings. Health is a value that most people accept without question. We tend to surrender our freedom of action to the doctor, whom we empower to do whatever he regards as necessary to make us well. On the other hand, "education" is a term whose content varies with the group using it. Since practically everyone has an opinion on what "education" is, since most people fancy themselves to be some sort of "educator," the teacher is open to attack. So, too, do the traditions of Protestantism and Judaism and the liberalizing trends within Roman Catholicism (occasioned by the deliberations of the second Vatican ecumenical council) make the role of the cleric extremely responsive to lay demands. These traditions allow considerable independence of personal belief and practice, and the religious specialist has become less and less the communicator of a deposit of unquestioned faith and more a first among equals. Moreover, the religious tradition itself has become increasingly suspect at a time when traditional involvements with the supernatural no longer occupy center stage. Consequently, ministers are buffeted by conflicting demands of parishioners who view themselves as no less competent than the minister to define the parameters of his role performance, especially since they employ him (at least within most Protestant denominations and in Judaism). Unable to act in the autonomous manner that was his hallmark, the minister is as hard put to confirm his identity as he is unwilling to surrender its determination to the laity. And therein is the crux of what has been called the "minister's dilemma."

Similarly when we look at the role of the soldier, we find it under considerable suspicion now that war as a "solution" to international animosities is viewed as untenable and the military superstructure appears to many as a quasi-government theatening to overwhelm its legally constituted civilian overseers. When even career soldiers question military actions, representatives of the armed forces find it difficult to convince the civil government, to which they must look for funding, of their utility, precisely because of the very sincere questioning of the military mandate in an age when nuclear holocaust threatens. In the wake of the changed energy situation, of the revelations of Watergate, when the national purpose itself seems unsure, the role of the soldier is, from the point of view of the larger society, anomalous.

To understand occupational control, then, we must see it as occurring not only through the operation of rules and sanctions within the occupation but also in the differential assessments of practitioner and layman of the rationales for the existence of ethical-legal functioning of the occupation, called license and mandate.

These illustrations serve as well to document the change in orientation toward work that has occurred over the past several centuries. It makes little difference whether one approaches work as a medieval craftsman or a forester in the heyday of the Protestant ethic might have. It is clear that there was a time when work was viewed as a calling. To interfere with the work of another was an affront not merely to the individual involved but to the divine plan for God's creatures. Yet previous discussion has suggested that a major problem faced by occupations in the modern world is the maintenance of integrity against the inroads of those outside the occupation. It could therefore be asserted that the degree to which occupational groups are concerned about lay interference is indicative of the concomitant decline of the sanctity attached to work. A contemporary perception of work as unfilfilling or irksome is the antithesis of a joyful response to divine command. Lay encroachment upon the territory of an occupation is in its way a symptom of the secularization of society. In an age that blandly announces the death of God, how sacred is work?

SUMMARY

This chapter has presented a series of dimensions along which occupations can be studied. These dimensions are (1) the "natural history" orientation, (2) the social organization of the occupation, (3) the "work drama" orientation, (4) work groups and colleague groups, (5) the culture of the occupation, and (6) occupational control. These approaches to the analysis of occupations are not mutually exclusive; they overlap and represent only different foci of attention, requiring different sorts of analytical schemes. However, when taken together, their use provides one with the breadth of perspective necessary to make some sense both of occupations as social systems and of their interface with the social order in which they are found and of which they are so crucial a component.

4

OCCUPATIONS IN PROCESS: PROFESSIONALIZATION

A NUMBER OF CONCEPTS has so far been suggested as being useful in the analysis of the history, structure, and dynamics of an occupation. However, a variable crucial to the understanding of work has not yet been considered explicitly. If the attempt to deal with change is a key problem of the human condition, it becomes imperative to develop some perception of the operation of change in the world of work because of the part played by work in shaping—and changing—our very humanity. Of course, in so doing we learn more about the nature of work as well.

By now it should be evident that occupations differ with respect to several variables, including the essentiality and prestige of the craft, rules and perceptions governing entry into and retention in the occupation, the length and intensity of training necessray to practice the skill, the breadth of license and mandate, the degree of autonomy in conduct, status and authority systems, and the nature of collegial relationships. Were one to *compare* occupations along these lines, as well as others not mentioned, one would find that they can be ranged along a continuum, with "the job" at one end and "the professions" at the other. Gross has termed this continuum the "axis of profession-alization."[1] Now, of course, no work role is wholly one or the other; the boundaries of every work role are permeable, so that we find elements of "the job" intruding on occupations that claim professional status, and we find, too, that many occupations presume that there are, or at least spend a good deal of time trying to find or justify, aspects of "the profession" in "the job." "The job" and "the pro-fession," then, represent types or models whose attributes can serve as guides for the observation of occupations in the real world.[2] If we can understand the differences between these polar types and how they shade into each other as we move along the continuum, we shall be better able to account for the impact of change on work.

PROFESSIONS

In popular usage, at least, professions loom as the pinnacle of work roles, the goal toward which any individual should aspire. The thought of "my son the doctor" should presumably fill the heart of a dutiful parent with greater enthusiasm than "my son the male nurse." The distinction between job and profession is not simply one of purpose, as if the professional serves others while the jobholder works solely for monetary reward. Nor is the professional any more com-mitted to what he does than is the jobholder. Nor does the pro-fessional necessarily see farther in terms of goals or aspirations or find his work more agreeable than the person who works at a job. Rather, the distinction is best seen in the German term for pro-fessions, *freier Beruf*, "free calling." The idea of "freedom" meant originally that a person who was drawn to what today is regarded as a profession was not in some way indentured to another or less than a citizen of his particular political commonwealth. But the professional

---

[1]Edward Gross, *Work and Society* (New York: Crowell, 1958), pp. 77–86.

[2]Max Weber called these models "ideal types." See Lewis A. Coser, *Masters of Sociological Thought* (New York: Harcourt Brace Jovanovich, 1971), pp. 223–24. Herbert Blumer referred to them as "sensitizing concepts." Herbert Blumer, "What Is Wrong with Social Theory?" *American Sociological Review* 19 (February, 1954): 3–10.

was—and is—free in another, more important sense. The professional is an autonomous person, in principle responsible to none save his peers. To the degree that a worker is constrained in the performance of his work by the controls and demands of others, that individual is less a professional.

If this be the case, the question may then be raised as to whether anyone is "truly" a professional, given the reciprocity of claims and obligations incumbent upon all actors in the work drama. In this context, the answer must be "no." But it must be remembered that we are dealing here with a model, which actual occupations can only approximate. It is the recognition by any occupation of the gap between the ideal and the actual that lies at the heart of the drive toward occupational change. It is this recognition, too, that suggests the explanatory utility of the professional model (and its converse, "job"). Pragmatically, the model "works" because it differentiates occupations in terms that serve to predict the behavior of people in or toward them.[3]

Freedom from interference, then, is the hallmark of the professional. In addition, however, "a profession is an occupation for which the necessary preliminary training is intellectual in character, involving knowledge and to some extent learning, as distinguished from mere skill; which is pursued largely for others, and not merely for one's self; and in which the financial return is not the accepted measure of success."[4] The professional is autonomous because long and arduous training has made him capable of "professing"; he is "the man who knows," competent to make final decisions that affect the behavior of others. Unlike other workers, the professional deals with unique cases and unique situations. Like that of other workers, his routine is the layman's emergency, but the professional, unlike others, cannot afford to routinize his work. Nor can he delegate the decision function; because his is the final decision, he alone is ultimately responsible for his actions, and so he must handle the "case" as a unit, from start to finish.

[3]Thus, occupations possess differences in prestige; these differences are in part explainable by this model. See Robert W. Hodge, Paul M. Siegel, and Peter H. Rossi, "Occupational Prestige in the United States," *American Journal of Sociology* 70 (November, 1964): 286–302.

[4]Louis D. Brandeis, *Business: A Profession* (Boston: Small, Maynard, 1914), p. 2

Although the professional deals with what Gross has called an "unstandardized product" as he handles individual problems,[5] his concern with the uniqueness of the client cannot obscure the necessity to gather information appropriate to the problem. For one thing, it would be intellectually and emotionally exhausting, let alone impossible, to empathize and identify with each person who comes to him. The problem of "transference"—identification with and feeling for the analyst, which patients receiving psychoanalytic therapy develop in the course of their treatment—extends to any therapeutic milieu. However, in addition, the professional cannot let his own predilections, prejudices, and idiosyncrasies intrude on his work. He may be repelled by what he sees or what he has to do, but he cannot shrink from the objectivity and ethical neutrality necessary to treatment. The professional is obligated not to behave like the social workers reported by Kuhn, who were obsequious to those who were their socio-economic equals or superiors but who chastised and victimized clients of lower socio-economic status.

In order to minimize the possibility of intruding his personal concerns, the professional approaches his client in terms of what Parsons refers to as "universalistic criteria."[6] He applies particular knowledge and techniques to all elements of a class exhibiting the same or similar characteristics, of which the person being treated is one member. That is, someone who comes to a physician seeking aid for a persistent pain in his lower right side should ideally be treated in terms of that pain rather than as someone of a particular skin color or residence who also happens to have a persistent pain in his lower right side. Likewise, although the professional, to be sure, interacts with the client personally, he does so rationally—according to rules of procedure appropriate to the specialty and the case. In other words, professional behavior requires that the particularity of the client be placed within a framework of efficiency and rationality and that attributes of the client that are irrelevant to treatment be "screened out" by the professional.

In order to act in this way, professionals are accorded the broadest license available to any worker to obtain and to keep dangerous

[5]Gross, *Work and Society,* p. 79.
[6]See Talcott Parsons, *The Social System* (Glencoe, Ill.: Free Press, 1951), pp. 428–79.

knowledge. Although it may be implicit in work to view today's emergency as merely routine, the "emergencies" with which the professional deals are linked to values of the highest priority—life and health, salvation and destiny, interpersonal equity—in human social life. He has not only license but the mandate to learn as much background information as possible, to develop a "case history"; otherwise the client-professional situation will remain just as unstructured, just as problematic to the professional as to the person who seeks his counsel. Of course, this creates problems. If I know quite a bit about you, if I have dangerous information, I am ethically bound not to reveal that information. But suppose my disclosure of the information might help in your treatment. To whom may it be revealed, how much of it may be revealed, and under what circumstances? It will be remembered that most occupations rest upon some bargain about information transfer. This is especially true of professions.

A case in point: An area of sociological interest that has emerged in recent years is medical sociology, which is concerned with, among other things, hospital administration, the relation between patient and doctor, social factors in illness, death as a social phenomenon, and the like. The medical sociologist must first convince physicians that he really is a scientist, worthy to work with the ancient and honorable craft of medicine. (This, incidentally, is a problem that faces occupations that aspire to professional status; the practitioner must convince the prospective client that he is in fact capable of doing what he claims to be able to do, that he is not flying false colors.) Once the sociologist of medicine has gained the confidence of his medical colleagues, he must then gain the confidence of his subject, be he patient, doctor, or administrator. In the process of gaining confidence the sociologist gathers data, presumably extends the boundaries of his body of knowledge, and adds to his expertise. However, should he attempt to communicate information gathered in confidence from a patient, let us say, to someone actually involved in a treatment situation, and if the subject learns of this, then the rapport that has been established between medical sociologist and subject breaks down.

The minister, too, wishes to lead the individual to better religious "health." This often involves some sort of confession or counseling. Yet, to reiterate, how can the minister know the sins of the person in the confessional unless he becomes, as it were, a specialist in sin? Fr. Jean Marie James, S.J., investigated conceptions of Catholic priests held by their parishioners. He found that the ones he interviewed were not so much concerned that a priest should fall from grace, for after all, a priest is a human being. They were far more apprehensive about confiding their innermost thoughts and their actions to a priest who appeared to demonstrate an inability to conform to the norms—humility and abstinence, for example—that governed priestly conduct.[7] The priest should ask no more of his flock than he is willing to give, runs the lay view.

A professional, then, is constrained by the nature of the emergencies with which he deals to see the client as moving in two worlds—the world of the client and the world of the professional. The professional uses his knowledge of the client to help to relate these two worlds. However, should the professional make too much of this knowledge he oversteps his license, and his professional status vis-à-vis the client/layman is lost.

Just as the professional is accorded the broadest license available in the work world, so also does he have the broadest mandate available to direct the behavior of others (including the lay client) in ways that he perceives to be necessary and functionally relevant to the resolution of the particular situation he has been called upon to treat. He may order about a wide variety of functionaries in an effort to realize his professional goals. License and mandate always define a "pecking order" of power—who may direct whom—because, as we have seen, the moral division of labor is so closely related to the functional and social divisions of labor. This is especially true at the professional pole of the "job-profession" continuum, precisely because professional specialties are so scarce and therefore so prestigeful. A doctor does not empty bedpans in a hospital. This is obvious. A doctor may prescribe medication but in most instances does not administer it. However, unless there is a doctor present on a hospital floor, there will be no medicine administered. A nurse may not take it upon herself either to order medicine or to go to the pharmacist and get it herself.

As the mandate of the professional to direct others is broader than

[7]Jean M. James, "The Social Role of the Priest," *American Catholic Sociological Review* 16 (June, 1955): 94–103.

that of any other occupation, so is his prerogative to *do* to his clients. It is the lot of the professional—both for good and for ill—to be charged with the right to do and say the most dangerous things: to cut, to dose, to reprimand, perhaps even to kill. That the doctor may kill, that the lawyer may lose a case, or that the professional may simply be wrong does not diminish the layman's faith in the professional. It is indeed faith, for the nature of the emergencies that bring one to a professional do not permit a detached assessment of the professional's competence, nor does the layman have the skills necessary to judge. To the extent that a person is unable to judge competence he becomes suspicious, and he is most likely to be suspicious of occupations that deal with personal and social well-being, because he knows so much less about them.

Because professional activities are highly valued and because the professional can so easily do irremediable harm to his client, the professional is in a remarkable position to exploit the client. That professionals by and large do not exploit clients is less an indication that they are more moral than others around them than a demonstration of their clear recognition that their prerogatives are built upon acceptance of their legitimacy by the larger community. Professionals recognize also that this community is suspicious and constantly evaluates professional performance. If the professional were not to keep his house in order, it might be done for him, however "ignorant" of competence the layman might be, less through legislation than through the formal and informal communication networks and referral systems that bring client and professional together.

THE IDEA OF THE PROFESSIONS: A CRITICISM

It is appropriate to note that, in viewing the professional as an autonomous personage performing his role subject only to peer influence, the sociologist may lose sight of the tacit bargain of legitimacy made between professional and layman. But it is clear that the professional, like the ideal-typical "jobholder," is limited in his performance by lay acceptance of professional role performance. Like the members of the nonprofessional occupations, the professional is able to keep the laity at a distance when the values

espoused by the profession are held to be important by the larger
society and when the professional's knowledge is not generally
available to the layman. This means that we must view any profession
not as a self-contained entity but as a framework composed of role
relationships in which the professional, like any other occupational
practitioner, not only shapes the character of the laity but is shaped by
it. The professional role must be viewed dynamically, as a function of
the degree to which the professional can mold his relationships with
clients. The model of "the professions" would then be viewed in a
broader social context than has frequently been the case in sociological research. Professional behavior is nothing more than a special
case of occupational behavior, differing from other cases only in
degree, not in kind. In fact, Harold Wilensky wonders whether all
occupations can or should even want to be professions.[8] Is it worth the
effort?

PROFESSIONALIZATION

That question having been raised, many occupations answer a
resounding "yes." To the degree that job-type occupations lack the
breadth of license and mandate, the freedom from restraint, the high
status, and the extensive moral leeway that derive from the functional
scarcity of a skill, the professional apex of the occupational pyramid
represents a goal that is apparently attainable and thought to be
worth winning. Thus we come upon the phenomenon of *professionalization*: attempts to reach professional status by occupations
that lack the credentials of autonomy and expertise.

Magali Sarfatti Larson has argued that the growth of the professions as a set of occupations is in fact a triumph of professionalization, what she calls a "collective mobility project".[9] By this
she means that over time occupations have attempted to assert a claim
over a particular area of knowledge and practice by a stress on
intelligence as both ideology and morality—that with expertise comes
a corresponding right to domination and power, a right to the free-

[8]Harold Wilensky, "The Professionalization of Everyone?" *American Journal
of Sociology* 70 (September, 1964), 137–58.
[9]Magali Sarfatti Larson, *The Rise of Professionalism: A Sociological Analysis*
(Berkeley: University of California Press, 1977), esp. pp. 66–244.

dom that expertise brings and which may not be challenged by those who do not have this knowledge. Out of the prestige that accrues to knowledge and the ability to use it derives prestige in the market-place. According to Larson "the rise of professionalism" coincides with the dominance of the capitalist economic order.[10]

Oswald Hall has discussed professionalization at length.[11] He argues that professionalization occurs in three ways. First, the members of the occupation attempt to improve their prestige. Second, they try to transfer unwanted duties from their occupation to others. Third, there is a continuous departure, or sloughing off, of persons at the most prestigious fringe of the occupation and a consequent severance of identification with the occupation by these persons.

Occupation members are concerned about their status and con-tinuously attempt to raise it, with the status of professional as the ostensible, and ultimate, goal. One obvious way of professionalizing is to change the name of one's occupation to one that at least connotes higher prestige. Thus the janitor becomes the "maintenance engi-neer" or "superintendent," the camp counselor becomes a "youth consultant," and the spectacle maker becomes the optometrist. Some-times occupations try to improve their relative status by borrowing from occupations that already possess more prestige. For example, in medieval times, when medical men were merely barber-surgeons with a status little better than that of the camp-follower, they sought to use the title "doctor" because it had already been made prestigious by its application to the fathers of the Church and the learned academicians (who of course were themselves clerics) of the newly emerging universities of Oxford and Padua and Salamanca. Later "medical doctors" acquired such prestige on their own that the insecure academics of our day seek to bask in this aura by using the title themselves.

Hall points out that a second device for raising occupational prestige is the formation of occupational associations, with all the ceremony and panoply of medieval guilds or contemporary Greek-

[10]*Ibid.*, pp. 136–58. See also Harry Braverman, *Labor and Monopoly Capital: The Degradation of Work in the Twentieth Century* (New York: Monthly Review Press, 1974).

[11]Oswald Hall, *Specialized Occupations and Industrial Unrest* (New Orleans: Tulane University, 1957), pp. 8–15, *et passim*.

letter organizations. Holding office in such an organization may
represent a means of occupational mobility alongside the more usual
method, developing increased competency. There may be an office
for every practitioner so inclined. Conventions of such organizations
may represent occasions for practitioners to escape the strictures and
routines of ordinary occupational life by engaging in fraternalisms
and the antics of individuals away from home for a while. Competition among organizations for members and degree of ostentation
serve as points of identification for practitioners of the aspiring
occupation.

Still another means of increasing status is to develop codes and
creeds of ethics to govern members. These codes set the occupation
off from its neighbor specialties by making its competencies clear, by
defining membership in it (which both keeps others away and wards
off the tendencies of occupational members to use this membership
for personal advantage), and by indicating a world view, or consciousness, through which other occupations may be approached and
through which a sufficiently high level of self-esteem on the part of
practitioners can be generated and maintained.

Occupations also attempt to raise status by trying to appeal to new
markets at a higher level of prestige. Advertising in the "better"
magazines, if not deemed unethical, and opening an office on the
"right side of town" at a "prestige address" are of this order. And
occupations may raise their status by laying greater claim to autonomy. The craft seeks increasing control over its use of time and its
manipulation of clients in ways heretofore held to be inappropriate
for the particular group.[12]

A greater claim to autonomy (Hall does not specifically use the
term, although it is implicit in his discussion) may also be made by an
aspiring occupation through a process by which it rids itself of
reprehensible or undesirable activities by attempting to charge others
lower in the skill hierarchy with these tasks. This effort to reassign
duties so that only the prestige-bearing activities of the occupation
remain may move the occupation toward professional status, but the
reallocation of "dirty work" and "nice work" (as Hall puts it) may leave
a group that feels itself to be victimized in its wake. In academia, for
example, assistant deans, deans of men or women, and registrars do

[12]Cf. Larson, *op. cit.*, pp. 159–207.

the collegiate "scut-work." Many of them are dissatisfied and restive. At the same time, the location of such groups lower on the prestige ladder frequently results in the appearance of new specialties, which eventually become occupations and later in their histories will themselves aspire to full professional standing. "Dirty work" tasks tend to recruit individuals of a socio-economic background lower that those who have sloughed off the task. The occupation thus relieved will be jealous of its own position and, through its code of ethics or occupational handbook, will seek to restrict membership to the performers of the more genteel tasks while simultaneously rejecting the performers of the more seamy occupational assignments. In short, occupations that strive to become professions constantly re-evaluate their duties, seeking to dismiss certain of them—emptying bedpans, sweeping floors, filing folders, grading papers—as beneath their dignity. Ultimately people are found to perform these tasks, and in time a new occupation may spring into being. College students have certainly discovered this. Across the country, "term-paper factories" have mushroomed and are doing a thriving business, even though some states have restricted their operation or prohibited it completely. Nevertheless, while the college student may balk at the writing of term papers, someone will be found who is eager to take up the task for an appropriate consideration.

Occupations also professionalize by laying claim to new tasks at the periphery of their skill level and then developing the competencies that are necessary. Those with the new skills then may break away from the existing occupation and enhance their status in the move. We find, then, a core of occupational skill with attrition at both upper and lower boundaries of the skill hierarchy—the former by default, the latter by design, as in the case of radiation protection.

Certainly, as occupations and the individuals within them jockey for more power, prestige, and opportunity for moral suasion, unrest is generated within the occupation. In fact, professionalization may be viewed as the control and channelling of this unrest. Such a view permits us to incorporate, and thereby review, the previous discussion. Groups and individuals desire improved prestige and will endeavor in many ways to maximize their collective life chance. At bottom, this involves dissatisfaction with the world as it appears to them. What is required, therefore, is the development of a view of the world as it could, or should, be. In occupations this involves the assumption and legitimation of monopolistic control over a specified type of service. This may be done, first of all, by the development of *esprit de corps* and morale within the group. (Remember that *esprit de corps* involves a feeling of identity with the group, while morale embodies conviction of the rectitude of the aims and aspirations of the group.) The inculcation in practitioners of these perspectives is accomplished through some sort of agitation, both interpersonally and symbolically. This may involve an occupational association, a change in name, or propaganda. The goal of this activity is to create within the practitioner the necessary sense of dissatisfaction with the occupation and sensitivity to its status with respect to other occupations. This felt unrest, the response to words and actions of peers, generates identification—i.e., *esprit* and morale—which in turn fosters a sense of collegiality (at least in the categorical sense). Dissent and unrest, which cluster about the nature of the work performed, the payment received for it, and the type of client or employer served by the workers, lead to the workers' pleas not only for upgrading but for greater autonomy in the structuring and control of work behavior.

Since it is the larger containing society that legitimizes any efforts to enhance status, one way of gaining the desired recognition is to present to the laity an image of indispensability by engendering the image of new needs. In other words, not only internal but also external unrest propels an occupation toward the professional end of the continuum. Again, propaganda efforts are of the essence; where there was no malady before, there must be one now, and it must be presented to others in the most somber colors and horrendous form. If there was no service before, it is not because there was no prior need; rather, it must be shown that the competent persons were previously unavailable. But, so the story goes, competent individuals are available now. In this manner, a new skill appears, and a new name to go with it. The legitimacy is further enhanced by the development of training programs, curricula, and formally chartered schools. At the same time, those practitioners who claim seniority or priority of membership attempt to limit what they practice to the prestigeful, refined, or elegant activities of their occupation by relinquishing the despised part of their duties, the dirty work, to other categories of workers. Eventually this restriction and the dissatisfaction that led to it are legitimized, and a new specialty, or perhaps a new profession, may have been born. It is this same process within an already established profession that leads to specialization, as individuals at the fringe of competencies take unto themselves new skills and assert their right to special, favored treatment. Or they may take over skills that no one else wants and make a virtue of necessity.

In this discussion of professions and professionalization, the notion of a continuum implies that occupations are at various stages along the road to professional status. It should be obvious that the same process occurs within the established professions. Thus the anesthesiologist was a "doctor without patients."[13] He was perceived merely as part of the equipment of an operating room until he was able to assert the legitimacy of his mandate with respect to the control of and research into the effects upon the human organism of depressant and stimulant drugs and to establish his right to the perquisites and prerogatives of specialization.

We close this section with a comment made earlier. A profession is simply a special case of occupational practice, different only in degree. Similarly, professionalization is a quite general phenomenon. It occurs in the occupational panorama wherever occupations try to better their lot, regardless of whether such actions ever eventuate in professional status.

THE ROLE OF POLITICAL BEHAVIOR IN OCCUPATIONS AND THE PROFESSIONS

Because of the nature of professionalization, it becomes appropriate to introduce the idea of occupational politics and to view its operation within the professions as a special case of the more general model. What will be said here can be inferred from much of what has gone before.

An occupational group may feel threatened in any of a variety of areas. It may feel itself to be a target of state regulation or assault by other occupational groups or by the laity. It may see new techniques, skills, and processes as encroaching on its traditional areas of oper-

[13]See Dan C. Lortie, "Anesthesia: From Nurse's Work to Medical Specialty," in E. Gartly Jaco, ed., *Patients, Physicians and Illness* (Glencoe, Ill.: Free Press, 1958), pp. 405–12.

ations; conversely, it may see its attempts to assimilate new skills and mark out new areas of operations as confronted with hostility from older, more entrenched occupational groups. The occupation may be threatened by dissenting elements within it. Or particular individuals, through nefarious or submarginal conduct, may have brought unfavorable publicity to the occupational group. Whatever may be the origin of the strain, its focus is the practitioner, and its essential element is a disruption of norms, expectations, and procedures, which make for group and interpersonal stability even at a time when the group may be undergoing rapid change, as in professionalization.

Whenever norms of a group are threatened, action toward integration inevitably follows. What solidarity remains will be expressed through sanctions of ostracism, disfranchisement, or expulsion from membership. Such formal, observable response to stress also serves to solidify group sentiment by focusing attention on a recognizable object of hostility. When attention is thus mobilized so that group action follows, perhaps through an occupational association or through the action of sociological colleagues, informal techniques of control can then be used to supplement formal control efforts.

Informal control involves the reintroduction of conformity by recalling the basic values of the group—the sacred myths, dogmas, and heroes through which the occupation recalls its past and marshals its forces to face the future. The formal occupational association and informal collegial relations serve to reduce tensions and to suggest appropriate courses of action by rewarding normative behavior and projecting an image through which the threatening influences can be viewed in "proper" perspective. Propaganda and techniques of influence—lobbying, for example—can be developed to grapple with the presumed invaders or new circumstances. Available ritual and ceremony may be invoked to stem the tide of opposition. Banquets, newsletters, impassioned oratory, and rallies may all be used to foster psychological unity within the occupation and to justify occupational behavior to outsiders.

While it is a unique case, the history of the International Typographical Union (ITU) indicates the part played by social-psychological mechanisms of conformity, as manifested in printers' political involvement in their union, in the maintenance not merely of union

solidarity but of the very solidarity of the occupation.[14] By the very
nature of their work, printers were required to be literate at a time
when intellectual acumen was not demanded of many crafts. The
history of printing suggests a skilled occupation perceived by others
as bordering on the professions. Consequently, printers have been
conscious of their skill and their presumed superiority to other skilled
trades; they have not been reticent in asserting this perception. The
result has been a militant stance toward other workers and toward
employers wherever printing has flourished. Nevertheless, Lipset,
Coleman, and Trow assert that, despite this militancy, the ITU is a
democratic union and has been since the formation of the union in
1852 from a number of secret societies. Union members exercise
remarkable independence in the determination of union policy. Each
plant local, or "chapel," is itself autonomous. There are many
communication networks within the chapel, and they are kept open
and functional as a matter of deliberate union policy. Second,
associated with each chapel are a number of informal clubs, which,
though ostensibly "social" in character, serve to induce in participants
a high degree of ideological sensitivity to union business and politics.
In fact, the authors found that such sensitivity was directly related to
intensity of participation. This concern and involvement are called
into action when employers or other unions threaten. Both the chapel
and the informal groups try to instill in union members a sense of
continuity with the past and an identity with the future. An ideology
built around these democratic values enjoys the support of both
conservative and liberal wings of union politics. The enemy is clearly
defined. The more the individual printer immerses himself in union
politics, the more he is felt to be conforming to the norms of union
democracy, and the more union solidarity is thought to be preserved.

The American Medical Association is another example. The organization until very recently has been able to induce conformity to its
view of medicine through the character of the sanctions that it could
impose. Since the AMA was presumed in principle to set the terms of

[14]Seymour Martin Lipset, Martin Trow, and James S. Coleman, *Union
Democracy: The Internal Politics of the International Typographical Union* (Glencoe,
Ill.: Free Press, 1956).

sociological colleagueship, it was thought to be the spokesman for and the creature of the sociological colleague group. When the AMA spoke, the profession itself was thought to be speaking. Changes now occurring in the medical profession with respect to the individuals attracted to it, perceptions of the physician's role, and attitudes toward medical care make the future of the American Medical Association as medicine's overriding representative unclear.

One major problem that confronts the professional association concerns the degree of autonomy that is or should be enjoyed by the professional. In theory, as we have seen, the professional claims autonomy as a condition of practice. Certainly, we act as if this were the case, notwithstanding the dictum about the reciprocal client-professional relation as a factor in the creation of autonomy. But, as we see the professional absorbed into a variety of bureaucratic and technical enterprises where his services presumably may be utilized more effectively, his demand for autonomy is usurped by the demands of the employing organization. The professional consequently begins to question the legitimacy of his mandate. The professional association must constantly reassure the professional of his worth. Of course, this involves personal tensions as the individual must rationalize or justify both loyalty to bureaucratic organization and to professional ethics; his self-image suffers accordingly. The industrial doctor is a case in point. Other physicians judge him to be an extremely low-status practitioner. He may once have been a doctor, but he has since degenerated. He receives a salary, not fees. He works a shift, not office hours. The doctor, on the other hand, feels himself to be a doctor, for he knows that licensure has legitimated his right to practice. But is he really a doctor when all he ever sees are patients with colds or broken arms or cut thumbs? His own professional organization assures him that he is indeed a physician, but when he is required to report to a director of plant safety or to the chief security officer, he wonders. And surely the laity—the workers in the factory or shop—do not confirm his identity; a nurse, they feel, could do just as well (and in many situations does).

The professor is yet another example. He feels that an ancient heritage and the learning he has acquired at great monetary and psychic cost entitle him to the label of professional. Although, historically, he has been underpaid—he likes to feel that no price can measure his usefulness—he has, at least since the Middle Ages, been autonomous. Now, when students seek to govern campuses as they participate in decisions about curricular matters and faculty appointments with a zeal far surpassing their former concerns with dormitory life-styles; when economic recession and cost-conscious legislatures and donors cut back aid to colleges and universities; when Ph.D's are unemployed and unionism rears its head amid the campus ivy; when even some colleges are unable to survive the economic crunch coupled with energy shortages, in turn coupled with wholesale departures of students—then organizations as traditional in academe as the American Association of University Professors find themselves beset by wholly unanticipated problems. And amid all this, the professor wonders about his own status—indeed, his very fate. How professional is he? How autonomous is he? Perhaps he is simply an employee whose problems can best be settled not with words but with the militancy of collective bargaining and the "withholding of services" (the phrase used by public employees of those political subdivisions that outlaw strikes). The contemporary professor is hard put to answer questions about his occupational legitimacy, and new organizations enter to fill the vacuum apparently left by the older, more traditional occupational groupings that seem unable to cope with an altered academic environment.

ILLUSTRATION: CHIROPRACTIC

Chiropractors base their form of therapy on the premise that an impairment of function of any of the twenty-four vertebrae of the spine will be transmitted along the nerve pathways that leave the spine and will ultimately affect any organ these nerves may reach. It follows, according to the chiropractic art, that bodily ills may be treated by manipulating the displaced vertebrae back into position. The Greek term for this pursuit is literally translated as "effective hand." The field was begun by Daniel David Palmer, an Iowa merchant, in 1895. In 1898 he established the Palmer College of Chiropractic in Davenport, Iowa, and in 1910 his textbook, *The Science, Art and Philosophy of Chiropractic*, appeared. His son and grandson carried on his work.

While orthodox chiropractic has always emphasized manipulation of the vertebrae as the principal approach to illness, in recent years some chiropractors have advocated that the field must keep pace with new technical and scientific advances, and so some practitioners broadened their treatment to include diathermy, exercise, the regulation of diet, and counseling. These differences in treatment have produced schisms within chiropractic, leading to two separate professional organizations. Those who restrict their practice to manipulation of the spinal vertebrae, the chiropractors known as "straights," belong to the International Chiropractors Association; those practitioners who add other techniques to the traditional form are members of the American Chiropractors Association (formerly the National Chiropractors Association) and are familiarly known as "mixers." The ICA accuses the ACA of having "sold out" to the medical opposition ranged against chiropractic, and the ACA charges the ICA with being primitive and unaware of change.

In 1980 sixteen colleges in the United States offered the Doctor of Chiropractic (DC) degree, requiring four years to complete and about four thousand hours in basic medical science and chiropractic subjects. All states now license chiropractors; the chiropractor passes the same basic science examination that is required for the certification of physicians. Since 1974 the American Medical Association and the U.S. Department of Health and Human Services have considerably relaxed their strictures against chiropractic; third-party payments for chiropractic treatment is an accepted part of U. S. health care. However, the Federal Government as well as the American Medical Association still regard the education received by the chiropractic student as inadequate and the students admitted to chiropractic schools as unqualified, even by the standards set by the schools themselves.

Therein lies the nub of the professional problems of the chiropractor. Regardless of the differences between "straights" and "mixers" with respect to treatment, practitioners are united in their view that the antipathy toward their professional advancement is attributable to the fears of orthodox medicine that chiropractic represents a threat to the prestige, the financial well-being, and even the supposedly "scientific" character of medicine. Chiropractors claim that, while medicine derides chiropractic as unabashed quackery, medical doctors have nevertheless incorporated chiropractic perspectives into their treatment programs without acknowledging their debt. Such an ideology provides a justification both for the professionalizing attempts of chiropractors—including general chiropractic publicity, frequent associational activity, lobbying for pro-chiropractic legislation, and stricter self regulation—and for their present status as a largely marginal, if parallel, healing orientation and an economically depressed social group. This ideology also provides them with a mandate, almost by default, to behave in ways that might appear to be ethically indefensible to occupations farther along the road to professional status—e.g., solicitation of patients, fee-splitting, advertising. The chiropractor might even risk legal difficulties through his practice, but his world view tells him that, despite hostility, all his troubles are to be endured because chiropractic "works" and is therefore worth doing, come what may. Medicine's vaunted claim to scientific impartiality is simply not so, the chiropractor asserts. The only avenue open to him, therefore, is to stand militantly for what he believes. Time and the support of loyal, cured, patients are on his side.

Thus, the chiropractor attempts to raise his status in the face of intense opposition by developing a self-image based on this opposition. He uses the imagery of an oppressed minority to foster relationships that legitimate his mobility aspirations as a normal part of "the American dream" and that justify his crusading stance.

However, increasing acceptance of chiropractic as a parallel, and hence "respectable" healing modality becomes itself a problem. Walter Wardwell suggests that were chiropractic to adopt what he calls a "limited practitioner" model—a practice independent of physicians but confined to neuromuscular and skeletal concerns—the chiropractic practitioner would have to surrender his claim to a different—and better—orientation to health and illness and thus become (says Wardwell) no different than dentists or podiatrists, operating within the same ideology and using the same rhetoric as the physician. This would mean a compromise of principles, with a consequent loss of *esprit*. Yet, if chiropractic is not to "fade away" or to become simply a medical specialty—both of which scenarios appear to him to be unlikely—the limited practitioner stance is the only viable alternative available to the occupation. Indeed, Wardwell regards such a stance as advantageous to chiropractors and to the health care system.[15]

[15]Walter I. Wardwell, "The Triumph of Chiropractic—And Then What?" *Journal of Sociology and Social Welfare,* 7 (May, 1980): 425–39.

ILLUSTRATION: SOCIAL WORK

Social workers like to perceive themselves as professionals. How-ever, the origin of the occupation in melioristic and reformistic activities has rendered social work suspect to many Americans. In addition, social workers have been hampered by their inability to develop a set of procedures that are wholly their own and are not also utilized in other fields. Few social workers have completed the two-year graduate training recommended for the field, and only one-third of all employed social workers are members of the National Association of Social Workers. Nevertheless, social workers claim professional standing for what they do because of the excellence connoted by that label. "In social work, being a 'pro' means more than earning money for the service you provide, because you can get a job in social services without being on the professional level." They assert that they in fact do possess their "own structure and body of knowledge, which has evolved from [the] social sciences and is based on democratic ideals or values."[16] Social-work organizations and journals argue for tightened educational standards, for greater recognition of the legitimacy of the Academy of Certified Social Workers (ACSW) as a certifying agency, and for increased freedom from bureaucratic and supervisory control. The possibility of further increments in professional standing is held to be a continuing occupational concern.

> Social work is already a profession; it has too many points of congruence with the model [of professions] to be classified otherwise. Social work is, however, seeking to rise within the professional hierarchy, so that it, too, might enjoy maximum prestige, authority, and monopoly, which presently belong to a few top professions.[17]

While an ideology of militant professionalism is fostered among social workers, the possibility of and hope for further mobility generate a very real dilemma for the practitioners. They recognize that increasing professional prestige and authority will change re-

---

[16]Kathlyn Gay, *Careers in Social Service* (New York: Messner, 1969), p. 38.

[17]Quoted in Nina Toren, "Semi-Professionalism and Social Work," in Amitai Etzioni, ed., *The Semi-Professions and their Organizations* (New York: Free Press, 1969), p. 145.

lationships with clients, agencies, and the like and will probably require rethinking of the social-action and social-reform components of social-work philosophy.[18] Yet, mindful of their origins, social workers are reluctant to divest themselves of this orientation even at the expense of professionalization.

ILLUSTRATION: LABORATORY TECHNICIAN TO MEDICAL TECHNOLOGIST

Prior to 1928, the qualifications of the laboratory technician were relatively unspecified. In that year the occupation first established an association with membership criteria that would both delimit the occupation with respect to other groups and at the same time deny membership to the unqualified, thus giving the members increased status. Self-identification was enhanced, and reliance upon previous occupational statuses was reduced, when the name of the occupation was changed from "laboratory technician" to "medical technologist" (1934). With the establishment of a code of ethics ("standards") in 1936, additional criteria for practice were introduced, along with an ideology to guide public response to practitioners and to assert the utility of the occupation for the more effective conduct of healing activities—that is, to provide *esprit* and morale. Political agitation for recognition of the occupation by private and public bodies was carried on concurrently with the development of training facilities controlled by the occupational association and the elaboration of working relations with allied occupations, such as those of the physician and the clinical pathologist. Having passed through this sequence, medical technology appears to be headed for professional standing.

PROFESSIONALIZATION AND THE STATE

As we have seen, a profession may claim a mandate on the basis of access to a specialized body of knowledge, the larger society may accept the validity of that mandate, but it is the state as disinterested

[18]See Ernest Greenwood, "Attributes of a Profession," *Social Work* 2 (July, 1957): 45–55.

observer that licenses both profession and practitioner. When once the state confers that license upon an aspirant profession, the professionalization process is complete. L. H. Orzack has observed a new relation between occupations and the state, in which the state actually intervenes to stimulate or force professionalization: what he calls "professions by fiat".[19]

For some time Orzack has been interested in attempts by the European Economic Community (the E. E. C.) to harmonize variations among member nations in the regulations governing entry into professions and professional certification and practice. Each of the states developed its own approach to the licensing of professions; the EEC hoped the generation of common standards that would apply to all nations of the Community would permit the free migration of professionals from one country to another. According to Orzack, dentistry presented a particularly difficult problem.

> A dental profession separate from medicine does not exist [in Italy] and the flow of individuals without discriminatory treatment to and from that country thereby confronts a lack of institutionally-defined roles. As one British dental leader noted: "United Kingdom dentists cannot practice in Italy except as quacks and hirelings". Italian dentists, all of whom are medical doctors, are not qualified to practice in other countries of the Common Market where qualification in a dental school is obligatory, nor can graduates from schools in other countries practice dentistry in Italy in the absence of a medical qualification. This slowed preparation [of standards for transnational accreditation of dental practitioners] and led finally to the unheralded order of the Common Market to Italy to *create a separate profession of dentistry* [italics ours].[20]

Italy tended to view dentistry as a branch of medicine; other member states did not. Orzack describes the process that led eventually to the issuance in 1978 of EEC Directives for Dentists, which defined the basic dental diploma, specified the titles under which practitioners could work in member countries, identified orthodontics and oral surgery as "advanced specialties in certain member

[19]Louis H. Orzack, "New Profession By Fiat: Italian Dentistry and the European Common Market," *Social Science and Medicine* 15A (1981): 807–816.
[20]*Ibid.*, pp. 807–808.

countries"²¹ and, in essence, required Italy within six years to create a new program of training and institutional structures to contain a profession of dentistry separate and distinct from that of medicine.

Medical doctors practicing dentistry at first resisted the creation of a specialty, although the Italian Association of Medical Dentists (A. M. D. I.) came grudgingly to espouse the reform of training. Neither the Ministry of Education nor university faculties responded to the Directives for Dentists. Nor could the Ministry of Health, despite favorable discussion, nor political parties acting through Parliament effect the necessary changes. In the spring of 1979, representatives of medical-dental educators and the Italian Medical Association agreed to seek the intercession of the President of the Italian Republic. The outcome is problematic at best. If Italy does not meet the deadline, further delays must be secured. Migration of dental specialists will be blocked. Perhaps the EEC may level economic or other sanctions against Italy.

Though other professions—accountancy, architecture, optometry and pharmacy, for example—await a similar action by the EEC, Orzack uses the example of dentistry in Italy to illustrate the point that, whatever may be the impetus for change from within an occupation—of which professionalization may be one form of change—professions are very much "communities within communities". The political order is the ultimate grantor of legitimacy; it can destroy as well as create. We have seen the role played by government with respect to nurses and the laboratory technician/medical technologist. Now we have a case in which governments both transnational and national officiate at the birth of a profession—in fact, cause it into being. "When the cross-national study of professions is undertaken, intricate relations between professions and governmental institutions can become more clear."²² The need for comparative sociological study of professional specialties (as, indeed, for so much of organized social life) to supplement the relative insularity of most sociological research—sociology confined to a single country in North America or to English- or French-speaking North America—is obvious. As Orzack puts it: "The unusual instance of an international governmental authority seeking to force changes in the

²¹*Ibid.,* p. 813.
²²*Ibid.,* p. 814.

structure of a profession by impelling action by the government of a sovereign nation highlights the need for further cross-national analysis of the relations between professional and political systems. Whether health professions are more susceptible to international harmonization than technical, scientific, financial or design professions remains an open question, until such research occurs."[23]

SUMMARY

In this chapter the professions were considered as a special case of occupations, but nonetheless as a goal toward which many occupations strive with unremitting effort. The process by which occupations try to acquire professional status, professionalization, was examined, and the operation of mechanisms of control in the process was discussed.

The treatment of occupations up to this point has moved from the historical to the interpersonal to the organizational aspects of work. Ultimately, the focus has been upon groups and their placement within two social structures—that of the occupation, and the more extensive and inclusive one outside the occupation. Thus, while we have considered "work," we have encountered the "worker" of our title only tangentially. In the next chapter our interest shifts. We look at workers.

[23]*Ibid.*, p. 807. See also Louis H. Orzack, "Educators, Practitioners and Politicians in the European Common Market," *Higher Education* 9 (1980): 307–23.

5

WORK AND THE SELF

[A] man's work is one of the more important parts of his social identity, of his self; indeed, of his fate in the one life he has to live, for there is something almost as irrevocable about choice of occupation as there is about choice of a mate.

THE TITLE OF THIS CHAPTER, as well as the lines above, is taken from a classic paper by Everett C. Hughes.[1] His argument there is simple but enormous in its implications. Work is so fundamental to the life of man, says Hughes, that we cannot understand the human condition unless we can make some sense of the ways in which man comes to terms with his work; these terms provide clues to the ways in which men live out their lives and see their destinies. Indeed, for many, work becomes a "central life interest" in which the concerns of the work place intrude on and inform nonwork relationships. We shift in this chapter from an examination of occupations as ongoing social structures to the impact of work on the individual. If work is inescapable, how do men learn to live with it, perhaps to structure

---

[1]Everett C. Hughes, "Work and the Self," in John H. Rohrer and Muzafer Sherif, eds., *Social Psychology at the Crossroads* (New York: Harper, 1951), pp. 313–23.

work in their terms, and even—when all is said and done—to regard their work as not only daily tribute to necessity but an enhancement of life?

RECRUITMENT TO WORK

Since the founding of America, a basic premise of the American dream has been the idea that no man in this country need be fettered by caste or class, that achievement in the occupation of one's choice is dependent solely upon initiative and ability. Therefore, perhaps the most heinous sin that could be committed by an American (and the least forgivable) is the admission of failure to achieve, with the concomitant renunciation of the success orientation altogether. Nevertheless, fulfillment of the dream is still elusive for many. Rapid technological growth, the explosion of knowledge, and changes in social needs and goals have changed the occupational options open to individuals from generation to generation. Ethnicity, income level, intellectual ability, availability of training, or cultural impoverishment may serve as a bar to achievement despite the apparent societal commitment to that idea. Finally, because occupational choice often must be made early in the life of the individual, persons may not have the knowledge necessary to choose wisely, may not be aware of the opportunities open to them—or may have the choices made for them.

Cicourel and Kitsuse,[2] in a study of a large suburban high school, pointed out that the assessments of motivation and ability made by school guidance counselors may serve to "stigmatize" or mark pupils for particular kinds of high school experiences—college-preparatory programs as against industrial-arts or business programs—and for particular post-high school work possibilities. In a high school that is committed to using the best available indicators of success in the search for talent, the authors report, counselors' evaluations may be made in terms wholly specific to the individual: e.g., his conformity to school norms, the extent to which he causes "trouble" for authorities, indications of ethnicity, or other "problems" as defined by the counselor. These diagnoses may bear little relation to the student's

---

[2]Aaron V. Cicourel and John I. Kitsuse, *The Educational Decision Makers* (Indianapolis: Bobbs-Merrill, 1963).

performance, but they still serve to direct him into channels of acceptance, sponsorship, and recognition that may structure his future as inescapably as a magnet rearranges iron filings. A student—indeed, anyone—who is told often enough that he is inept, "will never amount to anything," or, conversely, "is such a fine boy" will eventually come to view himself in these terms and to act accordingly. For if men define situations as real, said sociologist W.I. Thomas, they are real in their consequences.

The problem of occupational choice is compounded by the degree of commitment required by different occupations and the irrevocability of this commitment, once made. The prospective physician must make his commitment early, in the first year or two of collegiate undergraduate training, and once he decides on medicine it is difficult for him to change his occupational course except to pathology, dentistry, or research, because the specialized character of the training has little applicability to other fields. Medicine, then, tends to be a first-choice occupation; early commitment requires it. On the other hand, many liberal-arts fields, such as sociology, tend to be second- or even third-choice occupations because the skills acquired elsewhere can easily be applied to disciplines in the liberal-arts tradition. Persons who find themselves unhappy in one area may shift to another with little loss of time, momentum toward a degree or certification, or ego. Sometimes an individual finds that time itself is his enemy. He has been in a field of endeavor for so long, in fact has come to see himself as a practitioner in that field, that it would be difficult if not impossible for him to "start all over again," and any change would force him to divest himself of whatever benefits he has gained up to now—seniority, retirement security, prestige. However, such "retooling" may be mandated by changes in technology, the skill base, or social values: He may simply be "displaced" or declared obsolete. The person has no choice but to commit himself anew. Continued failure brings continued recommitment, with progressively diminished return on both the temporal and the psychological investment.

When sociologists have studied particular occupations they have of course been interested in the kinds of individuals who come to the occupation and the manner in which man and job mesh. However, sociologists have confined their more general interest in recruitment, the linkage between individual and occupation, to inferences from data on occupational mobility, on differential changes over time, of participation in census categories of occupations. That is to say, if we know what kinds of people participated in an occupation from 1920 to 1940, and if we know, further, that the participants changed from 1960 to 1980, we may infer that the recruitment base of the occupation changed during these two twenty-year periods, even though we may not be able to talk about the dynamics of the process.

Warner and Abegglen studied the occupational origins (occupation of father) of some 8,300 business chief executives in 1952 and compared them with origins of a similar group studied in 1928.[3] They found that the business leaders of 1952 tended to be recruited from lower occupational categories than those of 1928. The difference is even more striking when leaders' occupations in 1928 and 1952 are compared with those of their grandfathers, especially paternal grandfathers. In other words, it may be inferred that business leadership has recruited more widely in recent decades. However, other studies indicate that a son can expect to do no better than his father, and perhaps not so well. Therefore, Chinoy urged far more intensive study before definitive statements about mobility trends (and, hence, statements about the attractive power of occupations) are made.[4] Nosow and Form suggest that definitive statistics do not exist because of (1) the lack of fixed occupational categories to provide long-term measurement; (2) the fact that good measurements are hard to obtain, and disagreements over their interpretation abound; and (3) these statistics must be interpreted in the light of gross historical changes, which, they say, is difficult to do.[5]

The best study that now exists is an intensive analysis of the American occupational structure conducted by Blau and Duncan.[6] Based on data collected from a representative sample of twenty thousand Americans, aged twenty to sixty-four, the study was administered through the cooperation of the Bureau of the Census. The

[3]W. Lloyd Warner and James C. Abegglen, *Occupational Mobility in American Business and Industry* (Minneapolis: University of Minnesota Press, 1955).

[4]Ely Chinoy, "Social Mobility Trends in the United States," *American Sociological Review* 20 (April, 1955): 180–86.

[5]Sigmund Nosow and William H. Form, eds., *Men, Work and Society* (New York: Basic Books, 1962), pp. 335 ff.

[6]Peter M. Blau and Otis Dudley Duncan, with the collaboration of Andrea Tyree, *The American Occupational Structure* (New York: Wiley, 1967), esp. Chapters 2 and 12.

findings are many. Principally, we may note that the data indicated no decrease in mobility within the occupational structure. However, men who start their careers in manual work are less likely to achieve an occupational status different from their fathers' than are those who start their working lives on farms or at a high blue-collar level; these findings suggest the continued importance of education and ethnicity in achievement. Diversified living and educational experiences give these men a greater advantage in the occupational race. Urban living is directly related to occupational attainment; those born in cities fare better, all other things being equal, than do migrants to cities or those who remain in rural areas.

Analyzing recruitment to occupations, Blau and Duncan examine their data in terms of a flow of men from occupational origins to occupational destinations. They find upward mobility, but of very short social distance; i.e., most occupational movement is between occupations that differ very little in socio-economic status. Thus recruitment to self-employed groups, what Blau and Duncan term free professionals, farmers, and proprietors, occurs primarily from within their ranks and with very little outflow. The occupations with high recruitment levels, which simultaneously send large numbers to other occupations—occupations having the least occupational inheritance—lie at the lowest status levels (as Blau and Duncan define them) of white-collar, blue-collar, and farm strata. These are retail salesmen, clerical workers, service and nonfarm laborers. Thus, they claim, there is a direct relationship between the flow of men leaving an occupation and the inflow or recruitment. These are channels for upward mobility as well as refuges for the downwardly mobile. Demand for occupational services and superior employment conditions also encourages entry into an occupation and reduces outflow. The American dream is therefore still capable of realization, at least for whites, as long as one can attain as much education as is available. Blacks, however, still face an uncertain occupational future, even when education is held constant. Indeed, their opportunities for movement seem to have deteriorated at the very time their "inalienable rights" as citizens have been confirmed in law.

Thus the linkage of man to occupation is neither so random nor so rational as Americans, nurtured in an egalitarian ethic, would like to admit. In fact, the question could be raised whether recruitment can be wholly open and choice completely free so long as occupations differ in the abilities required for effective performance. And of course the answer must be that the man-job nexus cannot be fortuitous precisely because of demands by occupations for different "kinds" of people. Perhaps all that can be asked is that what differences there are in the skills of people, and the prestige increments accorded these differences, not be made a matter of inheritance, open only to particular groups. Rather, they should be viewed as shaped by the requirements of a highly complex technology and operating in such a way that men, equal under law, are able to find congenial work and to do their work unencumbered by their social histories. Yet even now men do achieve and find challenge in what they do. This recognition gives hope, but at the same time it serves to indicate what has yet to be accomplished for many of our citizens.

THE MEANING OF WORK

Although man and occupation are eventually brought together, it does not follow that the meeting is necessarily a happy one or that the relationship that ensues will result in anything more than a marriage of convenience. One man's "chore" or "daily grind" or, simply, "job" may be another's sport or consuming passion or "calling," with all the religious conviction and dedication implied by the term.

At the very beginning of this book we had occasion to examine different conceptions of work through history. It is not necessary to reiterate all the changes here, but only to note that work today receives a "bad press." The economic historian John U. Nef has suggested that the conquest of the material world, which brought the comfort and luxury of an expanded standard of living, substituted quantity and utility for beauty and the conscious cultivation of morality.[7] Work was dehumanized.

Putting it somewhat differently, Adriano Tilgher, author of the classic book on the subject, noted that when work lost its religious imperative, as the Renaissance merged into modern times, work also lost its power to ennoble. He said that men no longer seek work done

---

[7] John U. Nef, *Cultural Foundations of Industrial Civilization* (Cambridge, England: Cambridge University Press, 1958).

well for the sheer satisfaction it affords. Western man is no longer interested in the beautiful but expends his energies in sport and play and ostentation in order to find the refreshment of spirit that work once provided. People who work mindlessly have their lives created for them from the opinions of others and become as automatic in response as the machines they tend.

Harvey Swados argues that, for all the money it may bring to a man, work is slavery. A person who curls up after dinner with a full attaché case and a pad of yellow paper or who sits at his typewriter pecking insights at 1:45 in the morning is chained to his work as surely as is a man at an automobile assembly line. The industrial worker is not being absorbed by the "middle class," according to Swados; rather, the white collar is slowly assuming a bluish tint. The slavery of work plays no favorites; the agony is intense whether it is felt in the ghetto of Detroit or the suburbanized "ghetto" of Glen Cove, New York, or Marin County, California.[8] And when even sexual activity is represented in marriage manuals to be work, to be doggedly pursued *on schedule*, how little valued has work become then?[9]

The meanings that work—a specific occupational task or work "in general"—assume for the individual derive from two sources. Early socialization experiences provide the origins of reactions toward work. As a person is prepared for appropriate adult role performance through interaction in his family of orientation, with peers and adults in his community and his school, he learns to place a value on work behavior as others approach him in situations demanding increasing responsibility for productivity. The praise or blame, affection or anger, leveled at the growing child in such transactions as "picking up the toys," "setting the table," "going to the store for mother," and later part-time jobs enables him to assess his performance from the perspective of others, particularly those others, like parents, whom he regards as significant for conduct. As the person matures, these perspectives are internalized, and he takes

[8]Harvey Swados, "The Myth of the Happy Worker," *The Nation* 185 (August 17, 1957): 65–68.

[9]Lionel S. Lewis and Dennis Brisset, "Sex as Work: A Study of Avocational Counseling," *Social Problems* 15 (Summer, 1967): 8–18. See also Horace Miner, "Body Ritual Among the Nacirema," *American Anthropologist* 58 (June, 1956): 503–8, in which the author speaks of intercourse being "taboo as a topic and scheduled as an act."

upon himself the direction and evaluation of his own behavior, rather
than requiring direction by others. In work as in all other aspects of
human life, the sociologist claims, the child grows socially by ap-
proaching himself as others approach him. The consistency of
others toward him makes for consistency in his own behavior,
particularly as he develops an identity and concept of self.

In addition to incorporating others' evaluation of his work activities,
the maturing person internalizes others' attitudes toward work. If, for
example, a child's father seems to enjoy his work, the child senses this,
just as he quickly gets the sense of his father's impatience with and
disgust for an intolerable job. When a significant other is fired, the
child assimilates the fear and concern of that other; when someone
important to the child is rewarded for work well done, the child basks
in the feeling of well-being that is radiated.

The second source of work meanings is related to the work drama.
But here, too, socialization is involved, for socialization does not cease
with entry into adulthood; whenever a person tries out new interpersonal situations with new demands and obligations on the part of
the several participants, he is being socialized. People "on the job" in
both the intensive and the extensive work drama (insofar as the latter
may involve the specific individual) provide cues to their responses to
the work situation in both its technical and its affective components.
Few individuals can for long remain oblivious to the perceptions of
others. To the degree that these others are accepted as legitimate
communicators, their views are assimilated by the individual.

The culture of an occupation is validated "on the job." The culture,
too, embodies an attitude toward the work, but the attitude may
approach idealization as it seeks to give the work a prestige it might
not have "out there" in the real world. But at work, "out there," the
worker develops his own perceptions of his work, whether he be an
apprentice or a member of the "inner fraternity" of colleagues.
However valid these perceptions may be, he does in fact act as a result
of them, and his responses to the work will be colored accordingly.

For example, people who work together continuously over a long
period develop their own approaches to production; these approaches may not be supported by company policy, but, as we saw in
the example of the Voucher Check Filing Unit, they do permit the
maintenance of morale, and they get the job done efficiently. The
joking and the frequent trips to water cooler or lavatory may be

legitimized as conducive to production. Supervision may appear to be minimal or even absent. But should the way the work is handled be changed, through the introduction of more formal supervision or even by changing the structural conditions in which the work is carried on—moving filing cabinets, opening a door to an outer office that had previously been kept closed, tallying used rubber bands or paper clips—morale decreases, and new conceptions of work, mostly unfavorable, result.

To sum up to this point, then, the meaning of work for an individual results from his childhood and adult socialization experiences *and* the perceptions of the work world he has formed in the course of work, of being exposed to particular occupational cultures.

The meaning of work for the individual can be as varied as the gamut of human emotional responses. Factors that appear to structure work meanings, particularly as they are expressed in attitudes of satisfaction or dissatisfaction with the work, include absenteeism, achievement, advancement and promotion, a sense of alienation, job and career aspirations, degree of autonomy in work, automation, a sense of challenge, clarity of goals, education, job involvement, intellectual stimulation, social and occupational mobility opportunities provided by the job, personal and social motivations of the job, morale, needs, interpersonal relationships, organizational structure, salary, race, sex, ethnicity, job skills, status and prestige of the work, supervision, tenure, training, recognition provided by peers and superiors, conditions and hours of work, and performance and productivity.

Further, the meaning work has for the worker depends on his location within the functional division of labor. In 1952–53, Robert Dubin studied the extent to which work was viewed as more than a mandatory involvement in some enterprise and was in fact a "central life interest" among 1,200 workers in three plants in three Midwestern communities. [10] The plants, all in urban areas, were a manufacturer of industrial equipment, a maker of industrial, dress, and novelty gloves, and a producer of advertising items. Forty questions constituted a "central life-interest questionnaire" and were addressed to the respondent's preference for a particular locus in the com-

---

[10] Robert Dubin, "Industrial Workers' Worlds: A Study of the 'Central Life Interests' of Industrial Workers," *Social Problems* 3 (January, 1956): 131–42.

munity—work, nonwork, or indifferent (i.e., neutral)—for the conduct of some activity. A typical question was:

I would most hate
_____ missing a day's work
_____ missing a meeting of an organization I belong to
_____ missing almost anything I usually do

Analysis of 491 completed questionnaires led Dubin to conclude that
the primacy of work in the American experience appears to have
receded, at least for industrial workers. Perhaps work may still be a
means to an end, but work as an arena for satisfying social relationships is clearly outdistanced by relationships not involving the
work place. However—and this is an important proviso—when these
workers were asked about the centrality of organizational affiliation
in their lives, 61 per cent chose the work organization as the most
meaningful formal organizational structure in their lives. When
satisfactions involved in technical operations were considered, 63 per
cent were job-oriented; they found greatest satisfaction in performing
technical operations on the job as against a home shop in the
basement or the like. In other words, although work is no longer a
central concern for industrial workers, although they do not find it a
focus for meaningful interpersonal relations, nevertheless the formal
requirements of organizational life in industry—both interpersonally
and technologically—do provide a source of identification as the most
appropriate context in which organizational experience and technical
involvement can be realized. A man need not love what he does, but
the factory becomes the best place to do it. He certainly does not
organize his life out of an infatuation with work. He does not value it;
work is simply necessary.

Orzack attempted to apply Dubin's findings to professionals.[11] He
administered Dubin's central life-interest schedule to 150 registered
professional nurses employed in public and private hospitals and in a
state mental hospital in a Midwestern city. Scoring procedures were
identical to Dubin's. His findings using Dubin's analytical categories
are presented in Table 8. They indicate, according to Orzack, that
work does in fact loom as a dominant interest of professional nurses.

[11]Louis H. Orzack, "Work as a 'Central Life Interest' of Professionals," *Social
Problems* 7 (Fall, 1959): 125–32.

TABLE 8. TOTAL "CENTRAL LIFE INTERESTS" AND SUBORDINATE
EXPERIENCE PATTERNS FOR PROFESSIONAL NURSES AND INDUSTRIAL WORKERS

Pattern	Professional Nurses (Orzack) %	Industrial Workers (Dubin) %
Total "central life interest"		
Work	79	24
Nonwork	21	76
Informal relations		
Work	45	9
Nonwork	55	91
General relations (personal satisfactions)		
Work	67	15
Nonwork	33	85
Formal-organization relations		
Work	91	61
Nonwork	9	39
Technological relations		
Work	87	63
Nonwork	13	37
N	150	491

SOURCE: Louis H. Orzack, "Work as a 'Central Life Interest' of Professionals," *Social Problems* 7 (Fall, 1959): 127.

It serves as a focus for personal satisfactions as well as for most meaningful relations within a formal organizational context. That nurses do not find informal relations in work to the same extent as industrial workers may indicate that the professions in general strongly lack collegial relations, or this lack may be endemic to occupations composed largely of females, who, despite training, are socialized to find interpersonal satisfactions in nonwork situations. In any case, the saliency of work for the professional in contrast to the industrial worker suggests that more aspects of a professional's life are structured by his training, his ideological commitments, and his service orientation, thus rendering his life course more "vulnerable" to the demands of work. Work thus tends to have greater meaning or "centrality" for the professional. Consequently, to reiterate, the meaning of work varies with its place in the functional division of labor—i.e., with increments of indispensability (stemming, of course, from differences in skill and training).

But, however "central" or peripheral work may be to various groups, both studies point to the fact that in our society work is at least

valued as something necessary. The unemployed or "unem-
ployables"—derelicts, individuals with checkered work histories—frequently feel isolated from their fellows until they can get
work, for some work is better than no work at all. Friedman and
Havighurst indicate that all work provides common threads of
meaning even though a particular occupation may stress one or more
strands at the expense of others.[12] All work seems to provide income,
to regulate life activity, and to provide a source of identity, association, and meaningful experiences. Their study of five occupations that vary in skill, prestige, and commitment—steel workers,
coal miners, skilled craftsmen, retail salespeople, and physicians—
attest to these commonalities. Thus, the centrality of the meaning of
work in an occupation should not obscure the fact that all work does
possess meaning. As we remarked very early in this book, work is that
activity which permits a person to survive socially as well as physically.

THE PROCESS OF WORK: CAREERS

In *Centuries of Childhood*, a book that is both scholarly and a delight
to read, the French historian Philippe Ariès traces the image of the
family and the status of "child" over time.[13] He points out that the
boundary between "childhood" and "adulthood" varied in Europe
from century to century and from social group to social group. What
constituted appropriate role performance at any particular chronological age was a matter of biological development far less than of
social definition, and these definitions were far more flexible than
modern man might realize. In the course of his discussion, Ariès
asserts that the tendency to divide life into "ages" or "stages," even
when information on chronological age was missing or dismissed as
irrelevant, extends far back into antiquity. Life today, he says, is
viewed as a drama, a biosocial situation. But in the past, life was seen
to have a continuity in time, an inevitability that transcended the time
of man or of earth. The fragility of man's life in a period of high
mortality could only idealize a full life since life in the real world was

    [12]Eugene A. Friedman and Robert J. Havighurst, *The Meaning of Work and
Retirement* (Chicago: University of Chicago Press, 1954).
    [13]Philippe Ariès, *Centuries of Childhood*, trans. Robert Baldick (New York:
Knopf, 1962).

so tragically short, so frequently marred by illness, war, or starvation. Jaques's speech in Shakespeare's *As You Like It* (from which I quoted a few lines in connection with discussion of the work drama) typifies this concern with the ages of life. However old and anachronistic this concern may be, it nonetheless persists today, albeit in attenuated and secularized form. Educators have been interested in developmental tasks, psychologists in the psychology of development, and students of occupations in careers.

We may define a career as an orderly, predictable progression through a series of interconnected statuses. This status passage has become regularized over time so that many individuals will travel the same road with similar expectations, and it is legitimized within the occupations and groups where it occurs. Growing up about the career are various institutions (procedures) that facilitate—and deter or redirect—the passage. Thus we can talk about the career of the housewife, the nurse, the loyal member of the Veterans of Foreign Wars or the Elks, or the dying patient. A career, then, is socially defined and socially sanctioned. But it also has a subjective component. When a person recognizes himself as a participant in a career—and this point is crucial—his perception permits him to organize his life and interpret his experiences. Participation in careers of all sorts provides us with major segments of our identities—an awareness of who we are, where we have been, and where we can expect to go. Goffman sees the notion of career as linking the private world of the individual—his hopes and dreams and the personal stance he takes toward himself and his world—with the public world of norms, expectations, status, and other human beings. This linkage provides the concept with great analytic potential as the researcher moves from one "world" to the other. [14]

Both in the popular sense and in sociological thought, the concept of career has been most frequently applied to work. Individuals may work at a series of activities during their lives, but with no perception that they follow a career path. We might speak of the career of a dentist or an accountant but we would hardly speak of the career of a dishwasher or a hospital orderly. Unless the person and the containing social structure see some relation between the activities there

[14]Erving Goffman, *Asylums* (Garden City, N.Y.: Doubleday Anchor, 1961), p. 125.

is no career. Work at a particular job takes place in a relatively circumscribed time perspective; a sense of career involves expectations of and commitment to activities and outcomes at some future time, however ill defined it may be. And while work at a particular job may be viewed principally as a monetary matter, the assumption of career includes additionally a psychic overlay of expectations relative to increasing increments of prestige, responsibility, involvement, and, as it were, ego enhancement. The perception of an occupational career (to expand on a comment made earlier) permits an individual to tie his personal fate to socially sanctioned patterns of behavior. In so doing the participant finds meaning for himself and at the same time fixes a place in an ongoing social structure. "The concept 'career'" denotes the addition of the temporal dimension to the division of labor. [15]

Ultimately, what determines whether a series of related work activities will in fact be viewed as a career is its accessibility to the larger society and to the practitioner of the skill. The greater the popular awareness of a career path, the more intensive the training required by the specialty, and, thus, the more limited the access to it, the more can we expect the person to perceive his careerism. It then becomes possible to classify careers as in Figure 1, where a "public career" refers to a career whose path is clearly recognizable to nonpractitioners and the developmental stages can be readily identified; a "private career" refers to one whose characteristics are known

ACCESSIBILITY TO NONPRACTITIONER	ACCESSIBILITY TO PRACTITIONER	
	Open	Closed
Public	2	1
Private	3	4

FIGURE 1. Fourfold scheme for the classification of careers.

[15]Leonard D. Cain, Jr., "Life Course and Social Structure," in Robert E. L. Faris, ed., *Handbook of Modern Sociology* (Chicago: Rand McNally, 1964), p. 298.

only to its practitioners [16]; an "open career" denotes that little training is required to practice the specialty; and a "closed career" denotes a requirement of extensive training. [17] Thus a person in a career in cell 1 would exhibit the greatest sense of careerism because there is clear "public" confirmation of the career line and because the intensity of the training provides him with both a sense of expertise and his own model of where his occupational course is to take him. On the other hand, it can be expected that a practitioner of a career in cell 3 would exhibit the least sense of career, for he has no real model to follow, nor do people "outside" know what he is doing. It is interesting to note, further, that the prestige accorded an occupation by the sample of the American population studied by North and Hatt [18] is to some extent related to the location of the occupation along the "accessibility" dimensions schematized in Figure 1. (Of course, whether some of these occupations can be considered careers at all casts some doubt on the utility of this last assertion; it is nevertheless a tantalizing research possibility.) The kind of cross-classification suggested illustrates further the linkage between the individual worker, the social structure within which he carries out his work, and the symbolic frameworks which subsume both.

The ability of an individual to conceive of himself as pursuing a career becomes still more problematic when we note that the line between the private and the public career, as well as that between open and closed careers, is altogether fluid. The explosion of knowledge and the increasing complexity of the technological order transforms public into private careers, as Dubin points out. Changing organizational forms as well as the proliferation of the division of labor results in private careers that may have no relation to traditional careers. Individuals may not know either of the career alternatives open to them within a given occupation or of the potential of any particular private career or whether, in fact, the making of a career is even possible. This makes the development of an occupational identity difficult. One may identify with the organization for which

[16]Robert Dubin, *The World of Work* (Englewood Cliffs, N.J.: Prentice-Hall, 1958), pp. 277 ff.

[17]I am indebted to my colleagues Paul Dommermuth, David Larson, and Edward G. Ludwig for helping me to clarify this presentation.

[18]Cecil C. North and Paul K. Hatt, "Jobs and Occupations: A Popular Evaluation," *Public Opinion News* 9 (September, 1947): 3–13.

one works or the traditional career; he may identify himself as a member of the set of practitioners of the private career. But in either case the problems both of loyalty to colleagues and of survival within the occupation are evident. The worker must continually ask himself, "Who am I?" The desired confirmation from others may not be forthcoming. The attempts of occupations to professionalize may transform open careers into closed careers. Since professional status is related to the stringency of certification requirements, occupational organizations seek to increase such requirements, and the occupation is consequently changed as accessibility is controlled.

The problem of generating a self-concept geared to a sense of career is exacerbated still further when, for whatever reason, the demands of an occupation on a person change rapidly. A burgeoning technology, constant changes in assignment, in rules, in work place may not provide much sense of career. For this reason, lower-level skill categories of workers do not perceive the relatedness of their jobs or tasks in the same way as do workers upon whom demands are constant and the goals of work are explicit and traditional. Automobile workers live from day to day, hoping simply to remain employed and eke out enough seniority to avoid furlough. Their concern for the future is lived through their children, and success in their jobs is seen as an escape from the factory altogether or, at the least, earning enough to ensure that their sons will be able to avoid factory life.

When the sociologist gets down to the study of careers, however, the concept is employed with a good deal less precision than previous discussion indicated. *Career* is frequently used to refer to any pattern of occupational change of individuals or groups, without the orderly progression and the perception of relatedness between work tasks necessary to the strict construction of the term. In part, this imprecision stems from the zeal of specialists who know that they are pioneers and who seek their own professional legitimacy: There is so much to learn, and so quickly, that conceptual clarity must be subordinate to knowledge payoff. As well, this stems from the intellectual history with which the term is freighted.

Whether consciously or not, sociologists who study careers have been affected by the age-old interest in the "course of life" (a discussion of which began this section). The members of every society (that we know of) tend to differentiate statuses in terms of chrono-

logical or imputed biological age. So many of us, and so many
societies, are inclined to segment life in terms of temporal events that
are common to a people and often involve them collectively—circumcision, the first planting or the first snowfall of the year, menarche,
confirmation, bar mizvah, the first date, passing one's first road test,
marriage, death. Moreover, many of these events are invested with
religious significance, which gives them additional import. Consequently, it becomes very tempting, and perhaps inevitable, to think of
work life as a series of stages, each with its particular occurrences and
turning points. And it is not long before the sociologist undertakes to
compare and contrast occupations and categories of occupations in
terms of these purported stages.

Again, whether consciously or not, the terminology adopted by
psychologists interested in "life course" has been appropriated by
sociologists seeking to understand careers (as they define them).
While *career* as a concept has been mishandled in the process, the
return in understanding has nevertheless been considerable, for the
intimate relation between life and work has been revealed with
remarkable transparency. For example, in a series of works the
psychologist Charlotte D. Büler suggested that the lives of individuals
passed through a series of five stages,[19] as follows:

(1) growth and the preparation for self-determination (0–15 years)
(2) experimental or exploratory self-determination (15–25 years)
(3) goal-fulfillment and establishment (25–45 years)
(4) self-assessment and maintenance (45–65 years)
(5) restriction of accomplishment and decline (65–death)

Operating in the lives of both men and women, stage 1 involves the

[19]Charlotte D. Bühler, "The Curve of Life as Studied in Biographies,"
Journal of Applied Psychology 19 (1935): 405–9; *idem, Der menschliche Lebenslauf
als psychologisches Problem*, 2d ed. (Gottingen: Verlag für Psychologie, 1959);
idem, "Meaningful Living in the Mature Years," in Robert W. Kleemeier, ed.,
Aging and Leisure (New York: Oxford University Press, 1961), pp. 345–87; and
Charlotte Bühler and Fred Massarik, eds., *The Course of Human Life: A Study of
Goals in the Humanist Perspective* (New York: Springer, 1968). See Donald E.
Super, *The Psychology of Careers* (New York: Harper & Row, 1957), for
extensive discussion of Bühler's approach. Bühler's age ranges are approxi-
mations. She has used a variety of terms to characterize these stages, and so
have her interpreters. The discussion here is derived from Super and from
Althea J. Horner, "The Evolution of Goals in the Life of Clarence Darrow," in
Bühler and Massarik, eds., *Course of Human Life*, pp. 64–75.

person in the development of a self and the variety of role in-
cumbencies that go to make a functional adult in a complex society;
the person attempts to make a place for himself (herself) in his
associational and interpersonal life. Stage 2 carries this process on to
completion, as it were, as the person, now biologically mature, tries
out the roles that he has previously developed and internalizes the
behavioral constraints previously wielded by others. His experi-
mentation with roles, with interpersonal situations, is not merely a
matter of play or game but in earnest as he looks for an occupation,
for a mate, for meaningful fulfillment as budding adult. Stage 3
establishes the person in the world of the community, of work, in the
family, and he assumes a readily classifiable identity both in his own
eyes and in the eyes of others. He begins to get a sense of accomplishment, or frustration, as goals are met or unrealized. But
eventually the person must come to grips with the world as he finds it,
rather than as he wishes it to be. Thus in stage 4 he must reassess his
progress to date and make plans for whatever "future" there may be
so that he may at least "hold his own" and "keep things going," even if
hopes of greater glories must be set aside. Finally, in stage 5 there is
not only the physical diminution of vitality and exuberance but a
restriction of output, of responsibilities, and of social linkages until, in
senility, he may even lose responsibility for himself.

A sociological classification of the stages of work life proposed by
Delbert C. Miller and William H. Form parallels the psychological
classification of life course in general proposed by Bühler. These are
as follows:

(1) preparatory work period (0–14/15 years, approx.)
(2) initial work period (15–18/25)
(3) trial work period (18/25–34/35)   "ACTIVE
(4) stable work period (34/35–60/65)   WORK LIFE"
(5) retirement (60/65–death)

In stage 1 the child is socialized to work; he develops an orientation
toward work in the same way that he is socialized toward other values
and roles. In stage 2 the growing adolescent begins what Miller and
Form call the "active work life" by part-time or marginal employment.
This is a period of impermanence, which persists throughout the
person's formal educational experience. Work is assumed to be
temporary, and major concern is directed to the completion of school

requirements. Eventually school ends, and the person "goes to work." Stage 3 begins with full-time participation in the labor force and continues until the individual has found (often after considerable movement) a position that turns out to be relatively permanent—defined as one at which he remains for three years or longer. Stage 4 involves the worker in this more or less permanent position, in which he may remain until retirement or death—or until he enters another trial period ("I can't stand what I'm doing; I'm going to get out of this racket and try something else. I'm still young enough"). This is stage 4. Retirement (stage 5) brings the decline of work experiences.[20]

Since it is possible to isolate the stages of a person's work life, which parallel his biosocial life course, it then becomes intriguing to speculate on the different organization these stages might assume for different occupations. In other words, would occupations differ as to the length of any particular stage and the sequence of stages ($1 \blacktriangleright 2 \blacktriangleright 3 \blacktriangleright 4 \blacktriangleright 5$, as against $1 \blacktriangleright 2 \blacktriangleright 3 \blacktriangleright 2 \blacktriangleright 3 \blacktriangleright 5$), or might some stages be absent altogether? In fact, a number of sociologists, including Miller and Form, have investigated the presence of such differences. These have been called "career patterns." The first sociologist to demonstrate an interest in these patterns (even though he did not use the term) was Sorokin. In 1927, he attempted to show differential rates of inter-occupational mobility for different occupational strata, with mobility being inversely proportional to skill—i.e., the less the skill required by the occupation, the greater the job mobility of the practitioners of the occupation.[21] Accepting Sorokin's call for further research, Davidson and Anderson studied 1,165 males above the age of twenty in San Jose, California, during 1933–34 in an effort to develop, among other information, indicators of occupational mobility. They found that mobility differed by age and by occupational category.[22] Lipset and Bendix studied 935 males in Oakland, California, in 1948–49, and they, too, found different mobility rates for different occupational categories, but especially with respect to the manual-nonmanual distinction (much mobility within the sector but little between the

---

[20]Delbert C. Miller and William H. Form, *Industrial Sociology: The Sociology of Work Organizations*, 3d ed. (New York: Harper & Row, 1980), pp. 197–256.

[21]Pitirim A. Sorokin, *Social Mobility* (New York: Harper, 1927), pp. 424 ff.

[22]Percy E. Davidson and H. Dewey Anderson, *Occupational Mobility in an American Community* (Stanford, Calif.: Stanford University Press, 1937).

sectors).[23] But it is in the work of Form and Miller that patterns of job sequences for the variety of occupational categories within the American occupational structure is most clearly set forth.[24]

In 1946 Form and Miller obtained occupational histories from a sample of 276 Ohio male workers, the sample matching the employed Ohio population with respect to occupational distribution, age and sex distribution of the workers, and occupational distribution by sex. They found, among other things, that different occupational categories exhibited distinctive career patterns, in terms of time spent (in years) in the initial, trial, and stable work periods; and extent of mobility from job to job. With the current job of each respondent serving as the criterion for placing him in a particular occupational category—professional or clerical, for example—each job in his occupational history was categorized as belonging either to the initial, trial, or stable work period. The sequences of these periods were recorded and classified. Fourteen such sequences were identified. Seven of these sequences were termed stable or secure, while the remaining seven were termed insecure or unstable patterns of work.

Secure Patterns	*Insecure Patterns*
stable	trial-stable-trial
initial-stable-trial-stable	initial-trial-stable-trial
stable-trial-stable	initial-trial
initial-stable	trial
initial-trial-stable	stable-trial
initial-trial-stable-trial-stable	initial-stable-trial
trial-stable	trial-trial-trial-trial

When modal (or central) tendencies of respondents in the seven census categories of occupations were plotted, these occupational groupings were in fact found to exhibit different patterns of occupational movement and stability (or security).

[23]Seymour M. Lipset and Reinhard Bendix. "Social Mobility and Occupational Career Patterns: I. Stability of Jobholding." *American Journal of Sociology* 57 (January, 1952): 366–74; *idem,* "Social Mobility and Occupational Career Patterns: II. Social Mobility," *American Journal of Sociology* 57 (March, 1952): 494–504.

[24]William H. Form and Delbert C. Miller, "Occupational Career Pattern as a Sociological Instrument," *American Journal of Sociology* 54 (January, 1949): 317–29.

Although professional workers exhibited many different kinds of initial work experience, they moved to the professional level directly and tended to remain there. Proprietors, managers, and officials manifested considerable vertical mobility during the initial and trial work periods but thereafter remained stable. The pattern for clerical workers was marked by some movement prior to reaching clerical status but little movement thereafter. Skilled workers and foremen began their work lives largely as unskilled or semi-skilled laborers; when they reached their current skill level they remained quite stable, according to Form and Miller. Many of the semi-skilled workers began their work lives as domestic or personal service workers and thus displayed some vertical mobility, but once they reached semi-skilled status they rarely rose above it. Finally, unskilled and domestic workers showed little or no mobility; they held many trial jobs, and their stability at work was minimal.[25]

Building on their data along with that provided by other studies, Miller and Form later attempted to sketch the career of the "typical" worker in each category.[26] They argued that the stability of a particular career was predicated not merely on the "salability" or prestige of the skills of the practitioner but also on his social origins and the interpersonal climate in which he grew up. The higher the level of the father's occupation, the higher the probability of career stability. The greater the level of security at home and in interpersonal transactions involving the jobholder, the better his chance for a stable career pattern in his future work life.

Perhaps because the sociologists who have been interested in career patterns have been men, the career patterns of women have not been subjected to intensive study. Super suggested a series of career patterns for women, analogous to the Form-Miller types. He called them:

1. *The stable homemaking pattern.* Women marry while in school or college or shortly after completing their education. Marriage has been perceived as a logical next step, and the women have had little work experience.
2. *The conventional pattern.* The women leave school, go to work in some occupation requiring little or no additional training, and

[25]*Ibid.*, pp. 232–34.
[26]Miller and Form, *Industrial Sociology*, pp. 240–45.

then marry after a time. They then become full-time house-
wives. Thus, work may be thought of as a stopgap prior to
marriage in order to earn additional money or achieve independence from parents. Some women, however, may view
their work as their major interest. Super suggests that clerical
work, teaching, nursing, and secretarial work, are illustrative of
such work.

3. *The stable working pattern.* The woman enters the work force on
   completion of her education and begins a life work. While she
   may view it as preparatory to marriage or as continuing along
   with marriage, subsequent events (the nonappearance of "Prince
   Charming," for example) may alter this perception, a change to
   which it is often personally and socially difficult to adjust.

4. *The double-track pattern.* The woman works after completing her
   education, marries, and combines her work at home with work
   outside the home, occasionally ceasing outside work during
   pregnancy. This pattern is quite common at the upper and
   lower ends of the skill hierarchy

5. *The interrupted pattern.* The woman works, marries, and works
   again when time permits or interest or circumstance (divorce or
   widowhood) demands it.

6. *The unstable pattern.* The woman works, marries, works, and
   returns to homemaking, etc. Economic pressures may make
   work necessary despite the disinclination to work; when the
   pressures ease, work may cease. This is most often observed,
   says Super, among women at lower socio-economic levels.

7. *The multiple-trial pattern.* As for men, this consists of a series of
   unrelated jobs, making for no stability whatever; there is no
   sense of life work.[27]

Despite the paucity of studies of career patterns of women, it seems
reasonable to predict that, as larger numbers of women are absorbed
into the labor force *and* as the conventional wisdom regarding the
working woman is altered—that is, no longer the "convention"—
career patterns of women will more closely resemble those of men.[28]

[27]Super, *Psychology of Careers* (n. 19 *supra*), pp. 76–78.
[28]See Roslyn L. Feldberg and Evelyn Nakono Glenn, "Job Versus Gender
Models in the Sociology of Work," *Social Problems* 26 (June, 1979), 524–38.

CAREERS IN
SOCIAL-PSYCHOLOGICAL PERSPECTIVE

A discussion of careers would not be complete without focusing on their social-psychological dimension, to which we alluded earlier. To view careers solely as movement through a series of regularized work tasks, possibly bearing some relationship and, hence, some degree of reproducibility and predictability, is to view the individual worker as a kind of passive reactor to social situations in which he finds himself. If the individual initiates behavior as well as responds to the behavior of others, then the student of occupational careers must understand not only the change and stability implicit in the concept of "career" but the impact of temporal sequences upon the person and how the person modifies and reinterprets norm and sequence as he experiences them.

Strauss and Martin have suggested that movement through careers is analogous to a large old tree.[29] We see a heavy trunk with large branches, from which branches of smaller diameter radiate, culminating eventually in the smallest twigs. Because people have trod similar occupational paths, more or less standardized mobility paths tend to grow up within a career. These paths may be either horizontal or vertical and long or short in terms of time spent traversing them. A typical career consists of a series of moves both horizontally and vertically. Horizontal movements may provide breadth of experience or may serve to block further mobility, or both, whereas vertical movement suggests shifts in levels of competence, authority, and power. For example, within a company we may see vertical movement from section leader to department head within a given division, horizontal movement from department head in one division to a similar post in another, and, following this, vertical movement to division head or to a higher management level. The horizontal moves of an intern through the various staffs of a teaching hospital, then a vertical move to a residency, followed by a series of horizontal moves

---

[29]Anselm L. Strauss and Norman L. Martin, "Patterns of Mobility Within Industrial Organizations," *Journal of Business* 29 (April, 1956): 101–10. Although their discussion is limited to large-scale businesses, their approach is of such scope as to be highly suggestive of generalization to the class of stable careers. Aspects of this discussion has been elaborated in Barney G. Glaser and Anselm L. Strauss, *Status Passage* (Chicago: Aldine-Atherton, 1971).

as the physician (now emerged from student status) builds a practice, constitute another example. And the experience of an actor who exists for years at one "one-night stand" after another and eventually makes the "big time" of New York is still another example.

Within the total complex of statuses within a career, certain statuses operate as critical junctures or contingencies, passage through which may serve to modify or redirect all or a portion of ongoing occupational activity. The performance of the individual at these crucial turning points determines the type of career line along which he will move—whether to higher levels or to completion of his career at the level he now occupies. Is the person promoted to a higher management position, does the student pass his examinations and thereby become a candidate for an advanced degree?[30] These contingencies may be primarily testing situations:

> At the end of [medical school training, the individual] has earned his degree as a doctor of medicine, but he is a doctor in name only. It is during his internship year, the so-called fifth year of medical school, that he is pounded and sweated into the shape and substance of a competent physician. This year is the proving ground: for the first time he takes upon himself the burden of responsibility, and his handling of it determines his success or failure.[31]

The fledgling carpenter and the doctoral candidate are both apprentices, constantly being tested to determine whether they perform competently in terms of the norms of their craft. In a number of large companies the positions of assistant division manager or plant superintendent may serve this function. Management can directly observe the ability of the person to make decisions and effectively

---

[30]Some contingencies are situational, rather than being tied to a particular status. A pianist who loses an index finger, for example, can be said to have experienced a critical juncture in his career. The Austrian pianist Paul Wittgenstein (1887–1961) lost his right arm in World War I; were it not for music written especially for him (by Ravel and others) that provided him with a repertoire, he might never have performed his role. A minister who is dismissed from congregation after congregation may be required to restructure his occupational performance, regardless of the degree of theological commitment he entertains. Cf. Lee Braude, "Professional Autonomy and the Role of the Layman," *Social Forces* 39 (May, 1961): 297–301. Some contingencies, then, are (conceptually) independent of status.

[31]"Doctor X," *Intern* (New York: Harper & Row, 1965), p. 4.

interact with others, to take initiatives in relatively unstructured situations. These are characteristics demanded of higher management. Therefore, to the degree that the aspirant is effective in areas of limited scope, he will move to a higher niche in the organizational structure; should he fail to perform as expected he may either move horizontally for more testing and training, may be terminated altogether, or, what may be most dysfunctional to an individual who perceives himself to be both mobile and involved in a career, may spend the rest of his employment days in the firm at the same level. Many businesses give an individual seven years to move to "middle management" or face termination. Lawyers in Wall Street "law factories" have a similar period in which to be promoted to junior partnership; and the academic rank of assistant professor is notorious as a testing time, carrying with it an often explicit "up or out" proviso.

Of course, the amount of vertical and horizontal movement depends on the social and technical division of labor within the occupation and the corresponding status and authority system. Some occupations may require interchangeability. As we would expect, their technical division of labor is simple, the responsibilities and consequent rewards are meager from the perspective of the entire complex of work roles available to the individual in our society, and the resulting occupational organizational structure is relatively flat. Mobility is therefore largely horizontal. Conversely, in occupations with a highly developed technical division of labor, training and testing will emphasize technical competence, and movement is mostly vertical, since the occupational structure is organized in terms of acquired skills. And some occupations—particularly those in which skills rest on an intellectual substructure—will be a combination of both.

The speed at which one moves along a career path tends to proceed according to occupationally institutionalized timetables. Identifiable age ranges for each career point, and the time spent at each point, become part of the lore of an occupation. Just as there comes a time when it is either too early or too late to commit oneself to an occupation, so are there points at which a person may be judged to be too old or, for that matter, too young for a particular role performance. "He needs more seasoning." "He's been here too long to move him up." If an individual does not move out of a given career segment and into another by a particular age (or after a suitable time in the preceding slot), it is highly probable that any further movement may be blocked or at least slowed considerably.

In the "Professional Progress Chart," the aspiring minister, for example, is told somewhat facetiously—but not quite, for there is a grain or two of reality in all wit—the road he must take toward preferment to the highest clerical offices. He is further told how he may advance more rapidly: Make contacts, analyze the power structure, and relate cordially to it. "[Y]ou wait out the inescapable dreary years of your early career . . . you sedulously cultivate the power structure which controls preferment in your synod or conference or diocese. . . ."[32]

Because they recognize these timetables, the practitioners of the occupation know that others have passed this way before. The fate of others provides a series of benchmarks by which current role incumbents may assess their own movement and potential for advancement. An individual who does not proceed through the career at the legitimized pace may assume, first, that he has not met appropriate criteria for movement—somebody up there does *not* like him—and, second, that his potential for further movement is limited. As occupations set the terms by which achievement is measured, so do occupations define when noteworthy accomplishments (with their attendant mobility) ought to occur. Distinguished contributions in the natural and physical sciences must occur early—the earlier the better—in order for subsequent mobility to be both vertical and rapid; in the humanities and social sciences, most mobility during the early years of the career is horizontal, for "ripening" must occur (according to the folklore) before "seminal work," and rapid upward mobility occurs later. Individuals who opt for management tend to move early and rapidly toward the top.

Thus, careers have built into them the possibility of failure. The nature of this failure may be in level of achievement or productivity or inappropriate meshing of achievement and time (e.g., "too little and too late" or, for that matter, precocity—"ahead of his time," a prophet without honor, "upstart"). But failure is a crucial career contingency, and occupations must be able to cope with it at both the ideological and the interpersonal level. Robert Merton has observed that, given the avowedly Protestant origins of the United States and

[32]Charles M. Smith, *How to Become a Bishop Without Really Trying* (New York: Pocket Books, 1966), p. 134.

TABLE 9. PROFESSIONAL PROGRESS CHART

Age 26	Age 28	Age 30 or 31	Age 35–38	Age 43–50	Age 50–55
First miserable pastorate	Second miserable pastorate	County-seat parish or Grade B city church	First major-league pastorate or new suburban church with tremendous potential for growth	Second major-league pastorate or important board job or presidency of church-related college	Become bishop

SOURCE: Adapted from Charles M. Smith, *How to Become a Bishop Without Really Trying* (New York: Pocket Books, 1966), p. 130.

Canada and the resulting religious aura surrounding work, failure is not nearly so heinous a crime as the admission that one has failed. For then failure becomes a self-fulfilling prophecy: The recognition of failure brings further failure. And the coping mechanism reflects this. While failure may be a recognized outcome of movement through the occupation, the occupation must devise strategies for treating failure *as if* it were not. The victim must be "cooled out." Erving Goffman uses the term, which he borrowed from the argot of the confidence man, to refer to the attempt by organizations to render failure less disturbing.[33] With reference to the con man's operation, Goffman observes that the individual who has been deceived, "taken," by the con man suffers a predictable loss of self-esteem. Fearing that the disgruntled individual will go the police or otherwise create a disturbance, the criminal provides a mechanism whereby the person will be appeased, or "cooled out." An accomplice may remain behind to help the taken person redefine the situation as inevitable—to "take it like a man," go home and forget the entire matter. Goffman suggests that an organization, and by extension an occupation, must minimize the humiliation and loss of ego-strength attendant upon failure, so that the victim does no further damage either to himself or to the specialty. But at the same time the occupation must guard against charges of ineffective recruitment or unrealistic measures of achievement. Sometimes the latter charge is leveled at occupations by ethnic or linguistic minorities who feel impossible standards of success to be implicitly discriminatory.

[33]Erving Goffman, "On Cooling the Mark Out: Some Aspects of Adaptation to Failure," *Psychiatry* 15 (November, 1952): 451–63.

"Cooling out" is therefore subtle. Although one could be told outright that he is a failure or be fired or lose some sorts of privileges, it makes much more sense, at least in terms of protecting the integrity of the occupation, to be less open with the person. He may simply find further opportunities for upward mobility closed to him. He may find himself with new duties and perhaps a new job description but with little additional responsibility; that is, he may be "kicked upstairs." He may be ostracized physically by indefinite lateral movement away from his former base of operation. (For example, a police officer who has been too zealous in writing traffic tickets in the business or financial area of a city finds himself "sent to the sticks" to walk a solitary beat amid the vacant lots.) Or the person may find himself socially isolated. Thus, a rabbi commented on the vicissitudes of his career:

> *Rabbi*: I wanted to serve in a congregation that would be at least halfway responsive to my leadership, but they were completely unresponsive, not to me personally, but to what they knew I represented. . . .
>
> *Interviewer*: How did you gauge this responsiveness [of the congregants]?
>
> *Rabbi*: I gauged this responsiveness by the gauge which was the universal criterion. . . . If you suddenly stopped receiving calls, personal calls, or stopped receiving invitations to even general gatherings you knew that you were out, and once you were out socially you were on your way out physically.[34]

Similarly, students who fail their written examinations for the doctoral degree feel that the first indication of failure is deliberate avoidance by their professors. Sometimes the knowledge possessed by the person who fails may be utilized in essentially "noncombatant" or "limited service" capacities, as in the case of the flier who is grounded for failing his latest physical examination and is used as an airport operations officer or recruiter; or the soprano who fails to achieve star status but who is an excellent teacher of those who do. Some organizations run training programs to prepare employees for

[34]Lee Braude, "The Rabbi: A Study of the Relationship of Contingency Situations to Differential Career Structure" (unpublished Ph.D. dissertation, Department of Sociology, University of Chicago, 1964), p. 154.

failure. In short, because of the personal and occupational consequences, failure must be handled delicately, and usually is.

Although one cannot help but view failure negatively, given the orientation toward success and achievement that characterizes the socialization of people in North America, failure nevertheless does function positively for both work and workers. Becker and Strauss suggest that there are undesirable work tasks—dirty-work occupations—that no one may want but that must be performed as part of the total societal division of labor. Such occupations may for some be the only means of survival; railroad work gangs, for example, are often made up of Skid Row inhabitants. Thus the positions that may be filled by those who fail may not be regarded by them as such. The middle-class white person who becomes a counselor in a public employment agency may in a time of full employment look upon such a work task as beneath him. However, when jobs are scarce, the biweekly check may be very welcome. A black from the inner city may view such a job as an avenue to upward mobility. The transient, the individual who, disaffected with his life for the moment, seeks survival but with anonymity may usefully fill certain work roles, such as taxi driver or operator of an ice-cream truck or wagon. Of course, some persons may find themselves inescapably locked into such tasks when a return to something approximating their past behavior proves impossible because of illness, habituation to the current situation, or lack of access to the recruitment network.

The upwardly mobile individual pursuing his career—whether public or private, open or closed—recognizes that the patterns of movement within the occupation that have over time become standardized or traditional represents avenues of advancement. If the person is perceptive, he can, for the most part, determine the channels of progress appropriate to his own particular ambitions from cues that are generally available. These cues are aspects of the patterns themselves: the critical junctures and testing situations, the timetables for orderly progress through the occupation, and an awareness that certain career branches may slow down further advancement or may be dead ends altogether. If the occupation is relatively stable, this assessment may be made with considerable accuracy.

A crucial career contingency, with implications for the successful outcome of career movement, is the ability of the individual to acquire

a sponsor. A sponsor is one who occupies a superior status within the occupation and is able to pull the aspirant along with him. While the protégé may acquire from the sponsor much in the way of formal training and knowledge, of far more importance is the informal view of the occupation and his self within it that the newcomer assimilates. In daily interaction with his sponsor, the trainee learns the occupational culture, appropriate conduct, the very folklore of the occupation in a manner and with an intensity that could never be picked up in a classroom or other formal learning experience. Conversely, the sponsor sees his pupil and is able to assess both his competence and his interpersonal sophistication in a far wider context than would be possible in a structured relation. Thus, the procession of individuals along career lines is not only a matter of technical proficiency or commitment to occupational goals or even of being available and trained at the right time. A major influence determining who moves and how far is the conduct of the sponsor. In many instances, his presence is virtually a necessary condition for mobility.

As might be expected, the relation between sponsor and protégé tends to be reciprocal, for benefits accrue to both parties. The learner may complement the sponsor by being strong in an area of activity where the sponsor is weak. The novice may serve as secretary or confidant or detail man or adviser. Whatever his role, when the sponsor rises, so does the protégé. The sponsor may have a cadre of disciples about him, and their loyalty to him engenders his willingness to push to advance "his team" as he himself moves up. But the sponsor's efforts to benefit his protégés are not all that altruistic. His own reputation is at stake as well. If the sponsor sends well-trained and personable disciples out into the work world, his own distinction increases, and his particular point of view or style of work is spread more widely and perpetuated. If, on the other hand, the sponsor does not choose his disciples well or botches the job of indoctrination, his reputation will be tarnished by the examples he has unleashed. Of course, the sponsor himself may fail or may be lured to a more personally rewarding work place or even specialty, leaving his pupils defenseless. Such behavior is occupationally (as well as morally) indefensible, but it does happen.

The phenomenon of sponsorship is seen in the makeup of many sociological colleague groups and in the top echelons of business organizations. They are often composed of interlocking cliques of powerful sponsors and their adherents. It becomes important for the novice to "play his cards" properly by finding out who the members of this influential group are so that he might be able to choose a sponsor (and be accepted) from among them. It is up to him to assess the situation and to attach himself to an individual who could conceivably prove beneficial. Not only must he demonstrate the technical competencies that are necessary for advancement and that would bring him to the notice of potential sponsors; he must also exhibit the requisite social skills—ability to converse about trivia, ability to consume liquor, perhaps sexual prowess. Thus, the rational order that presumably underlies occupational placement is subverted to idiosyncratic and particularistic factors. Executives, trainees, apprentices, and students become concerned with developing their own positions and extending their power. Struggles may ensue that affect the career line and, perhaps, the occupation as well.

To sum up, then, from the sponsor the protégé learns the unwritten lore and self-presentation appropriate to the occupational role; thus the novice learns to share in the ethos of the occupation, and in the best way possible. If the sponsor is knowledgeable in his field of competence, if he is upwardly mobile in a field that seems to be relatively permanent, he can carry the protégé along with him. He will introduce the fledgling to people he "ought to know" and open doors providing situations for interaction that might not otherwise be accessible. The novice prospers and emerges from the testing situation implicit in sponsorship, no longer green and untried, to take a higher place in the occupational structure than might be possible were he to try for mobility without such aid. On the other hand, a sponsor who may not be meeting the occupational demands placed upon *him*, who may be isolated from his colleagues or in an unpopular or moribund specialty, is an unqualified danger, capable of pulling his disciple, however competent, out of the mobility race altogether.

THE DEVELOPMENT OF
A WORK IDENTITY

Ultimately, any consideration of work must focus on the relation between work and the individual. To be sure, this discussion has not

been absent in previous pages, but now we must focus explicitly on
that very intimate relation between performance in an occupation
and the person who performs, between work and the self.

Until recently, it was characteristic of sociologists to restrict their
treatment of socialization to the years of childhood. Thus, socialization was viewed solely as the process by which the growing child
developed a sense of self—i.e., the process by which the maturing
individual achieved the ability to look objectively at himself and to
regulate his responses to the world in terms of others' perceptions of
him. Increasingly, sociologists are examining any situation in which
an individual is prepared for a new status and learns the role
performance appropriate to that status as an instance of socialization.
Consequently, it becomes possible to conceive of life itself as one long
(and perhaps often agonizing) socialization experience.

What we are about to consider is relatively difficult to document
through empirically verified statements that derive from research.
Nevertheless, it is hoped that the ensuing discussion will suggest
phenomena of sufficient clarity to be identified as having happened
to each of us. Although you are asked to grant intuitively the
plausibility of the assertions to be offered, they are assertions that
should be easily demonstrable in the context of your own life course.[35]

We tend to think of ourselves in many ways: I am fat, I am thin, I
am handsome, I am ugly, I am intelligent, I am a nincompoop. We
have names that evoke responses in us. In addition to the family name
by which we are called, which in itself ties us to an entire social
heritage and a set of expectations and obligations implicit in that
history, we are of one sex or the other, we bask in the pride of
particular accomplishments—which can be named—and we work at
particular tasks. Whatever the criteria may be, we tend to name
ourselves in particular ways. And this act of naming—the acquisition
of identity—results in the classification through symbols of ourselves,
of the world and the ways in which we come to terms with that world.

---

[35]Much of the discussion that follows is predicated on the treatment
provided by Anselm L. Strauss in *Mirrors and Masks: The Search for Identity*
(Glencoe, Ill.: Free Press, 1959). See also Nelson N. Foote, "Identification as
the Basis for a Theory of Motivation," *American Sociological Review* 16
(February, 1951): 14–22; Nelson N. Foote and Leonard S. Cottrell, Jr., *Identity
and Interpersonal Competence* (Chicago: University of Chicago Press, 1955); and
Alex Inkeles. "Society, Social Structure, and Child Socialization," in John A.
Clausen, ed., *Socialization and Society* (Boston: Little, Brown, 1969), pp. 74–129.

All one need do is ask the question: Who am I? Answer the question, and the idea of identity should become clear. Anselm Strauss points out that, however elusive an identity may be, a central aspect is the individual's response to the appraisals he and others make of his conduct. From what he observes of himself in the mirror of others (including those situations in which he stands back and observes himself from their perspective), he fashions a kind of interpersonal mask through which he presents himself, as Goffman has put it, to · others and in terms of which he attempts to anticipate how others will respond to him in the future (which may be only seconds away).

For example, let us assume a male of acned face, portly frame, and—just to exaggerate the case—bowlegs. He is, as the saying goes, ugly as sin. People shy away from him on the street; their interaction with him is direct and brief when they must meet with him at all. There are some who even snicker when he appears. Eventually, such encounters lead the person to suggest to himself, as does Hamlet, that "man delights not in me nor woman neither." So the poor fellow withdraws, becomes defensive, and names—that is, identifies—himself as an "ugly duckling" who will never amount to much. Ah, but then he meets HER, and, for whatever reason, she sees beyond the obesity and the blackheads and the parenthetical shanks, and what she sees, together with her behavior in terms of what she sees, transforms him. "I am loved," says he. "I shall swing from the stars!" A new name—"Beloved"—brings a new stance toward self and world. The two marry and live happily ever after.

In the development of an identity, the part of the self that emerges when we name ourselves, work looms large. One of the most important names we provide for ourselves in North American society derives from the work we do. Indeed, Strauss has suggested that the shaping of one's work identity is the prototype of identity formation.

Central to the development of the work identity are those critical junctures or contingencies that not only serve to redirect ongoing activity (as discussed earlier in this chapter) but also force the person to realize that he is not the same person he was, that a redefinition of his situation is very much in order. He must question the nature of the change both interpersonally and against the backdrop of the standardized, or traditional, patterns of movement through the occupation. This means that, like the traveler who periodically compares his map with road signs and landmarks in order to note his progress, the worker must compare his progress with the progress of others *and* against the benchmarks or indicators of progress within the occupation. Thus, as medical students progress through their medical school training, they attempt to develop a perspective that will both guide their learning—what to learn and how to learn it—and indicate their growth:

> [These students] are, after all, engaged in a series of trials, reacting to the demands and constraints of their environment and estimating their success from cues given by grades, test questions, faculty perspectives, and the various events, scheduled and unscheduled, of the school year. . . . [T]he examinations at the end of each block of work continue to be the "traumatic" proving ground of student perspectives. This is so, not only because the penalty of failure is severe (repeating a course or possibly leaving medical school wth poor prospects of getting into another), but because test questions reveal to the students whether they are studying the "right" things, and discussion of tests in class or papers returned with comments indicate whether they are answering in the "right" way.[36]

These cues that are presented alter their perspectives and so change their identities through the four years of medical school. Similarly, Gouldner discusses the responses of a newly appointed plant manager to the cues provided by management, his former associates, and his new ones, as the manager attempts to define his new status.[37]

The individual must clarify to himself and to others the change in naming, identity, that has occurred. Thus, the newly crowned Henry V says to Falstaff:

> I know thee not, old man. Fall to thy prayers. . . .
> Presume not that I am the thing I was;
> For God doth know, so shall the world perceive,
> That I have turn'd away my former self.

Such clarification is aided considerably if there can be some sort of public proclamation of the change. On occasion, the person must

[36]Howard S. Becker, Blanche Geer, Everett C. Hughes, and Anselm L. Strauss, *Boys in White: Student Culture in Medical School* (Chicago: University of Chicago press, 1961), p. 159.

[37]Alvin Gouldner, *Patterns of Industrial Bureaucracy* (Glencoe, Ill.: Free Press, 1954), pp. 70 ff.

himself openly declare the change: "I'm a father!" "I got my license!" "The doctor says I can go home this afternoon!" More often than not, the social structure (of the occupation, of religion, or whatever) provides the opportunity as a by-product of the contingency. Graduates, in distinctive garb, are welcomed "to the company of scholars" in solemn convocation and, in front of those assembled, are given documentation of their arrival (the diploma). The king is crowned. The banns are published. The bishop places his consecrated hands upon the head of the new priest and ordains him to the service of his deity. The grades are posted. The latest promotions are announced in the company house organ.

The clarification further requires that the person be able to define—or have defined for him—the modifications in interaction that have resulted from the turning point. Often old relations must be sloughed off and new ones substituted. Sometimes the nature of an ongoing relationship must be redefined, as, for example, when a categorical colleague becomes a sociological colleague, or when an equal becomes a superior, or when, for that matter, an inferior overtakes and passes an individual who was once mentor or sponsor or role model—the student who rises to eminence in a field, leaving his teacher behind. (It should be noted that this is precisely the hope of teachers, especially at higher educational levels.) Receipt of a covered parking space—or loss of one—an invitation to move from the employees' cafeteria to the executive dining room, or the "feelers" of new job possibilities that often follow upon the publication of a well-reviewed book, all are examples of structurally provided definitions.

A change in identity thus brings a change in status. The recognition of this status shift, like the shift itself, may be sudden or gradual. But the preparation for that change is frequently long and arduous. In addition to the acquisition of necessary skills, it involves what has been called "anticipatory socialization."[38] This means that those who aspire to a particular status within some collectivity will orient themselves toward the norms and perspectives of that aggregation and attempt to assimilate them, at the same time rejecting the values of the grouping of which they are currently members and, by implication, their

[38]See Robert K. Merton, *Social Theory and Social Structure*, enlarged ed. (New York: Free Press, 1968), pp. 319–22.

current position within that group. Therefore, the substitution of new relations for old ones must begin long before the individual shifts his status. He may not in fact be permitted to initiate these changes by virtue of the status disparity; all that is necessary is that the individual behave *as if* the desired interaction were already taking place. His own definition of his altered interpersonal orientation will be communicated to his audiences—those whom he faces and those he leaves behind, as well as those who observe the change from the sidelines. To the extent that these several audiences legitimate the person's altered behavior, they will legitimate the mobility aspiration itself; conversely, as the individual receives the desired confirmation of actions, he will be more sure of the rightness of his upward thrust.

Of course, such a course is not without its dangers. The group that he leaves or to which he aspires may feel threatened or, perhaps, victimized. The individual may be ostracized; he may be denied entry by the reference group (the one above) and, having made public his intention to defect from the group of which he is now a (presumptive) member, he may not be permitted to return. His mobility drive may be stopped cold and the person forced to beat a hasty retreat out of the occupation altogether or at least drastically to revise his sense of career within it. Anticipatory socialization thus requires commitment over and above the commitment implicit in the intention to break new interpersonal ground in the service of higher occupational standing. One must also be willing to gamble his very occupational life on the assumption that his moves will be accepted; the individual who guesses wrongly may find himself without either his customary interpersonal anchorages or new ones, so that he may be totally alone.

The following quotations may serve to summarize what has been said up to this point:

> [A] career involves investment of substantial parts of one's life; commitments to particular tasks, colleagues and organizations; and claims to a particular type of identity and social reputation. Entry into a particular occupation or structure involves putting an irretrievable portion of time into a particular job. A realized misinvestment and attempts to correct it necessitate a new start. Such realization often comes only after a protracted period of reality testing when the person may be faced with the choice of continuing with something about which he is uneasy or trying something else which is an unknown quantity for him and where,

for all he knows, he may also be unhappy or unsuccessful. More
is involved than the sheer economics of investment of time.
Through commitment to a line of work a person becomes
committed to a particular social and personal identity. He has
held himself out to be a particular sort of person, to have a
particular set of prospects, to belong to certain indicated
groups.[39]

The decision, or the fact . . . of operating in a small or in a large
orbit involves the choice of significant others (reference groups),
the people on whose good opinion one stakes one's reputation;
those whom one can afford to pay less attention to; and those,
perhaps, from whom one must dissociate oneself. It involves, in
short, the choice of his closer colleagues. . . .
    Career is, in fact, a sort of running adjustment between a man
and the various facts of life and his [work] world. It involves the
running of risks, for his career is his ultimate enterprise, his
laying of his bets on his one and only life.[40]

To continue, the shaping of an identity is aided considerably when
the movement from status to status is regularized when identifiable
timetables of progression exist. The speed with which one moves can
be compared with that of individuals who have gone before. Noting
where he is on the career ladder, the individual can then make some
assumptions about the distance he has yet to travel to reach his goals
and the amount of time he has available to him to get where he wants
to go, as well as assess the alternative routes to these goals. As a
consequence of this evaluation, he can conceive of himself as a success
or a failure or somewhere along a continuum between these poles.
But the person's identity can never be, as it were, fully fleshed out,
because he cannot know in advance all the nuances of that career
however much he may be aware of what awaits him. Only those who
have gone through the recognized steps can guide and advise their
successors. And here enters the phenomenon of *coaching*.
    One way of looking at coaching is to think of it as the dynamic
aspect of sponsorship—that is, the role performance associated with

[39]Cyril Sofer, *Men in Mid-Career*, Vol. 4 in *Cambridge Studies in Sociology*
(Cambridge, England: Cambridge University Press, 1970), p. 270.
    [40]Everett C. Hughes, "The Making of a Physician," *Human Organization* 14
(Winter, 1955): 21–25.

the status of sponsor. However, coaching behavior is not limited to a sponsor; it occurs whenever someone seeks to move another along a series of steps of a character and sequence that are unclear to the initiate. Certainly, coaching is an aspect of the teaching situation, but, as Strauss points out, it can also be seen in the work of the confidence man, the revivalist seeking converts, the therapist helping an individual to overcome alcohol dependence, or the attorney maneuvering a reluctant witness into desired responses.[41] The coach knows the steps, can predict the changes that will occur, and will (presumably) aid the novice in interpreting his movement and the changes—both personal and interpersonal—that result from the movement. The learner relies on the coach to steer him correctly by lessening the ambiguities of status changes.

Coaching thus becomes fraught with danger. First, the candidate surrenders his autonomy to the coach in exchange for the correct interpretation of the indicators of change. The coach may prove false in that, consciously or otherwise, deliberately or not, he misinterprets the signals. He may move too fast or too slowly for the learner, perhaps forcing him over hurdles for which he is unprepared. Possibly the strategy of the coach may become overly standardized and insensitive to his student's needs; conversely, the student may surpass his mentor and threaten the coach's own survival. Or possibly the coach may end the coaching relationship before the learner is ready to be released. The coach on occasion might even refuse to relinquish the learner because the role of *guru* inflates his own sense of worth. And, of course, the learner might not let go.

In his discussion of coaching, Strauss has suggested that the process involves five interrelated components: prescription, schedule, challenge, trial, and accusation. "Prescriptions" are the drills or lessons or exercises—the methodical practice of the skills and attitudes that are prerequisite to further mobility and, hence, to the formation of a clear sense of occupational identity. This standardized practice may be the most clearly visible part of role learning: the seemingly endless scale-work that a soprano must master before she can confidently venture onstage; the typing of page upon page of dictation until the typist "gets up to speed"; the football player who must crash into that

---

[41]Strauss, *Mirrors and Masks* (n. 35 *supra*), pp. 109–24.

tackling dummy over and over again; the days of landing practice for a would-be pilot.

"Schedule" involves assumptions of timing: the speed of movement through the training situation, the appropriate points at which testing or practice or a hands-off policy on the part of the coach should occur.

"Challenge" is exactly that. The person being coached is pushed or cajoled or the physical and social space is manipulated so that the apprentice is dared to do, say, and think things that may be risky or even dangerous. But by meeting the challenge the individual demonstrates how far he has progressed in his acquisition of a new status. Now, of course, the individual may fail, and we have seen that failure must be handled delicately and judiciously. However, even failure may be used to teach necessary skills, suggest the route toward further progress, and provide clues as to how the challenge might be met in the future; even failure at something new indicates change.

"Trial" may be thought of as an extended challenge over time. It represents an experiment in role playing, in which the learner tries out the skills, the interpersonal stance, that he has learned to see if, in fact, he has internalized the required role performance. He is on his own, but not completely. The coach stands in the wings, ready to "bail him out" should he run into difficulties and thus cushion the trauma of failure. In any case, the coach is there to interpret behavior, to compare it with the benchmarks established by others in the same situation, and to use the trial as a preparation for the time when the novice will not have his coach with him to save him. "Trial" should be distinguished from "test"; the latter is institutionalized within the structure of the occupation, while the former is the prerogative of the coach. Sometimes, when the coaching process has become overly standardized, often because of the number of students who must be coached, there may be little difference between the two. Student teaching represents a trial; presenting a lesson with one's classmates as "students" is a test.

"Accusation" is essential in coaching, according to Strauss, because confrontations between coach and pupil force each of them to avow their intentions about the way things are going to the other and, inevitably, to themselves. The learner may be accused of sloughing off what has been learned, of not committing himself fully to the task at hand, of "goofing off." The coach, in turn, may be accused of betraying the learner or of having seduced him with unrealizable blandishments. Reconciliation may lead to further learning.

To sum up, an individual embarked on what he conceives to be a career is required to divest himself of old loyalties and practices, old ways of looking at his world, and to come up with new ones appropriate to a changed relationship to others. The coach guides or directs movement from one stage of learning to another and helps the person to evaluate what has happened along the way, in terms of both skills acquired and an altered view of self. He suggests alternative lines of action when they are present. For coaching to "work," there must be an element of trust on both sides and a willingness on the part of the pupil to commit himself to a destiny only dimly seen.

SUMMARY

Whenever one learns a work role or sets out along a path that may have the semblance of a career, he confronts the tasks of learning concepts, of assimilating aspects of an entirely new symbol system. Whenever symbols are learned, they tend to cluster about oneself as a symbol. The individual must therefore learn to see himself in new, perhaps untried or untested ways. New ideas mean that the individual is not who he was. And when that person learns to see himself in new ways, such that he can apply new labels to himself and his behavior, he has changed his identity. Who we are, as we have contended throughout the book, is in large measure a function of what we do. Therefore, it is at the social-psychological level, the conceptual or symbolic level, that work and the self meet, that the implications of work performance for the function of the individual are felt at the most personal level.

6

WORK AS A SOCIAL PROBLEM

LET US THINK of a social problem as the inability of one or more sectors of a population to act in habitual fashion with respect to some elements of the normative structure of the society. The interruption of ongoing behavior must first be *perceived* as taking place. It must then be *defined* as problematic; that is, it must be acknowledged that traditional ways of coping with the introduction have proved unavailing. It must then be *explained,* whether scientifically or from some other perspective (moralistic or theological, for example). Finally, *solutions* must be *proposed* in order to terminate the interruption and restore the normatively regulated routine.

Crime, opiate and alcohol addiction, and gambling perhaps come most readily to mind as illustrative of social problems that are felt to detract from the quality of life in North America. Yet environmental preservation, education, the plight of the young and the aged, the implications of the elusive search for world harmony, and the desire to remain healthy are additional examples of the problems associated

167

with a complex and rapidly changing society. Perhaps this latter group of "problems" may be of a less "sensational" character, less likely to create headlines or television "specials," but with these, as with the others, old orders break down and new methods must be found to cope with the altered social situation. It is becoming increasingly clear that work is assuming the dimensions of a "problem." To be sure, "work as a social problem" may be less notorious than others, but in the long run it may assume far greater import for the maintenance of the social system because it involves dearly held values and affects virtually every member of the populations of industrialized states.

COMPONENTS OF THE PROBLEM

Specialization. The essence of the problem of specialization was insightfully captured by that master humorist James Thurber in his short story "The Last Clock: A Fable for the Time, Such as It Is, of Man."[1] This is the story of an ogre who, having had anything he wanted, has suddenly acquired a taste—in the literal sense—for clocks. He has taken to eating clocks of varying size, shape, and complexity. The town, his ogredom, cannot provide enough clocks to assuage his insatiable hunger. He becomes ill. Terrified, his wife frantically calls for any and all who might be able to cure her husband. A doctor appears, but he soon decides "the case is not in my area." Next a "clockman" carrying a huge bag of tools is ushered in, but the case is not in his area, either; he says he is a "clogman" who can cure drains but not ogres. Beside herself, the ogress now calls in a general practitioner, who likewise declines to consider the case, because he treats only generals.

The ogress retires to consult a prodigiously large volume, *Who's Who in Areas.* "She soon [becomes] lost in a list of titles: clockmaker, clocksmith, clockwright, clockmonger, clockician, clockometrist, clockologist, and a hundred others dealing with clockness, clockism, clockship, clockdom, clockation, clockition, and clockhood." The ogre keeps on eating, so that both watches and clocks are rapidly disappearing. As a result, factories and stores close down, soft-boiled

[1]*New Yorker* 35 (February 21, 1959): 28–31.

eggs are hard, appointments are missed or not made at all, and everybody remains at home. A serious situation indeed!

The town council holds an emergency meeting to which, as expected, some members arrive late and some never appear. A "psychronologist," a "clockonomist," and a "clockosopher" are among those called upon to suggest solutions for the worsening crisis; each speaks in the language of his particular specialty, so that in the end, unintelligible to any but themselves, they can offer no solutions at all. As a last desperate measure, all the clockmakers in the town are enjoined from making any more clocks that could serve as food for the ogre.

While the clockmakers leave to look for other work, the ogre eats what appears to be the last clock remaining in the town and falls deathly ill. This time the ogress sends for the Chief Diagnostician of the Medical Academy, "a diagnostician familiar with so many areas that totality itself had become to him only a part of wholeness." But he proves unequal to the task because, of course, nothing like this has ever happened before: Who has ever eaten all the clocks in a town? So the problem of the town-without-clocks is carried to the Supreme Council, and various witnesses testify as to the implications of clocklessness, including the Celebrated Man in the Street, who suggests the use of sundials and is promptly dismissed from the stand. Finally, in an unanticipated moment of silence, the attention of all those in the Council chambers is arrested by the ticking of a clock—*the* last clock, it turns out—right on the wall behind the Chief Magistrate. The suggestion is promptly made that this last clock be placed in the clock tower of the town, where it might be seen by all the inhabitants. But there is even objection to this eminently sensible proposal. A specialist in antiques argues that this last clock is by definition a museum piece as well as an antique; it must therefore be allowed to run down and then be placed, with suitable ceremonies, in the town museum. The ogre dies, and this last clock in the town is placed in the museum. The town itself runs down and is buried by the sands of a nearby desert. Only eons later, when the town is discovered by a band of explorers from Venus (descendants of earthlings who had fled their planet centuries before), is the clock found and labeled an "antique mechanism. Function uncertain." The clock is carried back to Venus as a relic.

The growth of knowledge has brought with it an increase in the number and variety of work skills, with a consequent expansion of the division of labor. Work tasks could thus be spread across a population; this is one form of specialization. In addition, however, the requirements of rationality and efficiency that were generated by that same growth of knowledge demanded that existing skills be broken down into segments that could be easily learned, easily performed, and readily interchanged. So specialization suggests the proliferation of skills not only through expansion of the skill base but through segmentation. Thus, in the meat-packing industry we do not simply find an individual who dismembers the carcass of an animal; rather, the *Dictionary of Occupational Titles* tells us we shall find individuals with such skills as belly shaver, crotch buster, gut snatcher, snout puller, eyelid remover, hindlegs toenail puller, and frontlegs toenail puller. When skills are thus segmented, a single individual could focus his attention upon one task and learn all there is to know about it. He would become so completely involved with this task that eventually, as the popular saying has it, he would come to know more and more about less and less. He would develop a kind of occupational myopia. Skill segmentation can therefore generate the dilution of skills for any individual worker to the point where that single skill about which he knows so much may not be wanted at all. In a period of technological or economic change, a worker may be "diluted" right out of a job. So, it is not in the expansion of skills across a population that we encounter the problematic character of specialization but in the tendency for the individual's limited repertoire of skills to diminish still further when a particular task is emphasized at the expense of other tasks.

In the professions, which, by definition, deal with an unstandardized product, the difficulties and concerns of each individual who comes for service can be dealt with as a "case." The professional "works up" a history of these difficulties, and, so to speak, confronts them from start to finish. He works backward in time in order to develop some sense of the genesis of "the case" and then attempts some resolution of the situation as he faces toward the future. The professional, then, can see his client's problems as a totality and, by and large, need not be constrained by the exigencies of the particular moment when he encounters the individual-with-a-problem. However, in occupations that fall short of the ideal-typical model of *the profession* to the limiting case of *the job* at the other pole of that hypothetical continuum, time is all. Work takes on a routine character, and the worker knows the total product or output only partially. From the perspective of the particular set of bolts that *he* must tighten or the particular gasket that *he* must insert at so many to the minute, the worker may never see the complete entity on which he has worked. Consequently, it has become a commonplace to suggest, in the literature of sociology and elsewhere, that the nonprofessional subjected to a situation that is routine and in which outcomes can be controlled only partially is isolated, alienated, and even dehumanized. Whatever joy there can be in work is utterly lacking for him.

However, there is more to the problem of specialization. As the economic historian John U. Nef has argued, the specialization that was spawned by the Industrial Revolution, with the consequent growth of technology, led not only to the progressive estrangement of the worker from his work but also to the loss of a sense of and a concern for beauty in material culture. The potter at his wheel and the lacemaker and the carriage-builder could take pride in what they made, could see that it was aesthetically as well as functionally pleasing, because they could follow their work from concept to completion. They were, so to say, re-enacting the very mystery of Creation, partners with God in the beautification and refreshment of His world. But the division of a task into its component parts has prevented the worker from seeing beyond the immediate because he is geared to the pressure to produce in the here and now. Because he is not permitted to see beyond the demands of the moment, he has no idea, except perhaps in the most abstract sense, of what the finished material ought to be, or of his part in bringing the "creation" of this material to fruition. And if he cannot see what his labor will eventually bring forth, why then should he take pride in what he does? Why care whether it is beautiful or not, whether the item even operates or not? The worker is no longer a partner with God, for the Protestant Ethic, the intellectual tradition that shaped so much of Europe and North America, has been shorn of its religious significance and God has been dethroned. Specialization and secularization arose from the same set of ideas.

Thus, in the 1920's a Dutch social psychologist, Hendrik (Henri) deMan, could question whether there was in fact any joy in work, as in the 1950's Harvey Swados tried to puncture the "myth of the happy worker."[2] And in 1973 and 1974 we saw that workers at the Lordstown, Ohio, plant of Chevrolet protested through shutdown and slowdown the alienation they said they experienced as a result of assemblyline work. A twenty-year-old worker put it this way: "Every day I come out of there I feel ripped off. . . . A good day's work is being tired but not exhausted. . . . I don't even feel necessary."[3] And so, too, in 1973 Volvo revamped its auto manufacturing procedures to move from traditional assembly methods to "work teams" that would be responsible for the construction of a major segment of the automobile and would be trained, not only to produce that segment properly, but to see the integration of their work with those of other groups involved in manufacturing component segments of the car and putting them together.

Beauty and pride in craftsmanship are thus lost at the expense of efficiency. Utility becomes the norm by which one judges products and, by extension, people and the relationships into which people enter. And the worker, in such a view, becomes merely the cog in the gears of a machine over which he has no control. He becomes a means to an end; when he has outlived his usefulness as a "cog" or a "hand" he can then be replaced by someone presumably more fit or adaptable or pliant. Political movements that seek to appeal to the "proletariat" operate with such a perspective.

If the foregoing is in fact an accurate description of the matter, the question could then be asked whether the malaise of specialization is inevitable given the increasingly complex character of the functional division of labor. There is certainly no doubt that specialization through skill expansion will continue to be a consequence of any society in which the components of culture change rapidly. The proliferation of knowledge and the necessity to develop ways of dealing with that new knowledge suggest the permanence of that form of specialization as part of the social scene. But it is not such specialization that engenders dissatisfaction, since the education or preparation that is usually required embodies a creative outlet of its

---

[2]Henri deMan, *Joy in Work,* trans. Eden and Cedar Paul (New York: Holt, 1929), and Harvey Swados, "The Myth of the Happy Worker," *The Nation* 185 (August, 1957): 65–68.

[3]Stanley Aronowitz, *False Promises: The Shaping of American Working-Class Consciousness* (New York: McGraw-Hill, 1973), p. 21.

own. However, when we confront the specialization that takes place through the segmentation of skills, we then encounter dissatisfaction with the routine, apparently senseless, and debilitating effects of work. It is then that the worker appears to be the personification of the alienated man about whom Marx wrote so perceptively. So the question that must ultimately be addressed is whether or not specialization through segmentation is somehow inherently antagonistic to the achievement and maintenance of personal (and by implication social) well-being.

When viewed sociologically, such an assumption is misleading if not illogical. After all, it is human beings who bring meaning to a phenomenon, meaning that is based on prior experience and that suggests a particular disposition to act toward that phenomenon. Specialization has no "inherent" qualities except those we impute to it. The negative affect surrounding segmental specialization must then be viewed as part of a larger dilemma. Can work be freed of its negative emotional tone, the "bad press" it has acquired through the ages? Should work be regarded as something more than a means of earning money? Is it a divine curse because of the innate sinfulness of man or, on the contrary, can work be viewed as a necessary way of expressing one's individuality and vitality? Can "joy" somehow be returned to the work place?

Worker dissatisfaction and the meaning of work. A U.S. government task force report, *Work in America,* summarizes what is known about worker dissatisfaction. The level of satisfaction with one's work is directly related (there is a parallel change in two associated variables) to the level of:

(1) prestige of the job
(2) autonomy; control over the conditions of work
(3) cohesiveness of the work group, which facilitates interaction
(4) challenge and variety of the task
(5) employer concern and involvement of employees in decision-making
(6) wages, with respect to both amount and "relative deprivation" felt by the worker; his perception of adequacy of wages when compared with those of others performing similar tasks
(7) mobility potential of the job: workers want to feel that there exists in a job a potential for movement upward through the skill hierarchy, the occupational hierarchy, the organizational

structure in which the work is performed, or any combination
of the three
(8) satisfactory working conditions
(9) job security[4]

Such an enumeration suggests that at least a partial answer to the
problem of worker dissatisfaction may lie in rethinking the lessons of
Hawthorne.

Research conducted at the Hawthorne Works of the Western
Electric Company (the manufacturing arm of the American Telephone and Telegraph Corporation) in the late 'twenties and early
'thirties demonstrated, among other things, that productivity and
employee morale increased when the worker was led to think of
himself as someone in whom management was interested, that
company goals represented meaningful ends for employee as well as
employer, and, most important, that the individual could find satisfying interpersonal relationships at work. If, in other words, a worker
felt himself to be part of a viable group rather than an isolate among
isolates, a group whose members could work together toward goals
that made sense to them and that involved them in a real way in
contributing to the total progress of the organization, then output
increased, and with it worker satisfaction.

Such findings gave rise to the "human relations" movement in
industrial management, which led eventually to what has been
characterized as the "organization man" mentality. Anyone who
cannot conform to company demands and to a company life-style,
who will not keep the organization always in his thoughts by "playing
it the company way," will not be tolerated and will be ostracized until
he gets the message or eliminated altogether should he be unable to
interpret correctly the signals presented. If such an approach had its
excesses, the core notion still remains. When the worker can develop a
sense of "groupness" with its attendant morality of cooperation, then
the repetitive aspects of work can be made less onerous for any
person precisely because they will be shared by several, rather like the
interaction fostered among professional colleagues.[5]

[4]*Work in America: Report of a Special Task Force to the Secretary of Health,
Education, and Welfare* (Cambridge, Mass.: MIT Press, 1973), pp. 36–96. See
also Clark Kerr and Jerome M. Rosow, eds., *Work in America: The Decade Ahead*
(New York: Van Nostrand Reinhold Co., 1979).
[5]Kingsley Davis, *Human Society* (New York: Macmillan, 1949), p. 217.

Thus, Michel Crozier studied the work behavior of 350 workers in the Paris headquarters of six French insurance companies and found that the workers, who ranged from keypunch operators to managerial employees, valued a clearly defined stratification system because it apparently made them "freer."[6] They could be creative in structuring their work and work-related interpersonal lives because the limits to their behavior were clearly set forth; they knew what was expected vis-à-vis other work groups, and, once this was known, they did not have to be concerned about the work itself (the limits) and could devote their time to making the work situation tenable. Moreover, the presence of these hierarchical niches, which Crozier likens to little boxes, made for ease of worker interaction since they saw themselves in the same "box." They did not have to induce a feeling of community artificially and, possibly, risk too much self-revelation. A sense of involvement was provided by the common work situation and the common perceptions engendered therein; whatever additional commitments workers wished to make to each other depended on what they personally wished to bring into the work situation. The workers themselves would generate *Gemeinschaft* freely and creatively, rather than expect a pseudo-*Gemeinschaft* to be provided by a corporate "employee relations" group.

To cite another example, morale and efficiency increased when workers in a men's clothing factory were involved by management in discussions relative to factory automation and changes in method of payment. Discussion sessions were conducted for each group of workers performing the same task; in the very act of talking about the proposed changes, the employees came to perceive of themselves as participants in a common enterprise facing common problems, and their receptiveness to change increased as they became aware of the bonds that united them.[7]

And finally, as one of the results of negotiations between the United Auto Workers and the Chrysler Corporation in 1973, workers won the right to participate in experimental programs designed to reduce assembly-line tedium, all of which involved conscious group participation in the production process. Thus, according to the *New York Times*, workers were given the responsibility for turning out

---

[6]Michel Crozier, *The World of the Office Worker* (New York: Schocken, 1973).

[7]J. R. P. French *et al.*, "Employee Participation in a Program of Industrial Change," *Personnel* 35 (November–December, 1958): 16–29.

engines and could organize the task as they saw fit, supervising themselves and working at their own pace, with only the requirement that the engines be completed at a given time specified in their instructions.[8]

Concommitant with the necessity to generate a feeling of group involvement on the job is the necessity to reintroduce a concern with what is being produced, so that the worker is able to see his role in the total productive enterprise and can follow the process of production of the item from start to finish—again, as in professional conduct. This requires the recognition by both management and the worker that the work site does in fact represent the stage on which is played out a drama of far more import than that on the television screen or Off Broadway. Workers *do* structure the parameters of their work to a far greater extent than is realized. If they are explicitly charged with the development of a "work script" (as the term has been used in previous discussion), they can be expected to have a greater tendency to identify with each other, with the job, and with the employing organization. When the worker is thus able to define for himself his existence on the job and to specify the nature of the work-worker interface, when he can have some say in determining his contribution to production rather than simply being on the receiving end of directives from "on high," then involvement and concern with the ends of production—a quality product, if you will—might very well supplant the tedium that now obtains in so much of industrial work.[9]

But there is more to this than merely modifying the terms in which the individual-at-work approaches his peers and his task. When one encounters the following statement, voiced by a Lordstown worker—

[8]*New York Times*, Sunday, Sepember 23, 1973.

[9]See Cary L. Cooper and Enid Mumford, eds., *The Quality of Working Life in Western and Eastern Europe* (Westport, Conn.: Greenwood Press, 1979); Louis E. Davis and Albert B. Cherns, eds. with commentary, *The Quality of Working Life*, vol. I: *Problems, Prospects and the State of the Art* (New York: Free Press, 1975); *idem*, and associates, eds. with commentary, *The Quality of Working Life*, vol. II: *Cases and Commentary* (New York: Free Press, 1975); Robert M. Marsh and Hiroshi Mannari, *Modernization and the Japanese Factory* (Princeton, N.J.: Princeton University Press, 1976); Michael Poole, *Workers' Participation in Industry* (London: Routledge & Kegan Paul, 1975); Pehr G. Gyllenhammar, "The Team System at Volvo," (British) *SSRC Newsletter* 27 (April, 1975):8–9. A dissent to this is provided by Graham A. B. Edwards, "Volvo, Shut Up!" (Bradford, West Yorkshire: Bradford (University) Management Centre Discussion Paper, 1974).

"I am not going to bust my ass for anybody. I don't even bust my ass for myself, you know, working around the house"[10]—it is clear that we face a much more difficult problem: the modification of our very attitudes toward work itself.

In America's infancy the Puritans who first colonized the new land enshrined work as an end in itself. Men were to be measured in terms of the work they did and the amount of sweat, either implied or actual, expended in the accomplishment of that work. There was a wilderness to be won, and work very literally meant individual and social survival in a hard and often uncongenial environment. America's folk heroes—the Paul Bunyans, the Johnny Appleseeds and John Henrys and Mike Mageraks—were forged in the crucible of the "gospel of work." And "gospel" it was, for, as we have seen, the theology of Calvinist Protestantism reinforced the practicality of sheer physical survival with survival in the hereafter. Work was the key to the riddle of salvation. Benjamin Franklin, the archetypal man of the "Protestant Ethic," put it succinctly in his "Advice to a Young Tradesman":

> [T]he way to Wealth . . . is as plain as the Way to market. it depends chiefly on two Words, INDUSTRY and FRUGALITY; i.e. Waste neither Time nor Money, but make the best Use of both. He that gets all he can honestly, and saves all he gets (necessary Expenses excepted) will certainly become RICH; if that Being who governs the World, to whom all should look for a Blessing on their honest Endeavors, doth not in his wise Providence otherwise determine.[11]

Idleness was sinful, while work was the source of all the virtues.

But as wilderness gave way to cultivation, which in its turn surrendered to the urban sprawl, a religious legitimation for the efficacy of work as the source of survival in a hostile environment was displaced by a secularized conception of work as contributing to "survival" at an interpersonal level. New technological advances,

[10]Quoted in "Adam Smith," *Supermoney* (New York: Popular Library, 1972), p. 239.

[11]Benjamin Franklin's "Advice to a Young Tradesman" (1748) represents the Protestant Ethic incarnate. Weber quotes it extensively in *The Protestant Ethic* (p. 175). See Benjamin Franklin, *The Papers of Benjamin Franklin*, ed. Leonard W. Labaree and Whitefield J. Bell, Jr. (New Haven: Yale, 1959–), 3:306–8.

spawned by that same zeal to survive physically, were making it possible to produce goods more quickly and inexpensively than in the past. And work came increasingly to be seen as that activity which could generate money that, in turn, could provide more of the *things* then appearing in greater variety and quantity. These *things* would then serve to indicate one's socio-economic status relative to others and provide the cues to behavior of the participants in the status relation. So, at an accelerating pace, Americans consumed (and perhaps were consumed by) the products of a burgeoning technology. However, work became less a "central life interest" for large sectors of America's expanding population, because the individual was less able to see a direct relation between occupation and success as measured by the Protestant Ethic. With work shorn of its transcendent moral imperative, the person required others to legitimate his progress, which was itself measured differently. That is to say, it was one thing to clear a plot of ground and harvest the crop of that new farm or to produce an artifact or run an enterprise, earn money and return that money to the business; one could see the immediate effects of one's effort here on earth and, firm in the faith of a providential God, "feel" the effects one would reap in the hereafter. It was quite another thing, however, to work for a monetary reward, to see that reward solely in terms of the use to which it could be put, and then to use that money to accumulate personal property capable of enhancing oneself in the eyes of others—an indication of increasing status—but without knowing whether the status shift had in fact occurred until others had confirmed it by their behavior. No room for "feeling" here.

In time, then, the acquisition of money, rather than work, as a bridge to enhanced status became a dominant goal orientation of Americans. Money meant achievement, and it eventually made little difference whether that money was acquired by fair means or foul. The "robber barons" who despoiled the land or jockeys who "fixed" races or the "hot tip" resulting in windfall profits for a speculator in the stock market are examples. And if, at least theoretically, work was not the only way to accumulate wealth, it became less necessary to immerse oneself single-mindedly in the work one did. Work was downgraded in the American scheme of things, and new justifications for work (perhaps even a new definition) were required.

Such a justification emerges clearly from studies of worker satisfaction. While there is some relation between satisfaction with one's work and the skill level associated with that work—professionals and managers appear to exhibit greater satisfaction with their work because of its content than do semiskilled and many service workers— one consideration unmistakably appears to override all others. Work fills time. It gives a person the day-to-day continuity of routine. What is important is that there be something to do, rather than nothing at all, to structure at least a portion of one's day. As long as it is felt that there is some freedom, some room to maneuver, work is accepted; if there is in addition a sense of creativity, of contributing to an obvious productive outcome, work then becomes fulfilling.

While a conception of work as time-filling or time-serving may appear to be simplistic or naïve, when it is remembered that so much of work has become routine and repetitive, that the segmental specialization of work tasks and the bureaucratization of work organizations have given the worker a depersonalizing anonymity despite Hawthorne, in such circumstances it would seem almost inevitable that a perception of work as an anodyne to insecurity should have developed. Really, what alternatives were present when the human being was simply reduced, in the phrase of C. Wright Mills, to a niche in "the enormous file"?[12]

However, like any predisposition toward action, attitudes toward work are not irreversible; as they have been learned so can they be unlearned, or rendered more positive. At least some tentative suggestions in that direction can be advanced. A key to the problem is provided by the social philosopher Hannah Arendt in her volume *The Human Condition:* [W]e have proved ingenious enough to find ways to ease the toil and trouble of living to the point where an elimination of laboring from the range of human activities can no longer be regarded as utopian. For even now, laboring is too lofty, too ambitious a word for what we are doing, or think we are doing, in the world we have come to live in. The last stage of the laboring society, the society of job-holders, demands of its members a sheer automatic functioning, as though individual life had actually been submerged in the over-all life process of the species and the only active decision still required of the individual were to let go, so to speak, to abandon his individuality, the still individually sensed pain and trouble of living,

[12]C. Wright Mills, *White Collar* (New York: Oxford University Press, 1951), pp. 189–212.

and acquiesce in a dazed, "tranquilized," functional type of behavior. . . . It is quite conceivable that the modern age—which began
with such an unprecedented and promising outburst of human
[creative and manipulative] activity—may end in the deadliest, most
sterile passivity history has ever known.[13]

If what men do at their work is to be once more endowed with
meaning, then this activity must in fact be made active, as it once was.
At the risk of overromanticizing the prosaic, work must once again
become a kind of Hegelian confrontation between the worker, acting
to transform a piece of the world, and the world, which, in its way,
resists that effort.

Automation. It may possibly be ironic that automation, so often
regarded as being principally responsible for giving work its social-
problematic character, might very well offer a way by which the active
and manipulatory dimension of occupational involvement could be
restored to the work setting. If automation does in fact represent the
"Second Industrial Revolution," as has been suggested, then it becomes a matter of not merely coping with its implications but *using* it
in as socially and personally meaningful a fashion as possible.

Automation may be defined as the mechanized performance of an
activity that had previously required human performance of that
same activity. Thus, a bulldozer, a crane, and a postage meter could
be thought to be low-level examples of automation. The regulation by
a crew of five of an entire oil-refining process would represent a more
complex example. However, automation must further be distinguished from mechanization. The former implies the total substitution of the machine for the operator or operators. The latter
implies only that a machine assists, but does not replace, the worker in
easing production or performance or increasing the volume of what is
produced. Data-processing equipment or the "catalytic cracker" distil-
lation apparatus used in the petrochemical industry illustrates automation; an instrument that monitors the vital functions of several
patients in a hospital intensive-care facility is an example of mechanization. Or consider the superiority of the electric over the manual
typewriter for both ease of operation and elegance of the typed page;

---

[13]Hannah Arendt, *The Human Condition* (Chicago: University of Chicago
Press, 1958), p. 322.

or the mimeograph machine or xerography as a technique of duplication as against a piece of carbon paper used again and again.

Automated devices seem generally to take three forms:

(1) those that deal with the storage, retrieval, and dissemination of information
(2) those that transfer, position, and perform complex operations on material (sometimes called "Detroit automation," since such machines were developed for and are used extensively in automobile assembly)
(3) those that monitor and control ongoing processes (a furnace thermostat is a very simple illustration)

The use of such automated devices produces a very different kind of "scenery" for the work drama. There are fewer workers but more machines. These are likely to be quite complex and to dwarf in size those who oversee them. And the worker becomes much more passive; he watches dials, digital readouts, printouts, and cathode-ray display tubes and waits for them to yield necessary data or to signal that something is wrong that requires human intervention to correct.

But this raises a paradox. If, in order to make work meaningful to the worker, it is necessary to restore a sense of active involvement—or confrontation—with what the worker does, it would appear that the watch-and-wait stance required by automation would hardly be conducive to that end. Yet consider what we have already learned. First, jobs that rank high on autonomy, responsibility, and opportunities for interaction lead to greater worker satisfaction than jobs that rank low on these attributes. Second, because work is not an isolated activity because it is carried out within some organizational structure, the greater the degree of interaction between employee and employer—the greater the common participation in a commonly perceived enterprise—the more can we expect a worker to be satisfied with his work situation. And there are enough data to suggest that the paradox presumably implicit in automation just does not exist. Over time it is almost certain that the replacement of many monotonous and repetitive tasks by those requiring greater alertness and intellectual preparation, which automation requires, will ultimately benefit the worker. He will have to know more about the total productive process and to orient his behavior toward the totality rather than a piece of it. The greater responsibility that results from this widened breadth of perspective ought to generate a more positive identity and a greater pride in accomplishment. In short, a fundamental assumption of automation is that the worker must be both intellectually alive and "sharp." The necessity to deal with a wider range of behavioral alternatives forces the worker to become more intensively a part of what is going on around him, as represented by the data being registered before his eyes. So, while the worker may be seated quite comfortably, as distinct from the hammering or lifting or pulling, or at least perspiring, worker at the nonautomated machine, that individual will be engaged in what amounts to a dialogue with the machine.

Moreover, automation is precipitating new organizational responses to the man-machine interface. Trends toward increased job enlargement (requiring more of individuals so that repetition and monotony can be reduced), job redesign (changing the way people perform their work to take advantage of new technologies and at the same time increase opportunities for interaction among the workers), and heightened worker response to calls for joint labor-management planning for technological innovation are evident. Workers are participating in the structuring of their work to an extent that perhaps would have surprised and possibly delighted Hawthorne's workers and, as well, those who studied them.

One unanticipated consequence of the drive toward automation may be the intensification of professionalizing attempts on the part of occupations not usually conceived of in those terms. Whether such occupations do in fact "make it" as professionals, whether their attempts are legitimated by clients or others, is less important than the morale and *espirit de corps* that may be manifested by the members of the occupation as they strive to develop and assert their new image. Now, this does not mean that pitting one's head against a stone wall is a good thing because it develops stoicism. Rather, it means that the facts of social life—traditional distinctions between occupations and popular expectations of differential competency—are not easily transformed. Nevertheless, automation may propel an occupation farther along the road than might otherwise have been possible, with a consequent increment in both self-image and positive affect toward the occupation itself. And if, in the process, the model of the profession as developed by sociologists should need modification, the researcher should be equal to the task.

But there is another and possibly far more meaningful consequence of automation. In an automated situation the worker does not "produce"; the machine does that, while to all intents the worker monitors the process. He becomes essentially a manager as he becomes part of the decisionmaking process with respect to production. Hence, concerns about increasing worker output (raising the "bogey," improving worker efficiency, or restricting output, let us say), so characteristic of nonautomated work, are now transformed into concerns about the parameters under which the manchine—but not the worker—works. Because the worker is freed from the tyranny of the machine he is really better able to control the terms of his work as his role within the productive process shifts from an instrument of production in the classic Marxian sense to a determiner of production.

Such an outcome thrusts the blue-collar worker, at least, into a new relation with his white-collar co-worker. Richard A. Peterson cites a number of studies to document what he regards as a progressive process of what he calls blue-collar "embourgeoisment."[14] As we remarked earlier in this chapter, when work lost its moral force, the pursuit of things indicative of socio-ecomonic status became an end in itself. Within this context, Peterson addresses himself to blue-collar emulation of white-collar life-styles. He sees blue-collar workers' concern with their homes, their recreation, and their children as attempts to channel their perceptions of blocked mobility so as to minimize the status discrepancy and thereby suggest that the mobility they desired has occurred after all. We suggest that automation will accelerate this process. As the worker participates in output-related decisions, he stands in the same relationship to the work as do supervisors and administrators in the traditional organizational sense. Consequently, under automation the gap between the two statuses will narrow considerably, and embourgeoisment will acquire a work-centered legitimacy it did not previously possess. And as this gap narrows we may also expect the alienation experienced by the worker on the job to decrease because of his changed perception of his own position at work.

But what of the white-collar workers thus deprived of their superior position? They will require new rationalizations for new

[14]Richard A. Peterson, *The Dynamics of Industrial Society* (Indianapolis, Ind.: Bobbs-Merrill, 1973), pp. 29 ff.

definitions of their own status. In his classic study of white-collar workers, C. Wright Mills observed that these workers by and large identified with management or organization goals rather than with blue-collar workers (although, to be sure, white-collar unionization was increasing). White-collar work was seen as qualitatively different from blue-collar work.[15] But, as Blauner puts it, "Automation may eliminate the 'innate' hostility of men who work with their hands toward 'pencil-pushers' and administrators. And, conversely, white-collar employees will probably gain an enhanced understanding of, and respect for, the work of blue-collar men, since the office staff's contact with the plant and its production problems increases in automated firms, due to the greater need for checking and con- sultation."[16] With differences seemingly obliterated, the white-collar worker must search for new loyalties. It can be expected that white-collar workers will become a far more self-conscious group than Mills predicted, which will take the form of increased militancy at work—intensive unionization efforts, development of professionali- zing attempts—and heightened political involvement outside of work, in consumer and environmental protection, for example. And where the blue-collar worker complained of the tedium and monotony of work, we can expect the white-collar worker in the automated age to strike out at "the organization."

The Bureaucratization of Work. Max Weber asserted that the bureau- cracy was the social structure most characteristic of the modern world.[17] It developed out of the necessity to process people and things speedily, efficiently, rationally (according to rules, *ratio*), and inde- pendently of personal whim or caprice. While there have been bureaucratic structures throughout history, Weber argued that the demands of modern life, the fact that there is more to know and more to do, make the bureaucracy, a social organization that can get work done with a minimum of fuss and feathers, absolutely necessary. Its basis is the set of rules that structure the organization, that set the terms of interpersonal relations within it, and that obviate "the

[15]Mills, *White Collar,* pp. 244 ff.

[16]Robert Blauner, *Alienation and Freedom* (Chicago: University of Chicago Press, 1964), p. 180.

[17]Max Weber, "Bureaucracy," in H. H. Gerth and C. Wright Mills, eds., *From Max Weber: Essays in Sociology* (New York: Oxford University Press, 1946), pp. 196–244.

personal equation" or particularistic or idiosyncratic behavior on the part of worker or client that could stifle the efficiency of the organization:

Bureaucratization offers above all the optimum possibility for carrying through the principle of specializing administrative functions according to purely objective considerations. Individual performances are allocated to functionaries who have specialized training and who by constant practice learn more and more. The "objective" discharge of business primarily means a discharge of business according to calculable rules and "without regard to persons."[18]

The characteristics of the bureaucracy follow logically. It consists of a hierarchy of formally defined statuses (offices) with increments of authority and responsibility as one moves up the hierarchy. The office constitutes a full-time occupation, and individuals are recruited to the office and remain in it by virtue of their expertise. The responsibilities of office transcend the person who fills it; the military person is told to salute the rank, not the man. Appointment to a bureaucratic office (one cannot be elected, and thus the civil service is distinguished from the legislature) carries the presumption of lifetime tenure short of malfeasance—violating the rules, which, of course, must be substantiated through legal proceedings—or moral turpitude, and the possibilities of promotion "through the ranks," so long as one satisfies the criteria for promotion: "It's not who you know but what you know." Although Weber's formulation represents an ideal type, most formal organizations possess at least some of these ideal-typical attributes.

As these organizations have proliferated, more and more workers, spread from one pole to the other of the "job-profession" continuum, have been drawn into them. Heretofore independent practitioners, physicians are now as likely to be involved in group practice or in a clinic as they are to have their own practices. And in either case they are probably affiliated with a hospital. The late Erwin Smigel wrote of the operation of the Wall Street "legal factory" that brought lawyers of different types together under a comon organizational aegis. Some lawyers may be on salary in a corporation rather than being com-

[18]*Ibid.*, p. 215.

pensated through fees, as a free professional is. The small, independent proprietor is rapidly becoming a thing of the past as the "ma and pa store" is absorbed into supermarket or franchise chains. The technological strides that precipitated the spread of bureaucratic organizations and that resulted from that rise co-opted the skilled craftsmen who often worked alone or in small groups and made of them the "blue-collar workers" we know today. And certainly, the white-collar worker is a creation of the bureaucracy, for such workers came into being to fill the numberless offices in the bureaucratic structure made necessary by the growth of paperwork and administrative details generated by the very expansion of the structure, a kind of self-fulfilling prophecy. Work is thus increasingly a bureaucratized phenomenon.[19]

This means, first, that the opportunity for work resides in bureaucratic participation. If one wishes to work, he may be required to become part of an organization. The structure may own the tools required to work; and the more complex the tool the more likely is organizational ownership. After all, a scientist does not "own" his laboratory or atomic reactor. So, in virtually a pure Marxist sense, the worker in the bureaucracy is separated from his means of production, be they tools or techniques.

Second, the worker occupying a bureaucratic niche becomes so conversant with and so tied to "the rules" that "work to rule," a zealous inflexibility, may result in a standardized response to any situation, in what Veblen called a "trained incapacity" to react to changed situations. "This is the way we do it, and if you don't believe me, look here at § 443.52(d) of the *Manual of Procedure*." Discipline overcomes judgment, so that adherence to the rules sometimes borders on a ritualism that has made the "bureaucratic personality" an epithet in English. The bureaucrat is typified by Everett Hughes's description of the *Gleichschaltung*, the political coordination, of the German Statistical Office under the Nazis. Apparently undisturbed by the massacres of Jews, Poles, and others going on about him, the statistician dutifully records the macabre population changes and defines and redefines Jews by belief, by race, or by "blood," "because

[19]See Robert K. Merton, *Social Theory and Social Structure*, enlarged ed. (New York: Free Press, 1968), pp. 249–60, and Edward B. Shils, "Clerical Automation and White-Collar Organizing Drives," in Simon Marcson, ed., *Automation, Alienation, and Anomie* (New York: Harper & Row, 1970), pp. 259–71.

the needs of the State and the Party require it." Hughes's statistician has become so disciplined by his bureaucratic stance that he borders on an automaton.[20] And so we laugh at the bureaucrat. "Hurry up and wait." "When the civil servant died, emblazoned on his tombstone was the inscription: Do not fold, spindle, or mutilate." "There's the right way, the wrong way, and the army way."

Third, it follows that the bureaucrat is impersonal with his co-workers as with those he serves, his clients. He cannot afford to develop primary relations with his colleagues since they might detract from a single-minded dedication to his bureaucratic calling. He may have a great many secondary relations that he pursues avidly in the hope of an other-directed togetherness, but he is conditioned not to "open up," to reveal himself. The "organization man" is exceedingly lonely but finds solace in the pseudo-*Gemeinschaft* of others who are just as lonely as he. Today's worker is a member of Riesman's "lonely crowd."[21]

It is in this that a very real problem of work lies. How does the individual resist the absorptive power of bureaucratic life? How might he retain a sense of self in the face of demands for efficiency and discipline? It must of course be recognized that organizations are not absolutely rigid. Administrators are responsive to internal pressures for change and, in the face of white-collar unionization, are becoming increasingly so. As we have seen, the presence of cohesive work groups, of colleagueship, and of informal communication networks can to some extent insulate the individual from organizational im-peratives by reinterpreting them to the advantage of the worker. Herbert A. Shepard has suggested that the apparently debilitating effects of organizational life can be minimized if workers at all levels of the structure can be induced to see themselves as involved in a common enterprise, that the survival of each depends upon the survival of all. He argues that the typical perception of an organiza-tion as a dynamic of coercion and compromise can be changed to one of cooperation and consensus if concerned people at each level in the structure are willing to act as change agents, pulling others along with them. When those in power support and encourage efforts to create a

[20] Everett C. Hughes, "The *Gleichschaltung* of the German Statistical Year-book," *American Statistician* 9 (December, 1955): 8–11.

[21] David Riesman, in collaboration with Reuel Denney and Nathan Glazer, *The Lonely Crowd* (New Haven, Conn.: Yale University Press, 1950).

more responsive organization, all those involved in the organization should benefit by a more open environment that is better attuned to individual needs for self-actualization at work.[22]

However, a nagging question intrudes: How much ought we to rely on occupational behavior as a source of self-actualization or personal fulfillment? Perhaps all that can be asked of work is that it give us the means to "get our kicks" elsewhere. In responding to such a question we are led to consider the relation between work and nonwork and to approach once more the meaning of work.

Work and Nonwork. In speaking of nonwork, it should be noted first, I am *not* discussing unemployment. The perfection of automation will not spew vast hordes of workers from the work place to the employment agency or, worse yet, the gutter. A much more sanguine view is necessary. Certainly, the plaint of worker displacement by machine was voiced when the spinning jenny replaced the spinning wheel. In fact, mechanization opened far more jobs and gave rise to far more occupations than those displaced by the advent of the machine. We can expect the same results from automation. While there has been and will continue to be some short-run displacement, increasing use is being made of retraining programs and "displacement insurance." Those who can increase their skills in response to increased demand should fare well, although there is of course no guarantee that all who are displaced will return immediately to work.

What we are talking about, rather, is the new approach that will be necessary to deal with the increase in free, nonwork time that automation will bring in its wake. We will be faced with a redefinition of leisure and, by implication, of work itself.

Like work, leisure is a function of the value system of a particular society. From a sociological perspective, the emergence of the Protestant Ethic did more than merely make work a fundamental religious obligation, for such an obligation was, as we have seen, inherent in the Judaeo-Christian approach to work. Rather, for the first time in history, the Protestant Ethic gave moral leeway to competition. The seventeenth-century Puritan and the nineteenth-

[22]Herbert A. Shepard, "Changing Interpersonal and Intergroup Relationships in Organizations," in James G. March, ed., *Handbook of Organizations* (Chicago: Rand McNally, 1965), pp. 1115–43. See also Graham A. B. Edwards, "The Organisation of Work," [British] *SSRC Newsletter* 27 (April, 1975): 6–7.

century entrepreneur could not justify their presumed "election" to God's favor through some objective standard. They could only compare their acquisition of wealth with what others had acquired. Ultimately, this meant competition, a head-long race with others for an indication of divine blessing. And those who fared well in that race did so at the expense of others.

As Robert Merton and the Westleys have suggested, competition has intruded into every area of social life, so that it becomes easy to write about "the games people play."[23] What I win, you lose, and all's fair in love and war. Even the most influential sociology textbook ever written, *Introduction to the Science of Sociology*, by Park and Burgess, spoke of competition as the most universal and fundamental form of interaction.[24]

Now, such a world view was perfectly reasonable in an age of scarcity. It made work moral, it justified saving, and it made inequalities between individuals and groups morally legitimate. But what happens is a society like ours, where scarcity is no longer really a problem, where people appear to have all they need and want? There then opens for them, for us, a veritable "abyss of the impossible."[25] Nothing seems beyond our grasp, and we do not know how to handle such affluence. We practice "conspicuous consumption" as if consumption for its own sake will bring some sort of inner peace.[26] For obviously one can no longer point to consumption and competition as indicative of heavenly favor, since God has been declared dead in this post-Christian, let alone postindustrial, age. The result is a society that Etzioni labels inauthentic, a society in which the person feels acted upon rather than active, a society in which someone else, far off, seems to pull the levers that initiate behavior here.[27] The individual sees no hope of self-mastery.

While it is clear that energy shortages of greater or less scope are to

[23]William A. Westley and Margaret W. Westley, *The Emerging Worker* (Montreal: McGill-Queen's University Press, 1971), pp. 9–19, 128 ff.

[24]Robert E. Park and Ernest W. Burgess, *Introduction to the Science of Sociology* (Chicago: University of Chicago Press, 1921).

[25]Emile Durkheim, *Suicide*, trans. John A. Spaulding and George Simpson (Glencoe, Ill.: Free Press, 1951), pp. 246–58.

[26]Thorstein Veblen, *The Theory of the Leisure Class* (New York: Modern Library, 1934).

[27]Amitai Etzioni, *The Active Society: A Theory of Social and Political Processes* (New York: Free Press, 1968), pp. 617–66.

be reckoned with daily, and while a shift to the political right may be implied by the election of Ronald Reagan as U.S. president, it is as well evident that a philosophy of work based on the scarcity of things is out of date. College students are rejecting a competition-consumption orientation, for "living well" no longer means solely increased income or bureaucratic advancement. Even though enrollment in schools of business continues high, students are trying to find ways of coupling such training with possibilities of "helping"—in other words students and others are trying to find ways of being responsible and creative on their terms, to be free to determine their life course. Current concerns with environmental protection and with natural foods among vast sectors of the population can in one way be viewed as an attempt to "get back to basics," as many advertisements put it. The struggle for enactment of an equal-rights amendment in the U.S. Constitution is not yet over, despite the failure of sufficient States to ratify the amendment by the time limit of June, 1982. Thus, even though unemployment remains high and the memory of gasoline selling for less than a dollar a gallon remains vivid, there are nonetheless increasing signs of a deep-felt need to find and to articulate a set of values that assert the primacy of self- other relations creatively generated over the primacy of things.

So we need new values and motivations to cope with abundance and to bring such affluence within the range of all. Consider that in this century we have moved from a sixty-hour work week to a work week that ranges between thirty-five and forty hours. Perhaps by the year 2000 that figure will be halved. But as the time spent in gainful employment has decreased, nonwork time has acquired a character often attributed to work itself. It has become routinized and scheduled so that the cultivation of the good life, usually defined in terms of consumption, is felt to be a task to be pursued as avidly as is the paycheck. And it often costs more. Certainly if the job was a drudge and joyless, perhaps satisfaction could be found in the "do-it-yourself" of the home project: building a hi-fi receiver, adding an attic, or just fixing a leaking faucet. Perhaps one could shake off the tedium of work by taking to the open road in a recreation vehicle or modified jeep or plunging full-tilt into some hobby. Ideally, through such activities one ought to have been able to structure his work creatively, set his own pace, and follow through on a project. Yet even this amateurism came to be pursued with an intensity that demanded an uninterruptable schedule, a routine within it, and a kind of production quota—even for leisure. The vacation resort or "holiday camp" that literally programs every moment of relaxation so that the vacationer returns to his work to recuperate is simply a case in point. Leisure, too, is to be consumed, to be worked at.

Yet withal there is still the Puritan distrust of leisure, the lack of occupation or at least peoccupation is thought to be sinful. To be free of work, not to be obligated to perform some task can in a work-oriented society be psychologically disturbing, as studies of the retired have demonstrated. And assuredly, if leisure represents nothing more than the passivity of the spectator in front of his color television set or even in a "live" audience, it hardly merits a positive response. However satisfying the posture, the satisfaction ceases when the event is over. The person really changes little if at all. Then, if leisure is to be removed from an outdated philosophy of scarcity, it must be viewed as rewarding, satisfying, creative, self-actualizing, and self-involving. But so should employment. The orientation we propose brings us full circle to the definition of work proposed in Chapter 1.

The suggestion that work and leisure represent not a polarity but a fusion, that they are but two sides of the same coin, is not new. However, it becomes especially appropriate if work is viewed broadly as whatever a person does in order to survive socially as well as physically. So long as an individual attempts to maintain or to enhance any of the several statuses that he occupies by virtue of his group memberships, then he is working, and what he does is purposeful, whether or not he is paid for what he does, whether or not there is general social approval of what he does (thus some work is deviant but is work nonetheless). If a person can fulfill himself in an occupation, well and good, but if nonoccupational involvement performs this function, then let it be so.

Such a conception will certainly enable the society to better serve the retired. As our population grows older, there will be larger numbers of individuals no longer employed (in the traditional sense). Should the lack of remuneration for some meaningful activity consign the aged to a human scrap heap, to wait resignedly for the angel of death to tap them? The experience of living that the older person brings with him could be applied to innumerable tasks that need doing and that could provide a sense of real accomplishment for the person who chooses to perform them, despite the absence of monetary reward. This, too, is work.

So, too, does such a conception provide an appropriate optic to view nonmonetary work often performed by women. Traditional conceptions of work tend to disvalue such activities as housework, parenting, volunteer service—behavior that frequently engenders greater commitment, sense of satisfaction and involvement than does activity performed for some monetary end. "Woman's work" is frequently a pejorative term; it demeans and depreciates the person to whom it is applied. However, when viewed in the context suggested here, "woman's work" becomes but one of a number of categories of work—craftswork or professional work, for example—that would be studied and understood as one would attempt to learn of any of the varieties of work people do, and therefore shorn of the evaluative implications that confront far too often the work performed by women.

Living in a world of affluence requires freedom to be and freedom to do. Until we discover the discipline to accomplish this our ability to find meaning in the one life we have to live will be severely limited.

What are the implications of all this? These must be sought by the student of values, the social philosopher, the man of religion. This discussion admittedly has been speculative, and the sociologist must stop here. Were he to proceed further in this inquiry he would cease to be the objective searcher for the knowledge about human relationships that is his work, his identity, and his fulfillment.

SUGGESTED READING

CHAPTER 1

For material on the discipline of sociology, see Metta Spencer, *Foundations of Modern Sociology*, 3d ed. (Englewood Cliffs, N.J.: Prentice-Hall, 1982); and Lee Braude, *A Sense of Sociology*, rev. ed. (Melbourne, Fla.: Krieger, 1981).

On the history of work, see Adriano Tilgher, *Work: What It Has Meant to Men Through the Ages*, trans. Dorothy Canfield Fisher (New York: Harcourt, Brace, 1930); and Alan Richardson, *The Biblical Doctrine of Work* (London: SCM Press, 1963).

The relation between Protestantism and work has been the subject of controversy since Max Weber set forth his classic statement of the "Protestant Ethic." See Max Weber, *The Protestant Ethic and the Spirit of Capitalism*, trans. Talcott Parsons (New York: Scribners, 1930); R. H. Tawney, *Religion and the Rise of Capitalism* (New York: Harcourt, Brace, 1926); Ronald S. Wallace, *Calvin's Doctrine of the Christian Life* (Edinburgh: Oliver & Boyd, 1959); Kurt Samuelsson, *Religion and Economic Action*, trans. E. Geoffrey French (Stockholm: Scandinavian University Books, 1961); Talcott Parsons, *The Structure of Social Action* (New York: Macmillan, 1937), pp. 500–78; Irving M. Zeitlin, *Ideology and the Development of Sociological Theory*, 2d ed. (Englewood Cliffs, N.J.: Prentice-Hall, 1981), pp. 127–53; and S. N. Eisenstadt, ed., *The Protestant Ethic and Modernization: A Comparative View* (New York: Basic Books, 1968).

Benjamin Franklin's "Advice to a Young Tradesman" (1748) represents the Protestant Ethic incarnate; Weber quotes from it extensively in *The Protestant Ethic* (p. 175). See Benjamin Franklin, *The Papers of Benjamin Franklin*, ed. Leonard W. Labaree and Whitfield J. Bell, Jr. (New Haven: Yale University Press, 1959–   ), III:306–8.

The interaction of Protestantism, work, and achievement in modern society is explored in Robert K. Merton, *Social Theory and Social Structure*, enlarged ed. (New York: Free Press, 1968), pp. 185–248; Brian Jackson, *Working Class Community* (London: Routledge & Kegan Paul, 1968), pp. 94–98; Leonard I. Pearlin, Marian Radke Yarrow, and Harry A. Scarr, "Unintended Effects of Parental Aspirations: The Case of Children's Cheating," in *Life Cycle and Achievement in America*, ed. Rose Laub Coser (New York: Harper Torchbooks, 1969), pp. 84–104.

Although leisure is discussed more fully in Chapter 6, it is appropriate at this point to mention Nels Anderson, *Work and Leisure* (London: Routledge & Kegan Paul, 1961); Stanley Parker, *The Future of Work and Leisure* (New York: Praeger, 1971); *idem* and Michael A. Smith, "Work and Leisure," in Robert Dubin, ed., *Handbook of Work, Organization and Society* (Chicago: Rand McNally College Publishing Co., 1976), pp. 37–62.

Macroscopic analyses of work include Seymour Wolfbein, *Work in American Society* (Glenview, Ill.: Scott, Foresman, 1971); Peter M. Blau and Otis Dudley Duncan, with the collaboration of Andrea Tyree, *The American Occupational Structure* (New York: Wiley, 1967); Barbara Reskin and Frederick L. Campbell, "Physician Distribution Across Metropolitan Areas," *American Journal of Sociology* 79 (January, 1974): 981–98; Magali Sarfatti Larson, *The Rise of Professionalism: A Sociological Analysis* (Berkeley: University of California Press, 1977); and Robert M. Hauser and David L. Featherman, "Trends in the Occupational Mobility of U.S. Men, 1962–1970," *American Sociological Review* 38 (June, 1973): 302–11.

For cross-cultural studies of occupations, see Reinhard Bendix, *Work and Authority in Industry: Ideologies of Management in the Course of Industrialization* (New York: Wiley, 1956); Alvin W. Gouldner and Richard A. Peterson, *Technology and the Moral Order* (Indianapolis: Bobbs-Merrill, 1962); Alex Inkeles, "Industrial Man: The Relation of Status to Experience, Perception and Value," *American Journal of Sociology* 66 (July, 1960): 1–31; Seymour Martin Lipset and Reinhard Bendix, *Social Mobility in Industrial Society* (Berkeley: University of California Press, 1959); William H. Form, *Blue-Collar Stratification: Autoworkers in Four Countries* (Princeton, N.J.: Princeton University Press, 1976); Richard D. Lambert, *Workers, Factories and Social Change in India* (Princeton, N.J.: Princeton University Press, 1963); McKim Marriott, "Western Medicine in a Village of Northern India," in Benjamin D. Paul, ed., *Health, Culture and Community* (New York: Russell Sage Foundation, 1955), pp. 239–68; Mark G. Field, "Structured Strain in the Role of the Soviet Physician," *American Journal of Sociology* 58 (March, 1953): 493–502; Georges Friedmann, *The Anatomy of Work*, trans. Wyatt Rawson (London: Heinemann, 1961); Ephraim Yuchtman, "Reward Distribution and Work-Role Attractiveness in the Kibbutz; Reflections on Equity Theory," *American Sociological Review* 37 (October, 1972): 581–95; and Masako M. Osako, "Dilemmas of Japanese Professional Women," *Social Problems* 26 (October, 1978): 15–25.

Case studies of occupations include W. Fred Cottrell, *The Railroader* (Stanford, Calif.: Stanford University Press, 1940); Louis Kriesberg, "The

Retail Furrier: Concepts of Security and Success," *American Journal of Sociology* 57 (March, 1952): 478–85; Everett C. Hughes, "Personality Types and the Division of Labor," *American Journal of Sociology* 33 (March, 1928): 754–68; *idem, The Growth of an Institution: The Chicago Real Estate Board* (Chicago: Society for Social Research of the University of Chicago, 1931); Clifford R. Shaw, *The Jack Roller* (Chicago: University of Chicago Press, 1930); Oswald Hall, "The Informal Organization of the Medical Profession," *Canadian Journal of Economics and Political Science* 12 (February, 1946): 30–44; *idem,* "The Stages of a Medical Career," *American Journal of Sociology* 53 (March, 1948): 327–36; Eliot Freidson, *Profession of Medicine* (New York: Dodd, Mead, 1970); Ray Gold, "Janitors Versus Tenants: A Status-Income Dilemma," *American Journal of Sociology* 57 (March, 1952): 486–93; Joseph H. Fichter, *Religion as an Occupation: A Study in the Sociology of Professions* (South Bend, Ind.: University of Notre Dame Press, 1961); Stewart E. Perry, *San Francisco Scavengers: Dirty Work and the Pride of Ownership* (Berkeley: University of California Press, 1978); and Jeffrey W. Riemer, *Hard Hats: The Work World of Construction Workers* (Beverly Hills, Calif.: Sage, 1979).

Example of studies of the relation between occupations and other social structures include Frances Donovan, *The Saleslady* (Chicago: University of Chicago Press, 1929); Barney G. Glaser, *Organizational Scientists: Their Professional Careers* (Indianapolis: Bobbs-Merrill, 1964); Erwin O. Smigel, *The Wall Street Lawyer* (New York: Free Press, 1964); Christopher Beattie, Jacques Desy, and Stephen Longstaff, *Bureaucratic Careers: Anglophones and Francophones in the Canadian Public Service,* Documents of the Royal Commission on Bilingualism and Biculturalism, no. 11 (Ottawa: Information Canada, 1972); Robin F. Badgley and Samuel Wolfe, *Doctors' Strike: Medical Care and Conflict in Saskatchewan* (Toronto: Macmillian, 1967); Peter G. Hollowell, *The Lorry Driver* (London: Routledge & Kegan Paul, 1968); Helena Znaniecki Lopata, *Occupation: Housewife* (New York: Oxford University Press, 1971); Peter M. Blau, *The Organization of Academic Work* (New York: Wiley-Interscience, 1973); and Louis H. Orzack and Lester A. Janoff, "Sociological Perspectives of the Profession of Optometry: A New Look at Trends Since 1958," *American Journal of Optometrics and Physiological Optics* 53 (May, 1976): 259–69.

Studies of individuals at work are James M. Henslin, "Trust and the Cab Driver," in Marcello Truzzi, ed., *Sociology and Everyday Life* (Englewood Cliffs, N.J.,: Prentice-Hall, 1968), pp. 138–58; Everett C. Hughes, "Mistakes at Work," *Canadian Journal of Economics and Political Science* 17 (August, 1951): 320–27; Estelle Fuchs, *Teachers Talk* (Garden City, N.Y.: Doubleday Anchor, 1969); Fred L. Strodtbeck and Marvin B. Sussman, "Of Time, the City, and 'the One-Year Guarantee': The Relations Between Watch Owners and Repairers," *American Journal of Sociology* 61 (May, 1956); 602–9; Paul R. Dommermuth, "Retail Pharmacy: Work Perspectives and Social Structural Contingencies," expansion of a paper read before the annual meetings of the American Sociological Association, 1966; and Mason Griff, "The Commercial Artist," in Maurice Stein, Arthur J. Vidich, and David Manning White, eds., *Identity and Anxiety* (Glencoe, Ill.: Free Press, 1960), pp. 219–41.

The definition of work proposed in the text is discussed at somewhat greater length in Lee Braude, "Work: A Theoretical Clarification," *Sociological Quarterly* 4 (Autumn, 1963): 343–48.

A stimulating and provocative approach to an understanding of work is provided by Gale Miller, *It's A Living* (New York: St. Martin's Press, 1981).

The place of occupations in the developing nations is treated in Charles J. Erasmus, "An Anthropologist Looks at Technical Assistance," in Morton H. Fried, ed., *Readings in Anthropology*, 2d ed., 2 vols. (New York: Crowell, 1968), II: 565–82; Tyrell Burgess, Richard Layard and Pitambar Pant, *Manpower and Educational Development in India, 1961–1986* (Toronto: University of Toronto Press, 1968); and Christopher Howe, *Employment and Economic Growth in Urban China, 1944–1957* (Cambridge, England: Cambridge University Press, 1971).

The assumption that the distribution of occupations within a population is based on the functional scarcity of those occupations is derived from Kingsley Davis and Wilbert E. Moore, "Some Principles of Stratification," *American Sociological Review* 10 (April, 1945): 242–49, and the rejoinder that followed, Melvin M. Tumin, "Some Principles of Stratification: A Critical Analysis," *American Sociological Review* 19 (August, 1953): 387–94.

The discussion of the fine artist is based on Mason Griff, "The Recruitment and Socialization of Artists," in Milton C. Albrecht, James H. Barnett, and Mason Griff, eds., *The Sociology of Art and Literature: A Reader* (New York: Praeger, 1970), pp. 145–58; and Anselm L. Strauss, "The Art School and Its Students: A Study and an Interpretation," *loc. cit.*, pp. 159–77.

CHAPTER 2

Labor-force data are analyzed historically in Philip M. Hauser, "Labor Force," in Robert E. L. Faris, ed., *Handbook of Sociology* (Chciago: Rand McNally, 1964), pp. 160–90 (perhaps the most concise and readily understandable treatment of the labor-force concept available to the general reader); *The Statistical History of the United States* (Stamford, Conn.: Fairfield, 1965); and *A Century of Population Growth: 1790–1900* (Washington: U.S. Government Printing Office, 1909), pp. 42, 142–46.

Definitions appropriate to an understanding of labor-force data are presented in U.S. Bureau of the Census, *Statistical Abstract of the United States*, 102d ed. (Washington: U.S. Government Printing Office, 1981), pp. 375–76.

The relation between the development of the American nation and gross changes in U.S. population is discussed in Philip M. Hauser, "The Chaotic Society: Product of the Social Morphological Revolution," *American Sociological Review* 34 (February, 1969): 1–19. Implications of such changes, especially their influence on an emerging American system of values, are discussed in Max Lerner, *America as a Civilization*, 2 vols. (New York: Simon & Schuster, 1957); Seymour Martin Lipset, *The First New Nation* (New York: Basic Books, 1963); John Higham, "The Reorientation of American Culture in the 1890's," in John Weiss, ed. and intro., *The Origins of Modern Consciousness* (Detroit: Wayne State University Press, 1965), pp. 25–48; and David M. Potter, "The Quest for the National Character," in John Higham, ed., *The Reconstruction of American History* (New York: Harper, 1962), pp. 197–235.

Sociological interest in the city stems largely from the "classic" statement by Robert E. Park, Ernest W. Burgess, and Roderick D. McKenzie, *The City* (Chicago: University of Chicago Press, 1925), esp. Chapter II, "The Growth of the City: An Introduction to a Research Project" (pp. 47–62), which details the now classic "concentric zone theory of urban growth."

The implications of changes in census data dealing with occupations are discussed in Donald J. Bogue, *The Population of the United States* (Glencoe, Ill.:

Free Press, 1959), pp. 468–669; Thomas C. Fichandler, "The American Labor Force," in Sigmund Nosow and William H. Form, eds., *Man, Work and Society* (New York: Basic Books, 1962), pp. 97–111; Clarence D. Long, *The Labor Force Under Changing Income and Employment* (Princeton, N.J.: Princeton University Press, 1958), pp. 54–158; and Seymour L. Wolfbein, *Occupational Information: A Career Guidance View* (New York: Random House, 1968). The relevance of such changes for the aged is discussed in Fred Cottrell, *Aging and the Aged* (Dubuque, Iowa: Brown, 1974), esp. pp. 1–5, 22–32; and Fred C. Pampel, *Social Change and the Aged* (New York: D. C. Heath (Lexington Books), 1981). Finally, the significance of such changes for women and ethnic minorities is considered in Alva Myrdal and Viola Klein, *Women's Two Roles: Home and Work* (London: Routledge, 1968); the January, 1973, issue of the *American Journal of Sociology*, edited by Joan Huber, which dealt with "Changing Women in a Changing Society"; Joseph S. Himes, *Racial and Ethnic Minorities* (Dubuque, Iowa: Brown, 1974); Michael P. Fogarty, Rhona Rapoport, and Robert N. Rapoport, *Sex, Career and Family* (Beverly Hills, Calif.: Sage, 1971); Ronnie Steinberg Ratner, ed., *Equal Employment Policy for Women: Strategies for Implementation in the United States, Canada and Western Europe* (Philadelphia: Temple University Pess, 1980); Robert Calvert, Jr., *Equal Employment Opportunity for Minority Group College Graduates: Locating, Recruiting, Employing* (Garrett Park, Md.: Garrett Park Press, 1972); David H. Rosenbloom, *Federal Equal Employment Opportunity: Politics and Public Personnel Administration* (New York: Praeger, 1977); Kathleen Archibald, *Sex and the Public Service: A Report to the Public Service Commission of Canada* (Ottawa: Public Service Canada, 1973); and Phyllis Wallace, ed., *Equal Employment Opportunity and the AT&T Case* (Cambridge, Mass.: MIT Press, 1976).

The contribution of women in shaping the character of work in the United States is illustrated by: Thomas Dublin, *Women at Work: The Transformation of Work and Community in Lowell, Massachusetts, 1826–1860* (New York: Columbia University Press, 1979); Alice Kessler-Harris, *Women Have Always Worked: A Historical Overview* (Old Westbury, N.Y.: Feminist Press, 1981); Philip S. Foner, *Women and the American Labor Movement*, 2 vols. (New York: Free Press, 1979, 1980).

The voluminous literature on women at work is only suggested by: Ann H. Stromberg and Shirley Harkess, eds., *Women Working: Theories and Facts in Perspective* (Palo Alto: Mayfield, 1978); *Women Workers and Society: International Perspectives* (Geneva: International Labor Office, 1976); Cynthia B. Lloyd, Emily S. Andrews and Curtis L. Gilroy, eds., *Women in the Labor Market* (New York: Columbia University Press, 1979); Gillian Stevens and Monica Boyd, "The Importance of Mother: Labor Force Participation and Intergenerational Mobility of Women," *Social Forces* 59 (September, 1980): 186–99; Ian Watt, "Linkages Between Industrial Radicalism and the Domestic Role Among Working Women," *Sociological Review* (New Series) 28 (February, 1980): 55–74; and Helen MacGill Hughes, "Women in Academic Sociology, 1925–75," *Sociological Focus* 8 (August, 1975): 15–22.

CHAPTER 3

For examples of the variety of studies conducted within the Hughes perspective, see the following:

On *industry,* Ely Chinoy, *Automobile Workers and the American Dream* (New York: Random House, 1953); Jack Hass, "Learning Real Feelings: A Study of High Ironworkers' Reaction to Fear and Danger," *Sociology of Work and Occupations* 4 (May, 1977): 147–70; and Jack C. Ross and Raymond H. Wheeler, *Black Belonging: A Study of the Social Correlates of Work Relations Among Negroes* (Westport, Conn.: Greenwood, 1971).

On *professions,* Bud B. Khleif, "Professionalization of Psychiatric Residents," in Phyllis L. Stewart and Muriel G. Cantor, eds., *Varieties of Work Experience* (Cambridge, Mass.: Schenkman, 1974), pp. 301–12; Dan C. Lortie, "Laymen to Lawmen: Law School, Careers and Professional Socialization," *Harvard Educational Review* 29 (Fall, 1959): 352–69; and Ronny E. Turner, "The Black Minister: Uncle Tom or Abolitionist?" *Phylon* 34 (March, 1973): 86–95.

On *work within the bureaucratic setting,* Bernard H. Baum, *Decentralization of Authority in a Bureaucracy* (Englewood Cliffs, N.J.: Prentice-Hall, 1961); William J. Haga, George Graen, and Fred Dansereau, Jr., "Professionalism and Role-Making in a Service Organization: A Longitudinal Analysis," *American Sociological Review* 39 (February, 1974): 122–32; and Joseph J. Lengermann, "Professional Autonomy in Organizations: The Case of CPAs," in Stewart and Cantor, eds., *op. cit.,* pp. 173–87.

On *occupations exhibiting less structure than the preceding,* Howard S. Becker, "The Professional Dance Musician and His Audience," *American Journal of Sociology* 57 (September, 1951): 136–44; Harriet Zuckerman, "Nobel Laureates in Science: Patterns of Productivity, Collaboration, and Authorship," *American Sociological Review* 32 (June, 1967); 391–403; and James K. Skipper, Jr., and Charles H. McCaghy, "Stripteasers: The Anatomy and Career Contingencies of a Deviant Occupation," *Social Problems* 17 (Winter, 1970): 391–405.

For further examples of the "natural history" of an occupation, see Everett C. Hughes, "Professional and Career Problems of Sociology," in Everett C. Hughes, ed., *Men and their Work* (Glencoe, Ill.: Free Press, 1958), pp. 157–68; Frances Donovan, *The School Ma'am* (New York: Stokes, 1938); Clifton D. Bryant, "'Lease Hounds:' The Petroleum Landman," in Stewart and Cantor, eds., *op. cit.,* pp. 274–91; Edwin H. Sutherland, *The Professional Thief* (Chicago: University of Chicago Press, 1938); Eliot Freidson, *Profession of Medicine, supra;* Morris Janowitz, *The Professional Soldier* (Glencoe, Ill.: Free Press, 1960). Studies of the institutional complex surrounding work include Alvin W. Gouldner, *Patterns of Industrial Bureaucracy* (Glencoe, Ill.: Free Press, 1954); *idem, Wildcat Strike* (Yellow Springs, Ohio: Antioch Press, 1954); *idem,* "Cosmopolitans and Locals: Toward an Analysis of Latent Social Roles," *Administrative Science Quarterly* 2 (December, 1957): 282–306 and 2 (March, 1958): 444–80; Edward Gross, "Some Functional Consequences of Primary Controls in Formal Work Organizations," *American Sociological Review* 18 (August, 1953): 368–73; Ronald G. Corwin, *Militant Professionalism: A Study of Organizational Conflict in High Schools* (New York: Meredith, 1970); Theodore Caplow and Reece J. McGee, *The Academic Marketplace* (New York: Basic Books, 1958); Elizabeth G. Cohen, "Open-Space Schools: The Opportunity to Become Ambitious," *Sociology of Education* 46 (Spring, 1973): 143–61; Sarane S. Boocock, "The School as a Social Environment for Learning," *Sociology of Education* 46 (Winter, 1973): 15–50; Lee Sigelman, "Reporting the News: An Organizational Analysis," *American Journal of Sociology* 79 (July, 1973): 132–51;

Lloyd Rogler, "The Changing Role of a Political Boss," *American Sociological Review* 39 (February, 1974): 57–67; C. Forte, "Building a Catering Business," in *Studies in Business Organization* (New York: St. Martin's, 1967), pp. 1–24; Harold L. Wilensky, *Intellectuals in Labor Unions* (Glencoe, Ill.: Free Press, 1958); Robert W. Habenstein, "Sociology of Occupations: The Case of the American Funeral Director," in Arnold M. Rose, ed., *Human Behavior and Social Processes* (Boston: Houghton Mifflin, 1962), pp. 225–46; William Vega, "The Liberal Policeman: A Contradiction in Terms?" *Issues in Criminology* 4 (Fall, 1968): 15–33; Alan Gartner, *Paraprofessionals and Their Performance: A Survey of Education, Health and Social Service Programs* (New York: Praeger, 1971); and Waldo W. Burchard, "Role Conflicts of Military Chaplains," *American Sociological Review* 19 (October, 1954): 528–35.

Studies of occupational authority systems include Kenneth J. Reichstein, "Ambulance Chasing: A Case Study of Deviation and Control Within the Legal Profession," *Social Problems* 13 (Summer, 1965): 3–17; S. S. Blume and Ruth Sinclair, "Chemists in British Universities: A Study of the Reward System in Science," *American Sociological Review* 38 (February, 1973): 126–38; William H. Form, "Technology and Social Behavior of Workers in Four Countries: A Sociotechnical Perspective," *American Sociological Review* 37 (December, 1972): 727–38; Richard R. Myers, "Interpersonal Relations in the Building Industry," *Human Organization* 5 (Spring, 1946): 1–7; William D. Muller, *The "Kept Men"? The First Century of Trade Union Representation in the British House of Commons, 1874–1975* (Hassocks, Sussex: Harvester Press, 1977). Norman K. Denzin, "Incomplete Professionalization: The Case of Pharmacy," *Social Forces* 46 (March, 1968): 375–82; Bennie Graves, "Particularism, Exchange and Organizational Efficiency: A Case Study of a Construction Industry," *Social Forces* 49 (September, 1970): 72–81; Neal Shover, "The Social Organization of Burglary," *Social Problems* 20 (Spring, 1973): 499–514; Jerry D. Rose, "The Attribution of Responsibility for Organizational Failure," *Sociology and Social Research* 53 (April, 1969): 323–32; Ned Polsky, "The Hustler," *Social Problems* 12 (Summer, 1964): 4–15; Stephen J. Miller, "The Social Base of Sales Behavior," *ibid.*, 12:15–24; Donald E. Super, "The Professional Status and Affiliations of Vocational Counselors," in Henry Borow, ed., *Man in a World at Work* (Boston: Houghton Mifflin, 1964), 557–85; David J. Armor, *The American School Counselor: A Case Study in the Sociology of Professions* (New York: Russell Sage Foundation, 1969); Henry L. Mason, College and University Government: A Handbook of Principle and Practice, Tulane Studies in Political Science, no. 14 (New Orleans: Tulane University Press, 1972), pp. 47–55; and Elliott A. Krause, "Structured Strain in Marginal Professions: Rehabilitation Counseling," *Journal of Health and Human Behavior* 6 (Spring, 1965): 55–62.

Studies of the impact of informal, interpersonal, relations on the status and authority systems characteristic of a variety of work tasks and work structures are represented by the following: Hannah Meara, "Honor in Dirty Work: The Case of American Meat Cutters and Turkish Butchers," *Sociology of Work and Occupations* 1 (August, 1974): 259–81; Everett C. Hughes, "Comments on 'Honor in Dirty Work,'" *ibid.*: 284–87; Melville Dalton, "Conflicts Between Staff and Line Managerial Officers," *American Sociological Review* 15 (June, 1950): 342–51; Simon Marcson, "Organization and Authority in Industrial Research," *Social Forces* 40 (October, 1961): 72–80; Edward Gross, "Some Functional Consequences of Primary Controls in Formal Work Organiza-

tions," *American Sociological Review* 18 (August, 1953): 368–73; George Ritzer
and Harrison M. Trice, *An Occupation in Conflict: A Study of the Personnel
Manager* (Ithaca, N.Y.: Cornell University Press, 1969); Donald F. Rov,
"Efficiency and 'The Fix': Informal Intergroup Relations in a Piecework
Machine Shop," *American Journal of Sociology* 60 (November, 1954): 255–66;
James Coleman, Elihu Katz, and Herbert Menzel, "The Diffusion of an
Innovation Among Physicians," *Sociometry* 20 (December, 1957): 253–70;
James W. Dykens, Robert W. Hyde, Louis H. Orzack, and Richard H. York,
Strategies of Mental Hospital Change (Boston: Commonwealth of Masschusetts,
Department of Mental Health, 1964); and Robert Habenstein and Edwin A.
Christ, *Professionalizer, Traditionalizer, and Utilizer* (Columbia, Mo.: University
of Missouri Press, 1966).

On the relation between authority and power in occupations, see Robert
Dubin, *The World of Work* (Englewood Cliffs, N.J.: Prentice-Hall, 1958), pp.
27–123, for what is perhaps the most cogent discussion in the literature. See
also Perry Levinson and Jeffry Schiller, "Role Analysis of the Indigenous
Nonprofessional," *Social Work* 11 (July, 1966): 95–101; and James N. Baron
and William T. Bielby, "Workers and Machines: Dimensions and Determinants of Technical Relations in the Workplace," *American Sociological Review* 47
(April, 1982): 175–88.

The role of task essentiality and interchangeability in the determination of
power within an occupation or among them is suggested by Fred Reif and
Anselm Strauss, "The Impact of Rapid Discovery Upon the Scientist's
Career," *Social Problems* 12 (Winter, 1965): 297–311; Robert B. Faulkner,
"Orchestra Interaction: Some Features of Communication and Authority in
an Artistic Organization," *Sociological Quarterly* 14 (Spring, 1973): 147–57;
Michael S. Cline, "Community Factionalism and Teacher Survival in the
Alaskan Bush," *Human Organization* 33 (Spring, 1974): 102–6; Bruce H.
Mayhew and William A. Rushing, "Occupational Structure of Community
Hospitals," *Social Forces* 51 (June, 1973): 455–62; and Ralph H. Turner, "The
Navy Disbursing Officer as a Bureaucrat," *American Sociological Review* 12
(June, 1947): 342–48.

The following papers explore the relation between occupational task
complexity and power: Julius A. Roth, "Ritual and Magic in the Control of
Contagion," *American Sociological Review* 22 (June, 1957): 311–14; and Everett
C. Hughes, "Studying the Nurse's Work," in Everett C. Hughes, ed., *The
Sociological Eye*, 2 vols. (Chicago: Aldine-Atherton, 1971), II:311–15.

The relation between the power of an individual in an occupation and the
person's ability to legitimate his occupational performance is examined in
Manford H. Kuhn, "The Interview and the Professional Relationship," in
Arnold M. Rose, ed., *Human Relations and Social Processes, supra*, pp. 193–206;
Eliot Freidson, "Dilemmas in the Doctor-Patient Relationship," *ibid.*, pp.
207–24; Freidson, "Client Control and Medical Practice," *American Journal of
Sociology* 65 (January, 1960): 374–82; Lee Braude, "Professional Autonomy
and the Role of the Layman," *Social Forces* 39 (May, 1961): 297–301; Howard
S. Becker, "The Teacher in the Authority System of the Public Schools,"
Journal of Educational Sociology 27 (November, 1953): 128–41; and Ferris J.
Ritchey, "Physicians' Perceptions of the Suit-Prone Patient," *Human Organiza-
tion* 38 (Summer, 1979): 160–68.

See the following on the attempts of occupations to raise their status
through changes in job titles or through the use of jargon: Oswald Hall,

Specialized Occupations and Industrial Unrest (New Orleans: Tulane University, 1957), and Everett C. Hughes, "Education for a Profession," in Hughes, ed., *The Sociological Eye*, II:387–96. Work argots are discussed in Martin Meissner, "The Language of Work," in Dubin, ed., *Handbook of Work, Organization and Society, op. cit.*, pp. 205–79. Riemer, *supra*, provides a glossary of construction worker argot. General discussion on the role of argots and special languages in structuring group behavior can be found in Alfred R. Lindesmith and Anselm L. Strauss, *Social Psychology*, 3d ed. (New York: Holt, Rinehart, 1968), pp. 27–29; David W. Maurer, *The Whiz Mob* (New Haven, Conn.: College and University Press, 1964), pp. 200–215; and Paul Lehman, "Argot, Symbolic Deviance and Subcultural Delinquency," *American Sociological Review* 32 (April, 1967): 209–24.

On the work drama, see, for example, Alfred H. Stanton and Morris S. Schwartz, *The Mental Hospital* (New York: Basic Books, 1954), chaps. 8 through 10; W. Fred Cottrell, "Of Time and the Railroader," *American Sociological Review* 4 (April, 1939): 190–98; Howard S. Becker, Blanche Geer, Everett C. Hughes, and Anselm L. Strauss, *Boys in White: Student Culture in Medical School* (Chicago: University of Chicago Press, 1961); William Karracker, "Teamwork and Safety in Flight," *Human Organization* 17 (Fall, 1958): 3–8; Bennie Graves, "'Breaking Out': An Apprenticeship System Among Pipeline Construction Workers," *ibid.*, 17:9–13; Peter H. Mann, "The Status of the Marine Radioman: A British Contribution," *American Journal of Sociology* 63 (July, 1957), 39–41; Donald W. Ball, "An Abortion Clinic Ethnography," *Social Problems* 14 (Winter, 1967): 293–301; Walter I. Wardwell, "The Extra-Professional Role of the Lawyer," *American Journal of Sociology* 61 (January, 1956); 304–7; Peter M. Blau, "Cooperation and Competition in a Bureaucracy," *American Journal of Sociology* 59 (May, 1954): 530–35; Samuel W. Blizzard, "The Minister's Dilemma," *Christian Century* 73 (April 25, 1956): 508–10; David Riesman and Jeanne Watson, "The Sociability Project: A Chronicle of Frustration and Achievement," in Phillip E. Hammond, ed., *Sociologists at Work: Essays on the Craft of Social Research* (New York: Basic Books, 1964); Raymond W. Mack, "Ecological Patterns in an Industrial Shop," *Social Forces* 32 (May, 1954): 351–56; Samuel E. Wallace, *Skid Row as a Way of Life* (Totowa, N.J.: Bedminster, 1965); Gaye Tuchman, "Making News by Doing Work: Routinizing the Unexpected," *American Journal of Sociology* 79 (July, 1973): 110–31; Miriam Wagenschein, "Reality Shock: A Study of Beginning Elementary School Teachers," M.A. thesis, Department of Sociology, University of Chicago, 1950; George C. Homans, "Status Among Clerical Workers," *Human Organization* 12 (Spring, 1953): 5–10; and James P. Spradley and Brenda J. Mann, *The Cocktail Waitress: Woman's Work in a Man's World* (New York: Wiley, 1975).

That work groups are able to structure their work, perhaps in contravention of company policy, is nicely illustrated by Orvis Collins, Melville Dalton, and Donald Roy, "Restriction of Output and Social Cleavage in Industry," *Applied Anthropology* 5 (Summer, 1946): 1–14; Jason Ditton, "Baking Time," *Sociological Review* (New Series) 27 (February, 1979): 157–67; Fred E. Katz, "Explaining Informal Work Groups in Complex Organizations: The Case for Autonomy in Structure," *Administrative Science Quarterly* 10 (September, 1965): 204–23; and Donald F. Roy, "'Banana Time': Job Satisfaction and Informal Interaction," *Human Organization* 18 (Winter, 1959–60): 158–68.

The importance of secrecy in human affairs has been detailed by Simmel. See Kurt Wolff, ed. and trans., *The Sociology of Georg Simmel* (Glencoe, Ill.: Free Press, 1950), pp. 345–76.

Everett C. Hughes considers "Dilemmas and Contradictions of Status," *American Journal of Sociology* 50 (March, 1945): 353–59.

Implications of collegial control of work behavior are explored in Everett C. Hughes, "Mistakes at Work." *Canadian Journal of Economics and Political Science* 17 (August, 1951): 320–27; Dan C. Lortie, "Shared Ordeal and Induction to Work," in Howard S. Becker, Blanche Geer, David Riesman, and Robert S. Weiss, eds., *Institutions and the Person* (Chicago: Aldine, 1968); Everett C. Hughes, "Psychology: Science and/or Profession," *American Psychologist* 7 (August, 1952): 441–43; Edward Gross, "The Worker and Society," in Henry Borow, ed., *Man in a World of Work* (Boston: Houghton Mifflin, 1964), pp. 67–91, esp. pp. 85–91; Warren O. Hagstrom, "Anomy in Scientific Communities," *Social Problems* 12 (Fall, 1964): 186–95; Eliot Freidson and Buford Rhea, "Processes of Control in a Company of Equals," *Social Problems* 11 (Fall, 1963): 119–31; Jeffrey Leiter, "Perceived Teacher Autonomy and the Meaning of Organizational Control," *Sociological Quarterly* 22 (Spring, 1981): 225–39; Rosabeth Moss Kanter, *Men and Women of the Corporation* (New York: Basic Books, 1977); and Edwin M. Lemert, "The Behavior of the Systematic Check Forger," *Social Problems* 6 (Fall, 1958): 141–48.

Studies of occupational cultures include, for example, Sidney M. Peck, *The Rank and File Leader* (New Haven, Conn.: College and University Press, 1963); James H. Bryan, "Occupational Ideologies of Call Girls," *Social Problems* 13 (Spring, 1966): 441–50; S. Kirson Weinberg and Henry Arond, "The Occupational Culture of the Boxer," *American Journal of Sociology* 57 (March, 1952): 460–69; William Kornhauser, "The Negro Union Official: A Study of Sponsorship and Control," *ibid.*, 57:443–53; C. Wright Mills, "The Professional Ideology of Social Pathologists," *American Journal of Sociology* 49 (September, 1942): 165–80; Richard K. Kerckhoff, "The Profession of Marriage Counseling as Viewed by Members of Four Allied Professions: A Study in the Sociology of Occupations," *Marriage and Family Living* 15 (November, 1953): 340–44; Max Weber, "Science as a Vocation," in Gerth and Mills, *From Max Weber, supra,* pp. 129–58; Helen MacGill Hughes, "Maid of All Work or Departmental Sister-in-Law? The Faculty Wife Employed on Campus," *American Journal of Sociology* 78 (January, 1973): 767–72; Bernard R. Blishen, *Doctors and Doctrines: The Ideology of Medical Care in Canada* (Toronto: University of Toronto Press, 1969); Kanter, *supra;* Harold Cox, "Professional Orientation, Associational Membership and Teacher Militancy," *Sociological Inquiry* 50 (1980): 57–64; Eviatar Zerubavel, "Private Time and Public Time: The Temporal Structure of Social Accessibility and Professional Commitments," *Social Forces* 58 (September, 1979): 38–58; Joseph Gusfield and David Riesman, "Faculty Culture and Academic Careers: Some Sources of Innovation in Higher Education," *Sociology of Education* 37 (Summer, 1964): 281–305; David Riesman, Joseph Gusfield, and Zelda Gamson, *Academic Values and Mass Education* (Garden City, N. Y.: Doubleday Anchor, 1971), pp. 90–132; Donald I. Warren, "Social Relations of Peers in a Formal Organization Setting," *Administrative Science Quarterly* 11 (December, 1966): 440–78; and David J. Gregorio, "Enforcement Is the Name of the Game: An Essay on the Immigration Inspector at Work," *Sociological Focus* 11 (August, 1978): 235–46.

Herbert Blumer has used the terms *esprit de corps,* morale, and collective representations in his discussion of the development and social movements, to which the generation of an occupational culture bears a striking resemblance. See Herbert Blumer, "Collective Behavior," in Alfred McC. Lee, ed., *New Outline of the Principles of Sociology* (New York: Barnes & Noble, 1951), pp. 166–222. The idea of "collective representations" comes of course from Emile Durkheim, *The Elementary Forms of the Religious Life,* trans. J. W. Swain (Glencoe, Ill.: Free Press, 1947), pp. 427–47.

License, mandate and the moral division of labor have been considered extensively by Hughes and in Lee Braude, "Professional Autonomy and the Role of the Layman," *Social Forces* 39 (May, 1961): 297–301; Marie B. Haug and Marvin B. Sussman, "Professional Autonomy and the Revolt of the Client," *Social Problems* 17 (Fall, 1969): 153–61; Jerome Carlin, *Lawyers' Ethics* (New York: Russell Sage Foundation, 1966); Albert A. Blum *et al., White-Collar Workers* (New York: Random, 1971); and Howard M. Vollmer and Donald L. Mills, eds., *Professionalization* (Englewood Cliffs, N.J., Prentice-Hall, 1966), pp. 110–52.

On the military see, for example, Kurt Lang, "Military Organizations," in James G. March, ed., *Handbook of Organizations* (Chicago: Rand McNally, 1964), pp. 838–78; Neil Sheehan, Hedrick Smith, E. W. Kenworthy, and Fox Butterfield, eds., *The Pentagon Papers* (New York: Bantam, 1971); and Louis Zurcher, "The Navy Reservist: An Empirical Assessment of Ephemeral Role Enactment," *Social Forces* 55 (March, 1977): 753–68.

On education, see, for example, Joel E. Gerstl, "Education and the Sociology of Work," in Donald A. Hansen and Joel E. Gerstl, eds., *On Education: Sociological Perspectives* (New York: Wiley, 1967), pp. 224–61; and Sarane S. Boocock, *Sociology of Education,* 2d ed. (Boston: Houghton Mifflin, 1980), pp. 127–90.

On the ministry, see Jeffrey K. Hadden, *The Gathering Storm in the Churches* (Garden City, N.Y.: Doubleday, 1969); and Robert Wuthnow, "New Forms of Religion in the Seminary," in Charles Y. Glock, ed., *Religion in Sociological Perspective* (Belmont, Calif.: Wadsworth, 1973), 187–203; and Richard A. Schoenherr and Annemette Sorensen, "Social Change in Religious Organizations: Consequences of Clergy Decline in the U.S. Catholic Church," *Sociological Analysis* 43 (Spring, 1982): 23–52.

CHAPTER 4

For general works on professions see, for example, A. M. Carr-Saunders, *Professions: Their Organization and Place in Society* (Oxford: Clarendon Press, 1928); A. M. Carr-Saunders and P. A. Wilson, *The Professions* (Oxford: Clarendon Press, 1933); Morris L. Cogan, "Toward a Definition of Profession," *Harvard Educational Review* 23 (Winter, 1953): 35–39; William J. Goode, "Community Within a Community: The Professions," *American Sociological Review* 22 (April, 1957): 195–200; Ernest Greenwood, "Attributes of a Profession," *Social Work* 2 (July, 1957): 45–55; Eliot Freidson, ed., "Professions in Contemporary Society," *American Behavioral Scientist* 14 (March–April, 1971), entire issue; Wilbert E. Moore, *The Professions: Roles and Rules* (New York: Russell Sage Foundation, 1970); Everett C. Hughes, "The Professions in Society," *Canadian Journal of Economics and Political Science* 26 (February,

1960): 54–61; Talcott Parsons, "The Professions and Social Structure," *Social Forces* 17 (May, 1939): 457–67; Magali Sarfatti Larson, *The Rise of Professionalism: A Sociological Analysis, op. cit.;* A. G. Fielding and D. Portwood, "Professions and the State: Towards a Typology of Bureaucratic Professions," *Sociological Review* (New Series) 28 (February, 1980): 23–53; *idem,* "Privilege and the Professions," *Sociological Review* (New Series) 29 (November, 1981): 749–73; Roy Lewis and Angus Maude, *Professional People* (London: Phoenix House, 1952); Harold Wilensky, "The Professionalization of Everyone?" *American Journal of Sociology* 70 (September, 1964): 137–58; Marie R. Haug, "The Deprofessionalization of Everyone?" *Sociological Focus* 8 (January, 1975): 47–56; William J. Goode, "The Protection of the Inept," *American Sociological Review* 32 (February, 1967): 5–19; and Fred E. Katz, "Occupational Contact Networks," *Social Forces* 37 (October, 1958): 52–55.

Studies indicative of sociologists' interest in particular professions and would-be professions include: for medicine, Freidson, *Profession of Medicine, supra,* pp. 87–108; for sociology doctoral students, John Pease, "Faculty Influence and Professional Participation of Doctoral Students," *Sociological Inquiry* 37 (Winter, 1967): 63–70; for executives, William H. Whyte, Jr., *The Organization Man* (New York: Simon & Schuster, 1956), pp. 109–37; for prostitutes, James H. Bryan, "Apprenticeships in Prostitution," *Social Problems* 12 (Winter, 1965): 287–97; for optometrists, in addition to the paper by Orzack cited in the text, Louis H. Orzack and John R. Uglum, *Sociological Perspectives of the Profession of Optometry,* American Journal of Optometry and Archives of American Academy of Optometry Monographs, No. 250 (August, 1958); and for professional interaction involved in the treatment of tuberculosis, Robert L. Eichhorn and Jere A. Wysong, *Interagency Relations in the Provision of Health Services: Tuberculosis Control in a Metropolitan Region* (West Lafayette, Ind.: Institute for the Study of Social Change, Department of Sociology, Purdue University, 1968), pp. 72–112.

On the general topic of professionalization, see Howard M. Vollmer and Donald L. Mills, eds., *Professionalization* (Englewood Cliffs, N.J.: Prentice-Hall, 1966); Nelson N. Foote, "The Professionalization of Labor in Detroit," *American Journal of Sociology* 58 (January, 1953): 371–80; Everett C. Hughes, "Professions," *Daedalus* 92 (Fall, 1963): 655–68; and Bernard Barber, "Some Problems in the Sociology of the Professions," *Daedalus* 92 (Fall, 1963): 669–88.

An illustration of the process by which an occupation attempts to professionalize by laying claim to an emerging technology is provided by Howard Vollmer and Donald Mills, "Nuclear Technology and the Professionalization of Labor," *American Journal of Sociology* 67 (May, 1962): 690–96.

The following items attempt to relate professions and professionalization to more general theories of occupational evolution and change: Richard H. Hall, "Professionalization and Bureaucratization," *American Sociological Review* 33 (February, 1968): 92–104; William E. Snizek, "Hall's Professionalism Scale: A Reassessment," *American Sociological Review* 37 (February, 1972): 109–13; Eliot Freidson, *Doctoring Together: A Study of Professional Social Control* (New York: Elsevier, 1975); William J. Goode, "Encroachment, Charlatanism, and the Emergent Professions," *American Sociological Review* 25 (December, 1960): 902–14; Dietrich Rueschmeyer "Doctors and Lawyers: A Comment on the Theory of the Professions," in Eliot Freidson and Judith Lorber, eds., *Medical Men and their Work* (Chicago: Aldine-Atherton, 1972), pp. 5–19; Norman K.

Denzin, "Incomplete Professionalization: The Case of Pharmacy," *Social Forces* 46 (March, 1968): 375–82; William J. Goode, "The Librarian: From Occupation to Profession," *Library Quarterly* 31 (October, 1961): 306–18; and Geoffrey Millerson, *The Qualifying Associations: A Study in Professionalization* (London: Routledge & Kegan Paul, 1964).

On the role of political behavior in occupations and the professions, see, for example, Rue Bucher and Anselm Strauss, "Professions in Process," *American Journal of Sociology* 66 (January, 1961): 325–34; R. Carter, "Class Militancy and Union Character: A Study of the Association of Scientific Technical and Managerial Staffs," *Sociological Review* (New Series) 27 (May, 1979): 297–316; Adolf Sturmthal, "Comparative Essay," in Adolf Sturmthal, ed., *White-Collar Trade Unions* (Urbana, Ill.: University of Illinois Press, 1966), pp. 365–98; Stephen Cole, "Teachers' Strike: A Study of the Conversion of Predisposition into Action," *American Journal of Sociology* 74 (March, 1969): 506–20; William Kornhauser, *Scientists in Industry: Conflict and Accommodation* (Berkeley: University of California Press, 1962); and Ronald L. Akers and Richard Quinney, "Differential Organization of Health Professions: A Comparative Analysis," *American Sociological Review* 33 (February, 1968): 104–21.

On political behavior of the American Medical Association see, for example, Vollmer and Mills, *Professionalization*, pp. 173–76, 321–25, and Elton Rayack, *Professional Power and American Medicine* (Cleveland: World, 1967); and Jeffrey L. Berlant, *Profession and Monopoly: A Study of Medicine in the United States and Great Britain* (Berkeley: University of California Press, 1975).

On the absorption of professionals in large-scale organizations, see, for example, Barney G. Glaser, ed., *Organizational Careers: A Sourcebook for Theory* (Chicago: Aldine, 1968); Joe L. Spaeth, "Industrial Medicine: A Low-Status Branch of a Profession," unpublished master's thesis, Department of Sociology, University of Chicago, 1958; Charles E. Bidwell, ed., "New Research on the Academic Professions," *Sociology of Education* 47 (Winter, 1974), entire issue.

On chiropractors, see Sally F. Rosenthal, "Marginal or Mainstream: Two Studies of Contemporary Chiropractic," *Sociological Focus* 14 (October, 1981): 271–85; Walter I. Wardwell, "A Marginal Professional Role: The Chiropractor," *Social Forces* 30 (May, 1952): 339–48; *idem*, "The Reduction of Strain in a Marginal Social Role," *American Journal of Sociology* 61 (July, 1955): 16–25; and *idem*, "Limited Marginal and Quasi-Practitioners," in Howard E. Freeman, Sol Levine, and Leo G. Reeder, eds., *Handbook of Medical Sociology* (Englewood Cliffs, N.J.: Prentice-Hall, 1963), pp. 213–40.

On social work as an aspirant profession, see, for example, Nina Toren, "Semi-Professionalism and Social Work," in Amitai Etzioni, ed., *The Semi-Professions and their Organizations* (New York: Free Press, 1969), pp. 141–95; Frank M. Loewenberg, "Social Workers and Indigenous Nonprofessionals: Some Structural Dilemmas," *Social Work* 13 (July, 1968): 65–71; NASW Ad Hoc Committee on Advocacy, "The Social Worker as Advocate: Champion of Social Victims," *Social Work* 14 (April, 1969): 16–21; Harry Wasserman, "The Professional Social Worker in a Bureaucracy," *Social Work* 16 (January, 1971): 89–95; Arnulf M. Pins, "Changes in Social Work Education and their Implications for Practice," *Social Work* 16 (April, 1971): 5–15; Leslie Leighninger, "The Generalist-Specialist Debate in Social Work," *Social Service Review* 54 (March, 1980): 1–12; and Marquis E. Wallace, "Private Practice: A Nationwide Study," *Social Work* 27 (May, 1982): 262–67.

On medical technology, see Vollmer and Mills, *Professionalization,* pp. 19–21.

CHAPTER 5

The idea of work as a "central life interest" has been treated in two major papers: Robert Dubin, "Industrial Workers' Worlds: A Study of the 'Central Life Interests' of Industrial Workers," *Social Problems* 3 (January, 1956): 131–42; and Louis H. Orzack, "Work as a 'Central Life Interest' of Professionals," *Social Problems* 7 (Fall, 1959): 125–32.

Whether work well done is a bridge to status in a postindustrial society is considered by Paul Blumberg, "The Decline and Fall of the Status Symbol: Some Thoughts on Status in a Post-Industrial Society," *Social Problems* 21 (April, 1974): 480–98. See also Edward J. Walsh and Marylee C. Taylor, "Occupational Correlates of Multidimensional Self-Esteem: Comparisons Among Garbage Collectors, Bartenders, Professors and Other Workers," *Sociology and Social Research* 66 (April, 1982): 252–68.

The relation between socio-economic and other background factors and occupational achievement has been extensively studied. For example, see Carl J. Bajema, "A Note on the Interrelations Among Intellectual Ability, Educational Attainment, and Occupational Achievement: A Follow-up Study of a Male Kalamazoo Public School Population," *Sociology of Education* 41 (Summer, 1968): 317–19; Raymond Breton, *Social and Academic Factors in the Career Decisions of Canadian Youth* (Ottawa: Manpower and Immigration Program Development, 1972); Murray Milner, Jr., "Race, Education and Jobs: Trends, 1960–1970," *Sociology of Education* 46 (Summer, 1973): 280–98; Eldon l. Wegner, "The Effects of Upward Mobility: A Study of Working-Status College Students," *Sociology of Education* 46 (Summer, 1973): 263–79; James D. Stanfiel, "Socioeconomic Status as Related to Aptitude, Attrition and Achievement of College Students," *Sociology of Education* 46 (Fall, 1973): 480–88; Moshe Seymonov and Ephraim Yuchtman-Yar, "Professional Sports as an Alternative Channel of Social Mobility," *Sociological Inquiry* 51 (1981): 47–53; and Therese L. Baker, "Class, Family, Education and the Process of Status Attainment: A Comparison of American and British Women College Graduates," *Sociological Quarterly* 23 (Winter, 1982): 17–32.

On occupational choice and recruitment, see Howard S. Becker, "Notes on the Concept of Commitment," *American Journal of Sociology* 66 (July, 1960): 32–40; Ann M. Heiss, "Berkeley Doctoral Students Appraise Their Academic Programs," *Educational Record* 48 (Winter, 1967): 30–44; Eli Ginzberg and John L. Herma, *Talent and Performance* (New York: Columbia University Press, 1964); Howard S. Becker and James Carper, "The Development of Identification with an Occupation," *American Journal of Sociology* 61 (January, 1956): 289–98; *idem,* "The Elements of Identification with an Occupation," *American Sociological Review* 21 (June, 1956): 341–48; Howard S. Becker and Anselm L. Strauss, "Careers, Personality and Adult Socialization," *American Journal of Sociology* 62 (November, 1956): 253–63; Everett C. Hughes, "The Making of a Physician," *Human Organization* 14 (Winter, 1955): 21–25; Norval D. Glenn and David Weiner, "Some Trends in the Social Origins of American Sociologists," *American Sociologist* 4 (November, 1969): 291–302; Carolyn C. Perrucci and Dena B. Targ, "Early Work Orientation and Later Situational

Factors as Elements of Work Commitment Among Married Women College Graduates," *Sociological Quarterly* 19 (Spring, 1978): 266–280; Nahum Z. Medalia, "On Becoming a College Teacher," in Kaoru Yamamoto, ed., *The College Student and His Culture: An Analysis* (Boston: Houghton Mifflin, 1968), pp. 291–302; W. Lloyd Warner, Paul P. Van Riper, Norman H. Martin, and Orvis F. Collins, *The American Federal Executive* (New Haven, Conn.: Yale University Press, 1963); David C. Beardslee and Donald D. O'Dowd, "Students and the Occupational World," in Nevitt Sanford, ed., *The American College: A Psychological and Social Interpretation of the Higher Learning* (New York: Wiley, 1962), pp. 597–626; Mary Glenn Wiley, Kathleen S. Crittenden and Laura D. Bing, "Becoming an Academic: Early vs. Later Professional Experiences," *Sociological Focus* 14 (April, 1981): 139–45; Ida Harper Simpson, Richard L. Simpson, Mark Evers and Sharon Sandomirsky Poss, "Occupational Recruitment, Retention and Labor Force Cohort Representation," *American Journal of Sociology* 87 (May, 1982): 1287–1313; and Seymour Warkov with Joseph Zelan, *Lawyers in the Making*, National Opinion Research Center Monographs in Social Research (Chicago: Aldine, 1965).

On the socialization of children and youth to appropriate work orientations, see Robert J. Havighurst, "Youth in Exploration and Man Emergent," in Henry Borow, ed., *Man in a World of Work* (Boston: Houghton Mifflin, 1964), pp. 215–36; Anne Roe, *The Psychology of Occupations* (New York: Wiley, 1956), pp. 251–73; Norman K. Denzin, "Play, Games and Interaction: The Contexts of Childhood Socialization," *Sociological Quarterly* 16 (Autumn, 1975): 458–78; Wilbert E. Moore, "Occupational Socialization," in David A. Goslin, ed., *Handbook of Socialization Theory and Research* (Chicago: Rand McNally, 1969), pp. 861–83; and Leonard D. Cain, Jr., "Life Course and Social Structure," in *Handbook of Modern Sociology* (Chicago: Rand McNally, 1964), pp. 272–309.

Studies of socialization "on the job" include, in addition to the Richards and Dobyns study of the voucher cage (discussed in the text), Bernard C. Rosen and Alan P. Bates, "The Structure of Socialization in Graduate School," *Sociological Inquiry* 37 (Winter, 1967): 71–84; Louis A. Zurcher, Jr., "The Naval Recruit Training Center: A Study of Role Assimilation in a Total Institution," *idem*, 37:85–98; Sanford Dornbusch, "The Military Academy as an Assimilating Institution," *Social Forces* 33 (May, 1955): 316–21; George C. Homans, "The Cash Posters: A Study of a Group of Working Girls," *American Sociological Review* 19 (December, 1954), 724–31; Vilhelm Aubert, "The Housemaid: An Occupational Role in Crisis," in Seymour Martin Lipset and Neil J. Smelser, eds., *Sociology: The Progress of a Decade* (Englewood Cliffs, N.J.: Prentice-Hall, 1961), pp. 414–21; John Van Maanen, "Breaking In: Socialization to Work," in Dubin, ed., *Handbook of Work, Organization and Society, op. cit.*, pp. 131–65; and Anne Roe, *The Making of a Scientist* (New York: Dodd, Mead, 1952).

On adult socialization, see Orville G. Brim, Jr., "Adult Socialization," in John A. Clausen, ed., *Socialization and Society* (Boston: Little, Brown, 1968), pp. 182–226.

For analysis of factors that appear to give meaning to work, see Harold L. Sheppard and Neal Q. Herrick, *Where Have All the Robots Gone?* (New York: Free Press, 1972); *Work in America: Report of a Special Task Force to the Secretary of Health, Education, and Welfare* (Cambridge, Mass.: MIT Press, 1973), pp. 1–23; Barry Gruenberg, "The Happy Worker: An Analysis of Educational and Occupational Differences in Determination of Job Satisfaction," *American*

Journal of Sociology 86 (September, 1980): 247–71; and Robert Dubin, R. Alan Hedley and Thomas C. Taveggian, "Attachment to Work," in Dubin, ed., *Handbook of Work, Organization and Society, op. cit.,* pp. 281–374.

The relation between work and sheer physical survival is examined by Harold L. Wilensky, "Varieties of Work Experience," in Borow, ed., *Man in a World at Work,* pp. 125–64, esp. pp. 136 ff. Wilensky also considers the relation between skills used by workers and their ability to perceive jobs fitting together as a career in "Work, Careers, and Social Integration," *International Social Science Journal* 12 (1960): 543–60, esp. pp. 554 ff. Ely Chinoy explores perceptions of careers among automobile workers in *Automobile Workers and the American Dream* (New York: Random House, 1955).

The idea that events common to the life of a group may serve to demarcate the passage of individuals from one status to another has been examined by Arnold van Gennep, *The Rites of Passage,* trans. Monika B. Vizedom and Gabrielle L. Caffee (Chicago: University of Chicago Press, 1960).

The career of an intern, seen as preparation for the career of physician, is described in "Doctor X," *Intern* (New York: Harper & Row, 1965).

Career timetables are discussed in Julius A. Roth, *Timetables: Structuring the Passage of Time in Hospital Treatment and Other Careers* (Indianapolis: Bobbs-Merrill, 1963); Barney G. Glaser, ed., *Organizational Careers* (Chicago: Aldine, 1968), Parts IV through IX; Everett C. Hughes, "Cycles, Turning Points and Careers," in Everett C. Hughes, ed., *Men and their Work* (Glencoe, Ill.: Free Press, 1958), pp. 11–22; and Howard S. Becker, "The Career of the Chicago Public School Teacher," *American Journal of Sociology* 57 (March, 1952): 470–77.

Failure as a career contingency is explored in David Mechanic, *Students Under Stress* (New York: Free Press of Glencoe, 1962), and Barney G. Glaser and Anselm L. Strauss, *Status Passage* (Chicago: Aldine-Atherton, 1971). That certain "dirty work" occupations may recruit those who have failed elsewhere is suggested in Howard S. Becker and Anselm L. Strauss, "Careers, Personality and Adult Socialization," *American Journal of Sociology* 62 (November, 1956): 253–63.

On sponsorship, see Glaser, *Organizational Careers,* pp. 211 ff; William Kornhauser, "The Negro Union Official: A Study of Sponsorship and Control," *American Journal of Sociology* 57 (March, 1952): 443–52; and Mark S. Granovetter, *Getting a Job: A Study of Contacts and Careers* (Cambridge, Mass.: Harvard University Press, 1974).

CHAPTER 6

On the problem of skill segmentation and specialization of work tasks, see, for example, Robert K. Merton, "Bureaucratic Structure and Personality," *Social Forces* 18 (May, 1940); 560–68; Thorstein Veblen, *The Instinct of Workmanship* (New York: Macmillan, 1914); and Rue Bucher and Anselm Strauss, "Professions in Process," *American Journal of Sociology* 66 (January, 1961): 325–34.

On the problem of alienation at work see, in addition to the materials cited in the text, Robert Blauner, *Alienation and Freedom* (Chicago: University of Chicago Press, 1964); T. B. Bottomore, ed., *Karl Marx: Early Writings* (New York: McGraw-Hill, 1956), pp. 121–33; Ada W. Finifter, ed., *Alienation and the*

Social System (New York: Wiley, 1972); David Jenkins, *Job Power* (Baltimore: Penguin, 1974), pp. 9–61; Robert A. Nisbet, *The Sociological Tradition* (New York: Basic Books, 1966); Charles R. Walker and Robert Guest, *The Man on the Assembly Line* (Cambridge, Mass.: Harvard University Press, 1952); and William Foote Whyte, *Organizational Behavior: Theory and Applications* (Homewood, Ill.: Irwin-Dorsey, 1969), pp. 91–127.

For material on the studies at the Hawthorne plant of Western Electric, see Alex Carey, "The Hawthorne Studies: A Radical Criticism," *American Sociological Review* 32 (June, 1967): 404–16; Henry A. Landsberger, *Hawthorne Revisited* (Ithaca, N.Y.: Cornell University Press, 1958); Fritz J. Roethlisberger and William Dickson, *Management and the Worker* (Cambridge, Mass.: Harvard University Press, 1939); Elton Mayo, *The Human Problems of an Industrial Civilization* (New York: Macmillan, 1933); George C. Homans, "The Western Electric Researches," in Schuyler Dean Hoslett, ed., *Human Factors in Management* (New York: Harper, 1951), pp. 210–41.

For material on the "human relations" movement in industry see William H. Whyte, Jr., *The Organization Man* (New York: Simon & Schuster, 1956), pp. 3–59; Charles B. Spaulding, *An Introduction to Industrial Sociology* (San Francisco: Chandler, 1961), pp. 214–87; and Edward Gross, "Industrial Relations," in Robert E. L. Faris, ed., *Handbook of Modern Sociology* (Chicago: Rand McNally, 1964), pp. 619–79.

On the place of work in the American experience, see Marcus Raskin, "A Subjective/Objective Rendering of Technology," *The Humanist* 33 (September-October, 1973): 25–27; Max Lerner, *America as a Civilization, supra,* I:207–352, II:465–540; Jack Barbash, "The Tensions of Work," *Dissent* 19 (Winter, 1972): 240–48; Daniel Bell, "Labor in the Post-Industrial Society," *ibid.* 19:163–89; and Eric Trist, Toward a Postindustrial Culture," in Dubin, ed., *Handbook of Work, Organization and Society, op. cit.,* pp. 1011–33.

The idea of automation as the "second industrial revolution" is discussed in Arthur J. Goldberg, "The Challenge of 'Industrial Revolution II,'" in Morris Philipson, ed., *Automation: Implications for the Future* (New York: Vintage, 1962), pp. 3–11, and Robert Dubin, "Automation: The Second Industrial Revolution," in Simon Marcson, ed., *Automation, Alienation and Anomie* (New York: Harper & Row, 1970), pp. 152–61.

The characteristics of automation have been discussed in Blauner, *Alienation and Freedom,* pp. 166–87; John Diebold, "Congressional Testimony," in Philipson, ed., *Automation: Implications for the Future,* pp. 12–76; Claudine Marenco, "The Effects of Rationalization of Clerical Work on the Attitudes and Behaviour of Employees," in Jack Stieber, ed. and intro., *Employment Problems of Automation and Advanced Technology: An International Perspective* (New York: St. Martin's, 1966), pp. 412–29; and Louis E. Davis and Jems E. Taylor, "Technology, Organization and Job Structure," in Dubin, ed., *Handbook of Work, Organization and Society,* pp. 379–419.

Implications of the possible responses of employers to automation have been treated in Charles R. Walker, ed., with the assistance of Adelaide G. Walker, *Technology, Industry and Man: The Age of Acceleration* (New York: McGraw-Hill, 1968); *Work in America, supra,* pp. 93–120; Richard J. Schonberger, "Toward a Greater Flexibility," *The Humanist* 33 (September–October, 1973): 35–37; Mitchell Fein, "The Myth of Job Enrichment," *ibid.,* 33:30–32; Charles C. Killingworth, "Industrial Relations and Automation," *Annals of the American Academy of Political and Social Science* 340 (March, 1962): 69–80;

Dorothy Wedderburn and Rosemary Crompton, *Workers' Attitudes and Technology*, Cambridge Papers in Sociology, no. 2 (Cambridge, England: Cambridge University Press, 1972); and Duncan Gallie, *In Search of the Working Class: Automation and Social Integration Within the Capitalist Enterprise* (Cambridge, England: Cambridge University Press, 1978).

Worker displacement in the age of automation is examined in Harold L. Sheppard, Louis A. Ferman, and Seymour Forber, *Too Old to Work—Too Young to Retire: A Case Study of a Permanent Plant Shutdown*, Report to a Special Committee on Unemployment Problems, U.S. Senate, 1960 (Washington: U.S. Government Printing Office, 1960); *The Aging Worker in the Canadian Economy* (Ottawa: Economics and Research Branch, Department of Labour, 1964); and Dorothy Wedderburn, *White-Collar Redundancy*, University of Cambridge Department of Economics Occasional Papers, no. 1 (Cambridge, England: Cambridge University Press, 1964).

On the relation between work and aging, see, in addition to previously cited material, Zena Smith Blau, "Structural Constraints on Friendships in Old Age," in Rose Laub Coser, ed., *Life Cycle and Achievement in America* (New York: Harper & Row, 1969), pp. 197–222; Herbert S. Parnes, ed., *Work and Retirement: A Longitudinal Study of Men* (Cambridge, Mass.: MIT Press, 1981); Harold L. Sheppard, ed., *Toward an Industrial Gerontology* (Cambridge, Mass.: Schenkman, 1972); *idem* and Sara E. Rix, *The Graying of Working America: The Coming Crisis in Retirement-Age Policy* (New York: Free Press, 1977).

In addition to the material on leisure suggested in Chapter 1, the work-leisure nexus is explored in Erwin O. Smigel, ed., *Work and Leisure: A Contemporary Social Problem* (New Haven, Conn.: College and University Press, 1963); *Leisure in Canada: Proceedings of the Montmorency Conference on Leisure, 1969* (Ottawa: Department of National Health and Welfare, 1973); Paul Goodman, "Leisure and Work," in Philipson, ed., *Automation: Implications for the Future, supra*, pp. 446–56; Everett C. Hughes, "Tarde's *Psychologie Economique:* An Unknown Classic by a Forgotten Sociologist," *American Journal of Sociology* 66 (May, 1961): 553–59; Bennett M. Berger, *Working-Class Suburb: A Study of Auto Workers in Suburbia* (Berkeley: University of California Press, 1960); John R. Seeley, *et al.*, *Crestwood Heights: A Study of the Culture of Suburban Life* (New York: Basic Books, 1956); Sebastian deGrazia, *Of Time, Work, and Leisure* (New York: Twentieth Century Fund, 1962); Johan Huizinga, *Homo Ludens: A Study of the Play Element in Culture* (Boston: Beacon, 1950); Roger Caillois, *Man, Play, and Games*, trans. Meyer Barash (New York: Free Press of Glencoe, 1961); Carol Kirsh, Brian Dixon, and Michael Bond, *A Leisure Study—Canada 1972* (Toronto: A E Design and Culturcan Publications for Arts and Culture Branch, Department of the Secretary of State, Government of Canada, 1973); and a special issue on the sociology of leisure of *Social Forces* 60 (December, 1981): 281–413.

INDEX